CCNP Self-Study

CCNP Flash Cards and Exam Practice Pack

Denise Donohue

Tim Sammut

Brent Stewart

D1340534

CCNP Flash Cards and Exam Practice Pack

Denise Donohue

Tim Sammut

Brent Stewart

Copyright© 2004 Cisco Systems, Inc.

Published by:
Cisco Press
800 East 96th Street
Indianapolis, IN 46240 USA

Printed in the United States of America   4 5 6 7 8 9 0

Library of Congress Cataloging-in-Publication Number: 20-03107963

ISBN: 1-58720-091-0

Fourth Printing December 2005

Trademark Acknowledgments

All terms mentioned in this book that are known to be trademarks or service marks have been appropriately capitalized. Cisco Press or Cisco Systems, Inc. cannot attest to the accuracy of this information. Use of a term in this book should not be regarded as affecting the validity of any trademark or service mark.

Warning and Disclaimer

This book is designed to provide information about the CCNP Certification Exams. Every effort has been made to make this book as complete and as accurate as possible, but no warranty or fitness is implied.

The information is provided on an "as is" basis. The author, Cisco Press, and Cisco Systems, Inc., shall have neither liability nor responsibility to any person or entity with respect to any loss or damages arising from the information contained in this book or from the use of the discs or programs that may accompany it.

The opinions expressed in this book belong to the author and are not necessarily those of Cisco Systems, Inc.

Corporate and Government Sales

Cisco Press offers excellent discounts on this book when ordered in quantity for bulk purchases or special sales.

For more information please contact: U.S. Corporate and Government Sales 1-800-382-3419
corpsales@pearsontechgroup.com

For sales outside the U.S. please contact: International Sales
international@pearsoned.com

Feedback Information

At Cisco Press, our goal is to create in-depth technical books of the highest quality and value. Each book is crafted with care and precision, undergoing rigorous development that involves the unique expertise of members from the professional technical community.

Readers' feedback is a natural continuation of this process. If you have any comments regarding how we could improve the quality of this book, or otherwise alter it to better suit your needs, you can contact us through e-mail at feedback@ciscopress.com. Please make sure to include the book title and ISBN in your message.

We greatly appreciate your assistance.

Publisher	John Wait
Editor-in-Chief	John Kane
Executive Editor	Brett Bartow
Acquisitions Editor	Michelle Grandin
Cisco Representative	Anthony Wolfenden
Cisco Press Program Manager	Sonia Torres Chavez
Manager, Marketing Communications, Cisco Systems	Scott Miller
Cisco Marketing Program Manager	Edie Quiroz
Production Manager	Patrick Kanouse
Senior Editor	Sheri Cain
Copy Editor	Kevin Kent
Technical Editors	Jay Swan
	Patrick Lao
	John Mistichelli
Media Developer	Brandon Penticuff
Team Coordinator	Tammi Barnett
Cover Designer	Louisa Adair
Composition	Mark Shirar

CISCO SYSTEMS

Corporate Headquarters
Cisco Systems, Inc.
170 West Tasman Drive
San Jose, CA 95134-1706
USA
www.cisco.com
Tel: 408 526-4000
    800 553-NETS (6387)
Fax: 408 526-4100

European Headquarters
Cisco Systems International BV
Haarlerbergpark
Haarlerbergweg 13-19
1101 CH Amsterdam
The Netherlands
www-europe.cisco.com
Tel: 31 0 20 357 1000
Fax: 31 0 20 357 1100

Americas Headquarters
Cisco Systems, Inc.
170 West Tasman Drive
San Jose, CA 95134-1706
USA
www.cisco.com
Tel: 408 526-7660
Fax: 408 527-0883

Asia Pacific Headquarters
Cisco Systems, Inc.
Capital Tower
168 Robinson Road
#22-01 to #29-01
Singapore 068912
www.cisco.com
Tel: +65 6317 7777
Fax: +65 6317 7799

Cisco Systems has more than 200 offices in the following countries and regions. Addresses, phone numbers, and fax numbers are listed on the
C i s c o . c o m   W e b   s i t e   a t   w w w . c i s c o . c o m / g o / o f f i c e s .

Argentina • Australia • Austria • Belgium • Brazil • Bulgaria • Canada • Chile • China PRC • Colombia • Costa Rica • Croatia • Czech Republic
Denmark • Dubai, UAE • Finland • France • Germany • Greece • Hong Kong SAR • Hungary • India • Indonesia • Ireland • Israel • Italy
Japan • Korea • Luxembourg • Malaysia • Mexico • The Netherlands • New Zealand • Norway • Peru • Philippines • Poland • Portugal
Puerto Rico • Romania • Russia • Saudi Arabia • Scotland • Singapore • Slovakia • Slovenia • South Africa • Spain • Sweden
Switzerland • Taiwan • Thailand • Turkey • Ukraine • United Kingdom • United States • Venezuela • Vietnam • Zimbabwe

About the Authors

Denise Donohue, CCIE No. 9566, is a certified Cisco Systems instructor, currently teaching at Global Knowledge. As a Global Knowledge employee, she participated in the development of ICND, BSCI, BCMSN, BCRAN, and CIT for Internet-based delivery. She served as SME (Subject Matter Expert) for the CD-based BSCI title. Recently, Denise worked under contract to Cisco as an SME on the BSCI 2.0 update and the CVOICE update. Prior to working for Global Knowledge, she co-owned a networking consultancy firm. Denise also holds the CCNP and MSCE certifications.

Tim Sammut, CCIE No. 6642, is a senior network consultant for Northrop Grumman Information Technology. Tim has served in key project roles involving technologies from LAN switching to security to SNA integration and has helped many organizations, ranging from 100 to 130,000 users, make the most of their network investment. Tim also holds the CISSP, CCIE Security, and CCIE Communication and Services certifications. He can be reached at tsammut@northropgrumman.com.

Brent Stewart is a certified Cisco Systems instructor, currently teaching at Global Knowledge. As a Global Knowledge employee, he participated in the development of ICND, BSCI, BCMSN, BCRAN, and CIT for Internet-based delivery and served as SME for the CD-based ICND and CIT titles. He helped author the BSCI 2.0 update and served as the lab development engineer. Prior to working for Global Knowledge, Brent owned an ISP and worked as an IT consultant. Brent holds the CCNP, CCDP, and MCSE certifications. Brent lives in Hickory, North Carolina, with his wife, Karen, and beautiful but mischievous children, Benjamin, Kaitlyn, and Madelyn.

About the Technical Reviewers

Patrick Lao, CCIE No. 4952, has been a technical education consultant with Internet Learning Solutions Group (ILSG) since March 1998. He received a B.S. in electrical engineering technology from Cal Poly Pomona University and an M.S. in telecommunications management from Golden Gate University. He has been a certified Cisco Systems instructor since 1998. His certifications include CCIP, CCNP, and CCDP. He has more than 17 years of industry experience in technical training and course development.

John Mistichelli, CCIE No. 7536, CCNP, CCDP, MCSE, CNE, is a self-employed consultant with more than 12 years of experience in the Information Technology profession. He regularly performs Cisco consulting and Cisco certified training. John teaches all the courses preparing a CCNP candidate for certification. He is a certified Cisco Systems instructor. John also designed, built, and operates a popular forum to aid CCIE candidates to certification (Routopia.com).

Jay Swan, CCNP, CCSP, teaches Cisco courses with Global Knowledge. He is a certified Cisco Systems instructor with a bachelor's and master's degrees from Stanford University. Prior to joining Global Knowledge, he worked in the ISP and higher education fields. He lives in southwestern Colorado, where he is an active trail runner, search-and-rescue volunteer, and martial-arts practitioner.

Dedications

Denise Donohue:

I dedicate this book to my husband, Kevin, and children Ryan, Caitlin, and Peter. They'll probably think it strange to see me without a computer attached to my hands and are long overdue for a good home-cooked meal. I'd also like to dedicate this book to all the people who have been so generous in sharing their knowledge with me over the years. I'm hoping this book will help return the favor by passing some of that knowledge along to the next crop of network engineers.

Tim Sammut:

This book, like my heart, is dedicated to my beautiful wife Diane. Her unwavering support and inspiration have given me the courage to complete many things, including this book.

Brent Stewart:

This book is dedicated to my wife, Karen, who through her love and support made this book possible. My children, Benjamin, Kaitlyn, and Madelyn, serve as constant inspiration for all my work. While I was working on this book, a lot of trains ran and dolls were fed without me. Finally, J.D. Wegner has been a mentor and example for many years, and his friendship will always mean the world to me.

Acknowledgments

Denise Donohue:

First, thanks to my co-authors Brent and Tim for doing a terrific job. Our technical editors, John, Jay, and Patrick, are top-notch and I appreciated your helpful comments. Cisco Press has been a pleasure to work with, and I thank you all for that.

Tim Sammut:

I would like to thank Michelle Grandin for giving me the chance to prove myself as a technical editor, and for encouraging me to take part in this book. I would also like to say thank you to the technical editors unfortunate enough to be tasked with correcting my technical and grammatical errors.

Brent Stewart:

Michelle Grandin at Cisco Press has been a wonderful editor. She has shown a lot of patience and has, at every point, been encouraging and supportive. Thanks also to Brett Bartow and John Kane, who introduced me to the publishing process and encouraged my dreams.

I'd like to thank the technical editors: Jay Swan, Patrick Lao, and John Mistichelli. This format demands brevity and focus, neither adjective normally attributed to me. Jay, Patrick, and John kept their sense of humor through my gaffes and patiently repaired each. I appreciate their hard work.

Table of Contents

Foreword   x

Introduction   xi

Part I: BSCI   3

Section 1   Advanced IP Addressing   5

Section 2   Routing Principles   31

Section 3   EIGRP   63

Section 4   OSPF   93

Section 5   Intermediate System-to-Intermediate System (IS-IS)   127

Section 6   Migrating and Redistributing Routes Between
Multiple IP Routing Protocols   159

Section 7   Border Gateway Protocol (BGP)   191

BSCI Quick Reference Sheets   223

Advanced IP Addressing Issues   222
Understanding IP Routing   226
Classful IP Routing   228
Classless IP Routing Protocols   228
Comparing RIP and IGRP   229
IP Routing Protocols   230
EIGRP   231
EIGRP Messages   232
EIGRP DUAL   233
Configuring EIGRP   235
Advanced EIGRP   235
OSPF Overview   237
Configuring Single Area OSPF   239
Low-Level OSPF   239
OSPF Network Types   240
OSPF Advertisements and Cost   242
OSPF Summarization   242
IS-IS   243
Optimizing Routing   246
BGP   249

Part II: BCMSN   255

Section 1   Implementing Switching in the Network   257

Section 2   Configuring VLANS and VTP   277

Section 3   Implementing and Tuning Spanning Tree Protocol   303

Section 4 Enhancing Spanning-Tree Protocol 327

Section 5 Multilayer Switching (MLS) 355

Section 6 Improving Network Availability 377

Section 7 Cisco AVVID Services and Applications 401

Section 8 Implementing QoS 425

BCMSN Quick Reference Sheets 449

The Evolving Network Model 448

Multilayer Switching 450

Catalyst Switch Basics 451

VLAN Implementation 451

Understanding the Spanning Tree Protocol 456

Spanning Tree Enhancements 459

Multilayer Switching 463

Inter-VLAN Routing 465

Multilayer Switch Reliability 465

Default Gateway Redundancy 466

IP Multicast and IP Telephony in a Switched Network 468

Implementing QoS in a Switched Network 472

Optimizing Performance of Campus Networks 476

Security in the Campus Network 477

Metro Ethernet 479

Metro Ethernet Tunneling Options 479

Part III: CIT 483

Section 1 Network Baselining and Troubleshooting Methodologies 485

Section 2 Troubleshooting TCP/IP 511

Section 3 Troubleshooting Switched Ethernet Networks 537

Section 4 Troubleshooting PPP 563

Section 5 Troubleshooting Frame Relay 589

CIT Quick Reference Sheets 615

Network Troubleshooting and Baselining 614

The General Troubleshooting Process 614

Gathering Symptoms 614

Guidelines for Network Documentation 614

Reasons to Baseline a Network 614

Steps in the Network Discovery Process 615

Network Topology Diagrams 615

Components of a Network Configuration Table 615

Important Points to Document for Ethernet Switches 615

Important Points to Document for Routers 615

Helpful Commands in Network Discovery and Documentation 616

Troubleshooting TCP/IP 616

Administrative Distance   616

Route Redistribution   617

IOS TCP/IP Troubleshooting Commands   618

Workstation Troubleshooting Commands   619

TCP/IP Debugging Commands   619

Troubleshooting Switched Ethernet Networks   620

Using SPAN and RSPAN   621

Troubleshooting Error Disabled Ports   621

Important Troubleshooting Commands   621

Debugging Commands   622

Troubleshooting PPP   622

Debugging PPP Connections   623

Client IP Address Assignment   623

Configuring and Tuning Multilink PPP   623

Verification of a PPP Configuration   624

Supporting Frame Relay   624

Configuring a Router to Interact with a Congested Frame Relay
Network   624

Viewing the Status of Frame Relay Connections   625

Debugging Frame Relay Connections   625

Part IV: BCRAN   627

Section 1   Wide-Area Network Technologies   629

Section 2   Configuring Asynchronous Serial Connections   651

Section 3   Configuring PPP with CHAP and PAP   673

Section 4   Dial-on-Demand Routing   695

Section 5   Configuration Frame Relay Connections   717

Section 6   Network Redundancy and Backup Connections   739

Section 7   Queuing and Compression   761

Section 8   Network Address Translation   783

Section 9   Cable and DSL Technologies 805

Section 10   Understanding Virtual Private Networks 849

BCRAN Quick Reference Sheets 891

Wide-Area Network Technologies   890

Working with Asynchronous Connections   890

Configuring PPP with PAP and CHAP   892

Configuring Dial-on-Demand Routing   895

Configuring Frame Relay   898

Network Redundancy and Backup Connections   900

Configuring Compression   902

Configuring Queuing   902

Configuring Network Address Translation (NAT)   905

Understanding DSL and Broadband Cable Technologies   909

Understanding Virtual Private Networks   911

Foreword

CCNP Flash Cards and Exam Practice Pack is a late-stage practice tool that provides you with a variety of proven exam-preparation methods, including physical and electronic flash cards, study- and practice-mode assessment tests, and review-oriented quick reference sheets. Together, these elements help you assess your knowledge of CCNP concepts and focus your practice on those areas where you need the most help. This book was developed in cooperation with the Cisco Internet Learning Solutions Group. Cisco Press books are the only self-study books authorized by Cisco Systems for CCNP exam preparation.

Cisco and Cisco Press present this material in a text-based format to provide another learning vehicle for our customers and the broader user community in general. Although a publication does not duplicate the instructor-led or e-learning environment, we acknowledge that not everyone responds in the same way to the same delivery mechanism. It is our intent that presenting this material through a Cisco Press publication will enhance the transfer of knowledge to a broad audience of networking professionals.

Cisco Press will present existing and future practice test products through these Flash Cards and Exam Practice Packs to help achieve the Cisco Internet Learning Solutions Group principal objectives: to educate the Cisco community of networking professionals and to enable that community to build and maintain reliable, scalable networks. The Cisco Career Certifications and classes that support these certifications are directed at meeting these objectives through a disciplined approach to progressive learning. In order to succeed on the Cisco Career Certifications exams, as well as in your daily job as a Cisco certified professional, we recommend a blended learning solution that combines instructor-led, e-learning, and self-study training with hands-on experience. Cisco Systems has created an authorized Cisco Learning Partner program to provide you with the most highly qualified instruction and invaluable hands-on experience in lab and simulation environments. To learn more about Cisco Learning Partner programs available in your area, please go to www.cisco.com/go/authorized/training.

The books Cisco Press creates, in partnership with Cisco Systems, meet the same standards for content quality demanded of the courses and certifications. Our intent is that you will find this and subsequent Cisco Press certification and training publications of value as you build your networking knowledge base.

Thomas M. Kelly
Vice President, Internet Learning Solutions Group
Cisco Systems, Inc.
May 2003

Introduction

Since the Cisco Systems, Inc. career certification programs were announced in 1998, they have been the most sought-after and prestigious certifications in the networking industry. For many, achieving one's CCNP certification is a crucial step in building a rewarding career in networking or obtaining career advancement.

Notorious as being some of the most difficult certifications in the networking industry, Cisco exams can cause much stress to the ill-prepared. Unlike other certification exams, the Cisco exams require that students truly understand the material instead of just memorizing answers. This pack has been designed to help you assess whether you are prepared to pass all four of the CCNP exams. This pack contains flash cards that assist in memorization, quick reference sheets that provide condensed exam information, and a powerful exam engine to help you determine if you are prepared for the actual exam.

The Purpose of Flash Cards

For years, flash cards have been recognized as a quick and effective study aid. They have been used to complement classroom training and significantly boost memory retention.

The flash cards in this pack serve as a final preparation tool for the CCNP exam. They work best when used in conjunction with official study aids for the CCNP exam. Table I-1 presents the required exams and recommended study for CCNP certification. Note that these cards and quick reference sheets can be used in conjunction with any other CCNP exam preparation book or course of study. They might also be useful to you as a quick desk or field reference guide. There's also a composite exam, 642-891, which covers BSCI and BCMSN. This exam can be taken in place of BSCI and BCMSN and as a CCNP recertification exam.

Table I-1 *Exams and Courses Required to Achieve CCNP Certification*

Certification	Exam Number	Name	Course Most Closely Matching Exam Requirements
CCNA	#640-801	CCNA exam	Introduction to Cisco Networking Technologies (INTRO) Interconnecting Cisco Network Devices (ICND)
CCNP	#642-801	BSCI exam	Building Scalable Cisco Internetworks (BSCI)
	#642-811	BCMSN exam	Building Cisco Multilayer Switched Networks (BCMSN)
	#642-821	BCRAN exam	Building Cisco Remote Access Networks (BCRAN)
	#642-831	CIT exam	Cisco Internetwork Troubleshooting (CIT)

Who These Flash Cards Are For

These flash cards are designed for network administrators, network engineers, Cisco Networking Academy Program students, and any professional or student looking to advance his or her career through achieving Cisco CCNP certification.

How To Use These Flash Cards

Review one section at a time, reading each flash card until you can answer it correctly on your own. When you can correctly answer every card in a given section, move on to the next.

These flash cards are a condensed form of study and review. Don't rush to move through each section. The amount of time you spend reviewing the cards directly affects how long you'll be able to retain the information needed to pass the test. The couple of days before your exam, review each section as a final refresher.

Although these flash cards are designed to be used as a final-stage study aid (30 days before the exam), they can also be used in the following situations:

- **Pre-study evaluation**—Before charting out your course of study, read one or two questions at the beginning and end of every section to gauge your competence in the specific areas.

- **Reinforcement of key topics**—After you complete your study in each area, read through the answer cards (on the left side of the pages) to identify key topics and reinforce concepts.

- **Identify areas for last-minute review**—In the days before an exam, review the study cards and carefully note your areas of weakness. Concentrate your remaining study time on these areas.

- **Post-study quiz**—By flipping through this book at random and viewing the questions on the right side of the pages, you can randomize your self-quiz to be sure you're prepared in all areas.

- **Desk reference or field guide to core concepts (quick reference sheets section only)**—Networking professionals, sales representatives, and help-desk technicians alike can benefit from a handy, simple-to-navigate book that outlines the major topics aligned with networking principles and CCNP certification.

Quick Reference Sheets

At the back of this book, you will find approximately 100 pages of quick reference sheets. These sheets serve as both a study guide for the CCNP exam and as a companion reference to the text. For readers who seek CCNP certification, these quick reference sheets are well suited to reinforce the concepts learned in the text rather than as a sole source of information. For readers who have either already obtained CCNP certification or simply need a basic overview, these sheets can serve as a standalone reference. A complete set of the notes can also be printed from the enclosed CD-ROM.

To remain consistent with the current versions of the BSCI, BCMSN, BCRAN, and CIT course material and the CCNP exam, the operating systems used in the quick reference sheets are Cisco IOS Version 12.1(18) for the routers and version 12.1(13) for the switches. The configuration commands should be the same or similar on other currently available platforms. The reader is encouraged to investigate the pecularities of each piece of software and hardware. Failure to do so can result in testing frustration or damage to your equipment or network.

Conventions Used in This Book

Some of the flash cards and quick reference sheets contain important Cisco IOS commands used in that section. Because the CCNP exam might test your knowledge of IOS commands, it's crucial that you understand the function of every command. The conventions used to present these commands are the same conventions used in the IOS Command Reference:

- Vertical bars (|) separate alternative, mutually exclusive elements.

- Square brackets ([]) indicate an optional element.

- Braces ({}) indicate a required choice.

- Braces within square brackets ([{}]) indicate a required choice within an optional element.

- **Bold** indicates commands and keywords that are entered literally as shown.

- *Italic* indicates arguments for which you supply values.

What Is Included on the CD-ROM

The CD-ROM includes copies of the 650+ flash cards and 100 quick reference sheets presented in the physical set, plus an additional set of more than 450 flash cards. Also included is an electronic version of the flash cards that runs on all Windows and Palm platforms. The CD-ROM allows you to shuffle the flash cards so that you can randomize your study. The CD-ROM also includes a powerful practice test engine designed to simulate each of the CCNP exams. The practice test engine will help you become familiar with the format of the exams and reinforce the knowledge needed to pass them.

Special Features

You might notice that some flash cards on the CD-ROM provide pointers to the quick reference sheets included on PDF, to provide you with an additional mode of reviewing. Additional CD-ROM features include the following:

- Palm Pilot format so that you can study for the CCNP tests on your Palm

- The ability to shuffle the flash cards as well as the option to review custom sets that focus your study on difficult terms, basic concepts, or a "final exam"

Part I

BSCI

Section 1
Advanced IP Addressing

Section 2
Routing Principles

Section 3
EIGRP

Section 4
OSPF

Section 5
Intermediate System-to-Intermediate System (IS-IS)

Section 6
Migrating and Redistributing Routes
Between Multiple IP Routing Protocols

Section 7
Border Gateway Protocol (BGP)

BSCI Quick Reference Sheets

Section 1

Advanced IP Addressing

Network scalability is the result of applying good design principles. Scalability comes from summarizing, and opportunities for summarization are presented by assigning IP addresses in a hierarchical manner. A scalable network should also conserve IP address space.

Summarization involves replacing many specific route advertisements with more general advertisements—instead of advertising 16 individual /24 routes, advertise them as a "block" using a /20. Summarization allows routers to conserve memory by minimizing the number of routes saved in the routing table. Summarization speeds convergence and reduces processor overhead because fewer routes need to be considered. Finally, summarization hides details (like a bouncing T1 going to a remote office) that could cause the network to reconverge.

In the mid-1990s, a serious concern arose that the IP address space would be consumed. The Internet community reacted with a two-pronged approach—enabling the more efficient use of IP address space by allowing arbitrary masks (called VLSM) as opposed to classful masks (called FLSM) and creating Network Address Translation (NAT) to allow a single address to replace a large set of addresses. These approaches have largely worked and helped to forestall the move to IPv6 for a number of years. Scalable networks create opportunities for the use of VLSM and NAT.

IPv4 uses a 32-bit address space, whereas IPv6 uses a 128-bit address space. IPv6 is being deployed because the demand for address space exceeds the supply. IPv6 also adds features that reflect the years of supporting the IPv4 Internet. In 2002, network equipment software (such as Cisco IOS) and operating systems (like Windows, Mac, and Linux) became available with support for IPv6.

Question 1

What are the benefits of hierarchical addressing?

Advanced IP
Addressing

Question 2

List three characteristics of a well-designed hierarchical network with IP addresses assigned to support summarization.

Advanced IP
Addressing

Question 1 Answer

Hierarchical addressing allows summarization, and summarization...

- Requires fewer CPU and memory resources
- Hides flapping lines
- Converges faster

Question 2 Answer

Scalability—The IP addressing plan anticipates growth and supports summarization.

Predictability—Backup paths should be known and sized to handle the traffic. Load-balanced lines allow a route to continue even if a member link fails and obviates the need to converge.

Flexibility—The design should gracefully handle mergers, divestitures, and reorganizations.

Question 3

How does NAT facilitate network mergers?

Question 4

What does "/22" mean?

Question 3 Answer

Each company might have chosen to use the 10/8 address space. NAT handles this by changing the source addresses going either way to a different network.

NAT would be an interim solution until the new division could be renumbered.

Question 4 Answer

The first 22 bits in the subnet mask are "on":

/22 = 11111111.11111111.11111100.00000000 = 255.255.252.0

Question 5

What range of addresses is summarized by 150.159.216.0/21?

Question 6

Your company is assigned four Class C networks:

200.39.32.0/24

200.39.33.0/24

200.39.34.0/24

200.39.35.0/24

Can these networks be summarized into one route advertisement? How?

Question 5 Answer

150.159.216.0 through 150.159.223.255.

Question 6 Answer

Yes, they can be summarized as 200.39.32.0/22.

Question 7

Your company is assigned four Class C networks:

200.39.32.0/24

200.39.33.0/24

200.39.34.0/24

200.39.35.0/24

Your company has 10 manufacturing plants, each of which needs 50 IP addresses. HQ needs an entire Class C unto itself, and of course, the point-to-point links from HQ to each plant must be numbered. Prepare an addressing plan.

Question 8

What are some advantages of route summarization?

Question 7 Answer

You can do this in many ways. HQ needs a /24, each manufacturing plant needs a /26, and the point-to-point links need /30s. One solution is shown here:

HQ	200.39.32.0/24
Plant 1	200.39.33.0/26
Plant 2	200.39.33.64/26
Plant 3	200.39.33.128/26
...	
Plant 9	200.39.35.0/26
Plant 10	200.39.35.64/26
Dedicated Links	200.39.35.128/30, 132/30, 136/30, etc.

Question 8 Answer

Route summarization

- Reduces the amount of memory needed to store routing information.
- Reduces processor utilization required to maintain routes.
- Reduces bandwidth required to transmit routing. information
- Hides bouncing lines (a T1 going up and down) from other parts of the network—the summary does not change.

Question 9

How does each of the following protocols support route summarization?

RIPv1

RIPv2

IGRP

EIGRP

OSPF

IS-IS

BGP

Question 10

What is the best summarization for

10.0.152.0/21

10.0.160.0/21

10.0.168.0/21

10.0.176.0/21

10.0.184.0/22

10.0.188.0/22

Question 9 Answer

Routing Protocol	Automatic at Classful Boundary?	Classless Summaries?	Location of Summary
RIPv1	Yes	No	NA
RIPv2	Yes*	Yes, with some restrictions	Any interface
IGRP	Yes	No	NA
EIGRP	Yes*	Yes	Any interface
OSPF	No	Yes	ABR or ASBR
IS-IS	No	Yes	L1/L2 IS
BGP	Yes*	Yes	Any router

* Can be disabled

Question 10 Answer

10.0.152.0/21 and 10.0.160.0/19

Question 11

Which of the following IPv6 address are legal?

- 1234:0000:5678:9abc:def0:0000:0000:4321
- abcd:1234::def0:5678::9012
- 5678:9fgh:babe:0101:abcd:1234:8765:4321
- 9012::1

Question 12

What is the broadcast IP address in IPv6?

Question 11 Answer

- 1234:0000:5678:9abc:def0:0000:0000:4321—Legal.

- abcd:1234::def0:5678::9012—Illegal; can use :: only once.

- 5678:9fgh:babe:0101:abcd:1234:8765:4321—Illegal; no such hex character *g* or *h*.

- 9012::1—Legal.

Question 12 Answer

IPv6 does not use broadcasts.

Question 13

IPv6 supports autoconfiguration of host devices. Describe the autoconfiguration process.

Question 14

Your router has an Ethernet0 interface (10.0.0.1/ 24) and a Serial0 interface (12.150.146.1/30). How would you configure NAT so that the internal traffic from the Ethernet network uses a global address in the 12.150.147.0/24 range?

Question 13 Answer

An IPv6-enabled host sends a Router Solicitation message when it boots.

The router responds with a router advertisement containing the network prefix in use on the local segment and other information, such as the address of a default gateway.

The host appends its link-layer address to the prefix, producing a 128-bit IPv6 address.

Question 14 Answer

```
access-list 7 permit 10.0.0.0 0.0.0.255
ip nat pool Translated 12.150.147.1 12.150.147.254
       prefix-length 24
ip nat inside source list 7 pool Translated
interface e0/0
       ip address 10.0.0.1 255.255.255.0
       ip nat inside
interface s0/0
       ip address 12.150.146.1 255.255.255.252
       ip nat outside
```

Question 15

In the context of NAT, what do *inside, outside, local,* and *global* mean?

Question 16

Your router has an Ethernet0 interface (10.0.0.1/24) and a Serial0 interface (12.150.146.1/30). What is the minimal configuration (using NAT with a route map) needed so that traffic from the Ethernet network uses a global address in the 12.150.147.0/24 range?

Question 15 Answer

- Inside and outside establish *location*.
    - — Inside addresses are the private side (**ip nat inside**).
    - — Outside addresses are the public side (**ip nat outside**).
- Local and global establish *point of view*.
    - — Local is the address as seen from inside.
    - — Global is the address as seen from outside.

If a PC is 10.0.0.2, but 200.1.7.50 from the Internet,

- 10.0.0.2 is the inside local address. It is located inside, and this is the address as seen from inside.
- 200.1.7.50 is the inside global address. It is located inside, and this is the address as seen from outside.

Question 16 Answer

```
access-list 7 permit 10.0.0.0 0.0.0.255
ip nat pool Test 12.150.147.1 12.150.147.254 prefix-length 24
ip nat inside source route-map Example pool Test
interface e0/0
        ip address 10.0.0.1 255.255.255.0
        ip nat inside
interface s0/0
        ip address 12.150.146.1 255.255.255.252
        ip nat outside
route-map Example permit 10
        match ip address 7
```

Question 17

What command verifies NAT translations?

Advanced IP Addressing

Question 18

What does NAT do?

Advanced IP Addressing

Question 17 Answer

```
show ip nat translation
```

Question 18 Answer

NAT hides your local IP address from the rest of the world. A router doing NAT changes the source IP address of an outbound packet. When a reply to that packet comes in to the router, the router replaces the original IP address.

Question 19

Advanced IP Addressing

When using route maps with NAT, the router creates "fully extended" entries in the NAT translation table. What information does the fully extended entry contain?

Question 20

Advanced IP Addressing

Summarize the following:

200.100.50.0/24

200.100.51.0/24

200.100.52.0/24

200.100.53.0/24

Question 19 Answer

Protocol, source and destination ports, inside local IP address, inside global IP address, outside local IP address, outside global IP address

Question 20 Answer

200.100.50.0/23

200.100.52.0/23

Question 21

What is the advantage of using a 6 to 4 tunnel over a manually configured tunnel when connecting IPv4 and IPv6 networks?

Question 22

What are the benefits of using a route map to define NAT as opposed to access lists?

Question 21 Answer

Tunnels encapsulate data from one protocol in packets that use addresses from the other protocol stack. A 6 to 4 tunnel is established dynamically and configures itself based on the existing IPv4 network configuration. Manually configured tunnels are static and must be set up by an administrator. 6 to 4 tunnels use an IPv6 address that begins with 2002. They then convert the destination IP address into hexadecimal and add that to the IPv6 address after the 2002. The remainder of the IPv6 address is padded out to 128 bits with zeros.

Question 22 Answer

Access lists build only simple NAT tables that identify inside local to inside global mappings.

Route maps build complete NAT tables that identify protocol, inside local IP and port, inside global IP and port, and outside global IP and port.

Route maps allow more flexibility in mappings (not just 1:1), and route map NAT tables facilitate troubleshooting.

Question 23

In the following configuration, what happens to traffic that doesn't come from the 10.0.0.0/24 network?

```
ip nat inside source route-map Cape pool Launch_Facility
route-map Cape permit 10
        match ip address 7
access-list 7 permit 10.0.0.0 0.0.0.255
```

Question 23 Answer

The source address is not translated, but the traffic still routes.

Section 2

Routing Principles

This section examines how routes are put into the routing table and how the router chooses between routes. Directly connected routes are automatically entered into the routing table. Two basic ways that remote routes are put into the routing table are through static routes and dynamic routing protocols. Static routes give the administrator ultimate control over how traffic is forwarded, but lack the flexibility to deal with changes in the network structure. Dynamic routing protocols allow the router to adapt to changes in the network, but with varying methods and features.

Dynamic routing protocols can be broadly grouped by their support for VLSM (classful or classless), speed of convergence, and their method of operation (distance vector or link-state).

Question 1

How would you create a static route to 172.16.0.0/16 using 192.168.39.32 as the next hop address?

Question 2

What is a default route? Is a default route static or dynamic?

Question 1 Answer

The command is

```
ip route [network] [mask] [next-hop]
```

so...

```
ip route 172.16.0.0 255.255.0.0 192.168.39.32
```

Question 2 Answer

A default route is one that should be used if a more exact match to the destination network cannot be found in the routing table. It is represented by 0.0.0.0/0.

Default routes can be statically configured or dynamically learned.

Question 3

A router needs to forward traffic to 207.87.193.1. Which of the following routes from its routing table would it use? Why?

Route	Next-Hop
0.0.0.0/0	192.168.39.32
207.87.0.0/16	192.168.1.1
207.87.192.0/24	192.168.6.1
207.87.193.0/24	192.168.7.1
207.87.194.0/24	192.168.8.1

Routing
Principles

Question 4

Define metric.

Routing
Principles

Question 3 Answer

207.87.193.0/24 with a next hop of 192.168.7.1

IP routers choose the best—most specific—path, which is to say the path with the longest prefix length.

Question 4 Answer

Metric is a number used by a routing protocol to rank path desirability. A lower number is a more desirable path.

Question 5

What is ODR?

Question 6

Does ODR support VLSM?

Question 5 Answer

On Demand Routing (ODR) is a classless routing protocol that takes advantage of Cisco Discovery Protocol (CDP) packets to learn about remote networks.

Question 6 Answer

Yes.

Question 7

How quickly does ODR converge?

Question 8

How do you configure an ODR stub router connected to the hub with a T1? What if it uses Frame Relay?

Question 7 Answer

Up to 60 seconds:

- ODR is used for only one hop.
- ODR uses CDP, and CDP packets go out every 60 seconds.
- ODR does not support change-based (Flash) updates.

Question 8 Answer

T1—No configuration is required; CDP is on by default.

Frame Relay—Some WAN encapsulations disable CDP by default, such as Frame Relay and ATM. Enable CDP on the interface with the command **cdp enable**.

Question 9

How do you configure an ODR hub router?

Question 10

What is the metric for ODR?

Question 9 Answer

```
router odr
```

Question 10 Answer

The hub router uses a metric of 1 for ODR routes.

Question 11

List the classful routing protocols.

Routing
Principles

Question 12

What distinguishes a classful routing protocol?

Routing
Principles

Question 11 Answer

RIPv1

IGRP

Question 12 Answer

Classful routing protocols are unable to carry the subnet mask associated with a route.

Question 13

What are the two rules of addressing when using classful routing protocols?

Question 14

A router is running RIPv1, no ip classless, and has the following routing table:

```
Gateway of last resort is 0.0.0.0 to network 0.0.0.0
    10.0.0.0/24 is subnetted, 2 networks
C       10.0.1.0/24 is directly connected, Ethernet0
R       10.0.2.0/24 [120/1] via 10.0.1.1, 00:00:27, Ethernet0
R   172.16.0.0/16 [120/2] via 10.0.1.1, 00:00:27, Ethernet0
C   192.168.1.0/24 is directly connected, Serial0
R*  0.0.0.0/0 [120/2] via 192.168.1.254, 00:00:27, Serial0
```

Which interface does it use to forward traffic to 10.254.0.1?

Question 13 Answer

All subnets within a classful network must use the same mask.

All subnets within a classful network must be contiguous.

Question 14 Answer

This traffic will be dropped because it is destined for an unknown subnet of a directly connected, classful network.

Question 15

A router is running RIPv1, ip classless, and has the following routing table:

```
Gateway of last resort is 0.0.0.0 to network 0.0.0.0
    10.0.0.0/24 is subnetted, 2 networks
C       10.0.1.0/24 is directly connected, Ethernet0
R       10.0.2.0/24 [120/1] via 10.0.1.1, 00:00:27, Ethernet0
R    172.16.0.0/16 [120/2] via 10.0.1.1, 00:00:27, Ethernet0
C    192.168.1.0/24 is directly connected, Serial0
R*   0.0.0.0/0 [120/2] via 192.168.1.254, 00:00:27, Serial0
```

Which interface does it use to forward traffic to 10.254.254.1?

Question 16

List the classless routing protocols.

Question 15 Answer

Serial0. The **ip classless** command causes the router to use the longest match for all traffic, even if it has a route to a subnet of that network. Thus, it follows the default path.

Question 16 Answer

RIPv2, EIGRP, OSPF, IS-IS, and BGP

Question 17

How is summarization supported with a classful routing protocol? With a classless routing protocol?

Question 18

Describe the RIPv2 configuration for a router that should not automatically summarize and has two interfaces numbered 172.27.5.1/24 and 10.200.200.1/24.

Question 17 Answer

Classful—Automatically summarizes at classful network boundaries and does not allow manual configuration of summary routes.

Classless—Can manually summarize routes using a mask other than the classfully assumed mask. Each classless routing protocol has its own rules about just how and where this can be done and how far you can summarize.

RIPv2 and EIGRP are classless, but automatically summarize at classful boundaries by default.

Question 18 Answer

```
router rip
 network 172.27.0.0
 network 10.0.0.0
 version 2
 no auto-summary
```

Question 19

How does a router use Administrative Distance (AD)?

Question 20

A router receives a prefix of 172.28.0.0/16 through EIGRP and 172.28.1.0/24 through RIPv2. Which path is put into the routing table? Which path is used to send traffic to 172.28.1.1 and why?

Question 19 Answer

Administrative Distance (AD) is a ranking given to each routing protocol. If the router receives the same prefix from two routing information sources, it takes the path advertised by the routing protocol with the lower AD.

Question 20 Answer

Both are put into the routing table (different prefixes).

The RIP route because it is more specific.

Question 21

How do you create a floating static route with an Administrative Distance of 175?

Question 22

Group the IP IGP protocols by method (distance vector, advanced distance vector, or link state).

Question 21 Answer

In the **ip route** command, use the option to specify an administrative distance. For example,

```
ip route 172.16.0.0 255.255.0.0 192.168.0.1 175
```

Question 22 Answer

Distance Vector	Advanced Distance Vector	Link State
RIP	EIGRP	OSPF
IGRP		IS-IS

Question 23

List the metric used by each IP IGP.

Question 24

Which IP routing protocols support VLSM and converge quickly?

Question 23 Answer

RIP—Hops

IGRP—Formula uses bandwidth and delay (load, reliability, MTU, and hops tracked but not used by default)

EIGRP—Formula uses bandwidth and delay (load, reliability, MTU, and hops tracked but not used by default)

OSPF—Cost, which Cisco sets to 100 Mb/BW

IS-IS—Cost, which Cisco sets to 10

Question 24 Answer

EIGRP, OSPF, and IS-IS

Question 25

When are static routes recommended?

Question 26

What advantages do dynamic routing protocols offer over static routes?

Question 25 Answer

When there is no advantage to dynamically learning routes (for example, there is only one path)

When there are insufficient router resources (processor, memory) to run a routing protocol

When low speed links make overhead of a routing protocol unattractive

When administrative control is needed

Question 26 Answer

Dynamic routing protocols can

- Detect down links and choose a new path
- Detect and use new paths
- Learn new paths from neighbors
- Pick a best path using a metric

Question 27

Classful routing protocols do not pass masks. How then are subnet masks communicated?

Question 28

Which classless IP routing protocols automatically summarize at classful network boundaries?

Question 27 Answer

If a router receives an advertisement for a subnet on an interface that *is* within the same classful network, it assumes that the advertised network uses the same mask as its own interface.

If a router receives an advertisement for a subnet on an interface that *is not* within the same classful network, it assumes the classful mask is being used.

BGP will also, under certain conditions, summarize networks injected into the BGP database by a local router.

Question 28 Answer

RIPv2 and EIGRP

Question 29

Describe RIPv2 in terms of metric, VLSM support, convergence speed, and communication method (broadcast, multicast, or unicast).

Question 29 Answer

RIPv2

Metric is hops (number of routers crossed)

VLSM support: Yes

Summarization: Automatic at classful boundaries by default, but arbitrary summarization supported

Convergence: Slow (minutes)

Communication method: Multicast

Section 3

EIGRP

EIGRP is a modern advanced distance-vector (also called hybrid) routing protocol that supports VLSM and converges quickly. Fast convergence and support for VLSM are the principal reasons for choosing a routing protocol, so EIGRP joins OSPF and IS-IS as a fine choice. The principle issue with EIGRP is that it is a Cisco proprietary protocol. However, EIGRP offers two advantages over OSPF and IS-IS: It is conservative of network resources, and it is easy to configure and support.

EIGRP discovers its neighboring routers using a hello packet. Route information (queries and updates) is specifically acknowledged by each neighbor with either a reply or ACK. Because each router is responsible for making sure its neighbors receive new routing information, the routing table doesn't have to be periodically rebroadcast. EIGRP conserves network bandwidth by advertising routes only at initial startup and thereafter only in the event of a change.

Separate from the routing table, EIGRP tracks its best path to a destination (successor) and alternate paths (feasible successors) that are computed to be loop free by the DUAL algorithm. If the successor is lost, the feasible successor can quickly be elevated to the routing table. Even when a feasible successor isn't available, neighbors can be quickly queried to discover a new alternate route. Not only is this methodology conservative of network bandwidth, but it also minimizes the information that is stored and processed on the router, thereby minimizing the use of processor and memory.

EIGRP is configured on a router in a manner very similar to RIP and IGRP. The commands are simple and familiar. Anyone who has configured and supported RIP or IGRP will quickly feel comfortable with EIGRP. EIGRP can, therefore, achieve results similar to OSPF, but put fewer personnel requirements on a business.

EIGRP does a number of smart things automatically. For example, it limits its traffic to no more than half the available bandwidth on each interface (this sounds like a lot, but no other routing protocol limits itself at all). One "gotcha" with EIGRP is that it automatically summarizes at classful network boundaries. In the modern era of classless routing and arbitrary summarization, it is generally better to disable this feature.

Question 1

How does EIGRP support summarization?

Question 2

What are feasible distance and advertised distance?

Question 1 Answer

EIGRP automatically summarizes at classful boundaries. (This can be disabled with the command **no auto-summary.**)

EIGRP allows arbitrary summarization on each interface.

Question 2 Answer

Feasible distance—Metric value to reach a destination network.

Advertised distance—Metric for a neighbor to reach a destination network;, used by DUAL to guarantee loop-free paths.

Question 3

What is an EIGRP "successor" and "feasible successor"?

EIGRP

Question 4

How is the EIGRP metric calculated by default?

EIGRP

Question 3 Answer

Successor—Next hop with the lowest metric to a destination. Put into the routing table.

Feasible successor—Next hop whose metric meets the feasibility rule, insuring a loop-free path, but whose metric is not as good as the successor's. Serves as backup path.

Question 4 Answer

Metric = [k1 * bandwidth + (k2 * bandwidth) / (256 − load) + k3 * delay] * [k5 / (reliability + k4)]

The default "k" values are k1 = 1, k2 = 0, k3 = 1, k4 = 0, and k5 = 0. The last section is dropped since k5 = 0; thus, the default is...

Metric = bandwidth + delay

Question 5

List the five EIGRP packet types and which are reliable.

Question 6

What conditions in hellos cause two EIGRP routers to *not* become adjacent?

Question 5 Answer

Hello

Update*

Query*

Reply*

ACK

* = Reliable

Question 6 Answer

Mismatched AS

Different constants (k1, k2, k3, k4, k5)

Primary IP addresses on different subnets

Question 7

By default, how often does EIGRP produce hellos? What is the hold timer set to?

EIGRP

Question 8

What is the function of the EIGRP hello packet?

EIGRP

Question 7 Answer

High-speed line (faster than T1)—Every 5 seconds.

Low-speed nonbroadcast multiaccess (NBMA) line (slower than T1)—Every 60 seconds.

Hold time is three times the hello interval.

Question 8 Answer

The EIGRP hello

- Introduces neighbors and starts route exchange.
- Serves as a keepalive, so that information does not have to be periodically retransmitted.

Question 9

Describe the EIGRP process of neighbor discovery and route exchange.

EIGRP

Question 10

What is EIGRP DUAL?

EIGRP

Question 9 Answer

1 Router A sends a hello.

2 Router B also sends a hello and responds with an update.

3 After hellos are exchanged, Router A accepts the UPDATE from Router B and ACKs the route information.

4 Router A sends an update.

5 Router B ACKs the route information.

Question 10 Answer

Diffusing update algorithm (DUAL) is EIGRP's way of selecting the best paths.

Question 11

How is an EIGRP feasible successor chosen?

Question 12

What does EIGRP do if a route is lost and no feasible successor is available?

Question 11 Answer

A feasible successor does not have the lowest metric, but does have an AD less than the FD of the successor.

Question 12 Answer

EIGRP sends a query to all neighbors to discover alternate paths.

Question 13

What is the assumed bandwidth of a serial line? How would you specify the correct bandwidth?

EIGRP

Question 14

A router in AS 5 has serial 0 with an IP address of 172.16.1.1 and serial 1 with the IP address 172.16.2.1. How would you configure EIGRP to be active on just s0?

EIGRP

Question 13 Answer

The assumed bandwidth for synchronous serial interfaces is 1544 Kbps, and 128 Kbps for synch/async serial interfaces. Change the interface bandwidth with this command:

```
router(config-if)# bandwidth [bandwidth in Kbps]
```

Question 14 Answer

There are three ways:

```
router eigrp 5
        network 172.16.0.0
        passive-interface s1
```

or

```
router eigrp 5
        network 172.16.1.1 0.0.0.0
```

or

```
router eigrp 5
        network 172.16.1.0 0.0.0.255
```

Question 15

What command verifies EIGRP routes in the routing table?

EIGRP

Question 16

What command shows the EIGRP topology table (including information about successors and feasible successors)?

EIGRP

Question 15 Answer

```
show ip route
show ip route eigrp (displays just the EIGRP routes)
```

Question 16 Answer

```
show ip eigrp topology
```

Question 17

How many more specific routes within the summarized range must exist for the summary to stay in the table?

Question 18

What metric is used for an EIGRP summary route?

Question 17 Answer

One

Question 18 Answer

The smallest metric of the routes being summarized

Question 19

What command disables EIGRP automatic route summarization?

EIGRP

Question 20

Your router is in EIGRP AS 5. How do you advertise a summary to 172.0.0.0/8 out an interface?

EIGRP

Question 19 Answer

```
router(config-router)# no auto-summary
```

Question 20 Answer

```
router(config-if)# ip summary-address eigrp 5 172.0.0.0
    255.0.0.0
```

Question 21

By default, EIGRP limits its packets to not overwhelm a link. It is the only routing protocol to do this. What percentage of link bandwidth does EIGRP burst up to? How would you configure it to use 65 percent of the bandwidth?

EIGRP

Question 22

What happens when EIGRP is "stuck in active?"

EIGRP

Question 21 Answer

EIGRP bursts up to 50 percent.

```
router(config-if)# ip bandwidth-percent eigrp [as-number] 65
```

Question 22 Answer

If EIGRP loses a path and has no feasible successor, it sends out queries. It is then in the active state for that network. EIGRP cannot choose a new path until all replies are received. If a neighbor is unable to respond, the router is "stuck in active."

Question 23

What can be done to prevent EIGRP "stuck in active?"

Question 24

What is the destination address of an EIGRP hello?

Question 23 Answer

You can either scope the query range by implementing summarization, or identify the router as EIGRP stub.

Question 24 Answer

Multicast 224.0.0.10

Question 25

If a router receives a query for a route from its successor, what does it do?

Question 26

What command is used to tell EIGRP to run on a particular interface?

Question 25 Answer

The query means that the successor has lost the route. If the router does not have a feasible successor for the route, it places the route in Active and sends a query to all other neighbors. When all responses are received, a reply is sent to the former successor. If the router does have a feasible successor for the route, it installs that in its routing table and replies to the query.

Question 26 Answer

```
router (config-router)# network [network_address]
{wildcard_mask}
```

Question 27

Summarization in EIGRP creates two routes on the router which performs the summarization. What are they?

EIGRP

Question 27 Answer

- The summarized route
- Route to Null0 for loop prevention

Section 4

OSPF

Open Shortest Path First (OSPF) Protocol is an "open" (non-proprietary) link-state routing protocol that supports VLSM and converges quickly. Many vendors support OSPF on different kinds of equipment, and OSPF offers many configuration choices so that it can be tuned to a particular environment. Having said that, OSPF is more complicated than either EIGRP or IS-IS.

Each OSPF router produces a Link State Advertisement (LSA) that lists its connected networks and neighbors. OSPF meets and greets its neighbors using a hello packet. After bidirection communication is verified, the routers exchange LSA information and run the Dijkstra algorithm to compute best paths. OSPF traffic (except for hello) is reliable, so the routing table doesn't have to be rebroadcast often. OSPF is conservative of bandwidth by advertising LSAs only at initial startup, every 30 minutes to keep them "fresh," and if a change occurs.

OSPF is aware of all paths from one point to another, so convergence involves switching from one path to another. OSPF eats up processor and memory resources, however, because it stores more data than other protocols and the process of resolving a new path is more computationally intense.

Question 1

What is an LSA?

OSPF

Question 2

What is an OSPF router that attaches to one area called?

What is an OPSF router that attaches to more than one area called?

What is an OSPF router that attaches to OSPF and to another routing protocol called?

OSPF

Question 1 Answer

A Link State Advertisement is an announcement a link-state router makes about the structure of the network. It describes links or interfaces, the states of the network links, and the cost of each link.

Question 2 Answer

Internal router

Area Border Router (ABR)

Autonomous System Boundary Router (ASBR)

Question 3

What is the function of an OSPF DR?

OSPF

Question 4

What values, if not identical, can cause two OSPF routers to not become adjacent?

OSPF

Question 3 Answer

An OSPF DR reduces the number of adjacencies that must be maintained on a multiaccess link.

Question 4 Answer

Timers

Area ID

Password

Stub area flag

Authentication password

Question 5

Aside from configuration parameters, what must be present in an OSPF hello for routers to become neighbors?

OSPF

Question 6

What does OSPF "two way" state signify?

OSPF

Question 5 Answer

That a router sees its router ID in the hello of another router (bidirectional communication demonstrated)

Question 6 Answer

Bidirectional communication (router sees itself listed as a neighbor from another router).

Question 7

What is the destination address of OSPF packets?

Question 8

What command allows you to see OSPF traffic and header information into or out of a router?

Question 7 Answer

All OSPF routers 224.0.0.5

All OSPF DRs 224.0.0.6

Question 8 Answer

debug ip ospf packet

Question 9

What configuration commands would you use to enable OSPF process number 1 and put only interface serial0/0 (172.16.0.1) into area 0?

Question 10

A router connects to the headquarters OSPF area 0, process number 1 (10.32.0.0/19), and to a division using area 2 (10.71.0.0/24). How would this router be configured to act as an OSPF ABR?

Question 9 Answer

```
router ospf 1
 network 172.16.0.1 0.0.0.0 area 0
```

Question 10 Answer

```
router ospf 1
 network 10.32.0.0 0.31.255.255 area 0
 network 10.71.0.0 0.0.0.255 area 2
```

Question 11

What command might be used to verify that an interface was in the correct OSPF area and to check timers?

OSPF

Question 12

What command might be used to list OSPF adjacencies?

OSPF

Question 11 Answer

```
show ip ospf interface
```

Question 12 Answer

```
show ip ospf neighbor
```

Question 13

How is OSPF Router ID (RID) determined?

OSPF

Question 14

Make a table. Compare the five OSPF nonbroadcast multiaccess (NBMA) network types in terms of RFC compliance, use of DR, method of neighbor discovery, and default hello time.

OSPF

Question 13 Answer

If one or more loopbacks are configured, RID is set to the highest active loopback IP address. Otherwise, RID is the highest IP address on any active interface. If a **router-id** command is used, it overrides all automatic methods.

Question 14 Answer

	RFC?	DR?	Neighbors	Hello (Seconds)
NBMA	Yes	Yes	Manual	30
Point-to-Multipoint	Yes	No	Discovered	30
Broadcast	No	Yes	Discovered	10
Point-to-Point	No	No	Discovered	10
P2MP Nonbroadcast	No	No	Manual	30

Question 15

How are the OSPF DR and BDR elected?

OSPF

Question 16

What is the default OSPF router priority? What does a priority of 0 mean?

OSPF

Question 15 Answer

If a DR or BDR election takes place, the winner is the device with the highest router priority.

If more than one device has the highest priority, the winner is the device with the highest RID.

Once a DR is elected, the same process determines the BDR.

Question 16 Answer

The default OSPF router priority is 1.

A priority of 0 means that a router removes itself from consideration in an election.

Question 17

What expectations does OSPF have of NBMA environments in terms of connectivity?

Question 18

An OSPF full-mesh Frame Relay network has 10 members. How many adjacencies are required if the network type is set to NBMA? What if the network type were set to point-to-multipoint (P2MP)?

Question 17 Answer

It assumes that all nodes are directly attached. This means that either a full mesh or a network type that doesn't use a DR should be used.

Question 18 Answer

NBMA uses one adjacency from each device to the DR and one to the BDR. In this case, that means 9 each for a total of 17.

Point-to-multipoint uses an adjacency along each permanent virtual circuit (PVC), (it treats the PVCs as a collection of point-to-point (P2P) links) so

n(n-1)/2 = 10(9)/2 = 90/2 = 45

Question 19

How is a router configured to support OSPF point-to-multipoint mode on a Frame Relay interface serial0/0?

OSPF

Question 20

What is the difference between OSPF type 1 and type 2 LSAs?

OSPF

Question 19 Answer

```
interface serial 0/0
 encapsulation frame-relay
 ip ospf network point-to-multipoint
```

Question 20 Answer

Type 1 describes a router and its directly connected networks. Type 1 LSAs are produced by every OSPF router.

Type 2 LSAs are produced by a DR and describe the connected multiaccess network.

Question 21

What is the difference between OSPF type 3/4 and type 5 LSAs?

Question 22

What is the difference between OSPF "O E1" and "O E2" routes? Which is the default?

Question 21 Answer

Types 3 and 4 summary LSAs are both produced by an ABR. Type 3 LSAs describe routes in other areas, and Type 4 LSAs advertise routes to ASBRs.

Type 5 LSAs are produced by an ASBR and describe routes outside the OSPF routing domain.

Question 22 Answer

Both types are external routes, advertised using type 5 LSAs:

- E1 routes accrue cost as they move through the OSPF routing domain; thus the metric increases at each hop.

- E2 routes (the default) do not accumulate cost; thus, the metric stays the same throughout the OSPF network.

Question 23

What is the difference between OSPF "O" and "O IA" routes?

OSPF

Question 24

How is the default OSPF cost on an interface changed?

OSPF

Question 23 Answer

Routes shown in the routing table as "O" are inside the area and were learned from type 1 or 2 LSAs.

Routes shown in the routing table as "O IA" are outside the area and were learned from type 3 LSAs.

Question 24 Answer

There are two ways:

```
router(config-router)# auto-cost reference-bandwidth
   [bandwidth]
```

or

```
router(config-if)# ip ospf cost [cost]
```

Question 25

What command summarizes 172.0.0.0/8 from OSPF area 7 to area 0? Where is it executed?

Question 26

What command summarizes external routes to 172.0.0.0/8 for introduction into OSPF? Where is it executed?

Question 25 Answer

At the ABR, type

```
router(config-router)# area 7 range 172.0.0.0 255.0.0.0
```

Question 26 Answer

At the ASBR, type

```
router(config-router)# summary-address 172.0.0.0 255.0.0.0
```

Question 27

List the OSPF packet types.

OSPF

Question 28

How is an OSPF packet identified at Layer 4?

OSPF

Question 27 Answer

Hello

Database description

Link-state request

Link-state update

Link-state acknowledgment

Question 28 Answer

OSPF runs on IP (protocol 89). All OSPF packets share a common header after the IP header.

Question 29

What does OSPF "full" state indicate?

OSPF

Question 30

What command would show the OSPF network type for interface serial0/0?

OSPF

Question 29 Answer

That a router has completed the update process and synchronized its database with another neighbor

Question 30 Answer

```
show ip ospf interface serial 0/0
```

Question 31

What is the default OSPF network type on a Frame Relay main interface? On a Frame Relay multipoint subinterface? On a Frame Relay point-to-point subinterface?

Question 31 Answer

Main interface—NBMA

Multipoint—NBMA

Point-to-Point—Point-to-point

Section 5

Intermediate System-to-Intermediate System (IS-IS)

Intermediate System-to-Intermediate System (IS-IS) is a routing protocol developed by the ISO. It is a link-state protocol and behaves much like Open Shortest Path First (OSPF). The two protocols have some significant differences, however.

IS-IS was developed as part of the Open System Interconnection (OSI) stack of protocols. It uses OSI protocols to deliver its packets and establish its adjacencies. IS-IS routers need to be assigned OSI addresses, which they use as a Router ID to create network structure.

IS-IS has been adapted to carry IP network information, and this form is called Integrated IS-IS. Integrated IS-IS has the most important characteristic necessary in a modern routing protocol: It supports VLSM and converges rapidly. It is also scalable to support very large networks.

Question 1

What type of company typically uses IS-IS?

IS-IS

Question 2

Describe IS-IS Level 1 routing.

IS-IS

Question 1 Answer

Large ISPs typically use IS-IS because it is scalable to very large networks.

Question 2 Answer

Level 1 routing is routing within an IS-IS area. Level 1 routing is done based on System ID. Any traffic bound for other areas is sent to a router that performs Level 2 functions.

Question 3
Describe IS-IS Level 2 routing.

IS-IS

Question 4
What is the role of a L1/L2 IS-IS router?

IS-IS

Question 3 Answer

Level 2 routing is routing between areas. Level 2-capable routers comprise the IS-IS backbone and can be in separate areas. Any traffic bound for other areas must go through a Level 2-capable router. Level 2 routing is based on area ID.

Question 4 Answer

A L1/L2 router performs both Level 1 and Level 2 routing functions. This type of router is equivalent to an Area Border Router (ABR) in OSPF. It communicates with Level 1 routers and also with Level 2-capable routers.

Question 5

Describe the differences in backbone requirements between OSPF and IS-IS.

IS-IS

Question 6

What are the three parts of the OSI address used by a Cisco router running IS-IS?

IS-IS

Question 5 Answer

OSPF requires that an area be defined as a backbone area and that each other area border that backbone area. Special configuration (a virtual link) is required for any area that does not border the backbone area. IS-IS backbone routers can reside in any area. There merely must be an unbroken chain of Level 2 or Level 1/2 routers in order for the backbone to function.

Question 6 Answer

The three parts are area address, system ID, and NSEL. The area address can be from 1 to 13 bytes in length. All routers in an area use the same area address. The system ID is 6 bytes in length and should be unique to each router. The NSEL is 1 byte long and always has a value of 00 for routers.

Question 7

A router has a Network Entity Title (NET) of 49.001a.1122.3344.5566.00. To what area does this router belong, and what is its system ID?

IS-IS

Question 8

How many NSAP addresses does a router with 8 serial and 2 Ethernet interfaces need if all the interfaces are running IS-IS?

IS-IS

Question 7 Answer

The area is 49.001a. The router's system ID is 1122.3344.5566. The easiest way to figure this out is to start from the right and work towards the left. The last two numbers of the NET are the NSEL; they are always 00 on a router. The next 12 numbers (separated into 3 groups of 4 numbers) are the system ID. On Cisco routers, the system ID is always this length—6 bytes. Anything to the left of the system ID is the area ID.

Question 8 Answer

IS-IS devices need only one NSAP address, regardless of how many interfaces they have (although they are allowed to have up to three to deal with migrations). The address is assigned to the device itself. Contrast this with IP, where each interface is assigned a unique IP address.

Question 9

Which of the following is a valid router NET address, and why?

- 2.49.0000.00c0.1234.00
- 40.0000.00c0.1234.56
- 1234.5678.90ab.cdef.0001.00

IS-IS

Question 10

Compare IS-IS routing between areas with IS-IS routing within an area.

IS-IS

Question 9 Answer

- 2.49.0000.00c0.1234.00 is *not* a valid NET address because the first number in the area address has to be at least one byte (two numbers) long.

- 40.0000.00c0.1234.56 is *not* a valid NET address because the last two numbers, the NSEL, must always be 00.

- 1234.5678.90ab.cdef.0001.00 is a valid NET address. The area ID is 1234.5678, and the system ID is 90ab.cdef.0001. The NSEL is 00.

Question 10 Answer

Inter-area, or Level 2, routing is done based on area ID. The SPF algorithm is run to determine the shortest path to other areas. Once the packet reaches the destination area, then intra-area, or Level 1, routing is done based on system ID. The SPF algorithm is run to determine the shortest path to each system in the area. Note that in IS-IS, the SPF algorithm does not calculate paths to IP networks, just areas and end systems. Thus, when the IP information changes, the SPF algorithm does not need to be recalculated.

Question 11

Describe the link-state databases maintained by a L1 router, a L2 router, and a L1/L2 router.

IS-IS

Question 12

In IS-IS routing, where are area boundaries? Where are they in OSPF routing?

IS-IS

Question 11 Answer

A L1 router maintains a database of all routers within the area and tags L1/L2 routers for use as default routes. A L2 router maintains a database of all the areas in the autonomous system and the closest next-hop L2 or L1/L2 router for each area. A L1/L2 router maintains two separate databases—a L1 database for intra-area routing and a L2 database for inter-area routing. It also advertises a default route into its area.

Question 12 Answer

In IS-IS, the area boundaries are on the links between routers. Area membership is assigned to a router as a whole. In OSPF, the area boundaries are within the router. Area membership is assigned on an interface-by-interface basis.

Question 13

What are the four types of IS-IS protocol data units (PDUs), and their use?

IS-IS

Question 14

What is the recommended network topology when using IS-IS in a Frame Relay network, and why?

IS-IS

Question 13 Answer

- **Hellos**—Establish and maintain adjacencies
- **LSP (Link State PDU)**—Advertises link-state information
- **CSNP (Complete Sequence Number PDU)**—An update containing the complete list of LSPs known to the router
- **PSNP (Partial Sequence Number PDU)**—Used to acknowledge a routing update (LSP) on point-to-point links and to request missing information about a route after receiving a CSNP

Question 14 Answer

Point-to-point, using subinterfaces. It is possible to run IS-IS in broadcast mode over Frame Relay; however, the network must be fully meshed, and CLNS must be mapped to each DLCI. If one PVC goes down and the network is no longer fully meshed, IS-IS does not work properly. For this reason, it is recommended to use point-to-point subinterfaces instead.

Question 15

If two Cisco routers are directly connected via an Ethernet link, belong to the same area, and both are L1/L2 routers, what types of adjacencies do they establish?

IS-IS

Question 16

Describe the role of the DIS in an IS-IS broadcast network.

IS-IS

Question 15 Answer

They establish both a L1 and a L2 adjacency, maintain a separate database for each level, and send each other both L1 and L2 types of hellos.

Question 16 Answer

The Designated IS (DIS) creates a logical router called a *pseudonode*. Each router on the LAN forms an adjacency to the pseudonode, as well as to each other. The DIS generates one advertisement for the entire LAN network, on behalf of the pseudonode, rather than each router's advertising the same LAN network. Other routers in the area use the pseudonode's LSP in their SPF calculations for that network. The DIS also ensures that all the routers on the LAN maintain synchronized databases by sending periodic CSNPs out onto the LAN (every 10 seconds by default).

Question 17

What criteria are used in electing the DIS?

IS-IS

Question 18

How often are hellos sent on an IS-IS point-to-point link?

IS-IS

Question 17 Answer

An IS-IS DIS is elected based on highest priority value, and then on highest SNPA address (typically the MAC address). The priority is assigned to each interface and has a default value of 64. Priority can be configured; the range is 1–127. In case of a tie, the router with the highest SPNA address for that interface is elected the DIS. No backup DIS exists.

Question 18 Answer

Hellos are exchanged every 10 seconds on a point-to-point link, by default.

Question 19

How often are hellos sent on an IS-IS broadcast link?

IS-IS

Question 20

When using Integrated IS-IS, you are routing IP network information. Why then does the router still need a NET address?

IS-IS

Question 19 Answer

Hellos are exchanged every 10 seconds on a broadcast link by all routers except the DIS. The DIS sends a hello every 3.3 seconds.

Question 20 Answer

Because Integrated IS-IS uses a CLNS address to identify the router. SPF calculations are based on system ID and area ID, not IP subnet. Only a partial route calculation is done if IP routing information changes. Routers form CLNS adjacencies based on area ID and IS type; the IP subnet does not even have to match on both sides of a connection for the routers to form an adjacency. If the IP subnet doesn't match, IP does not work properly, however.

Question 21

What command displays the IS-IS adjacencies formed by the router?

Question 22

What command displays the result of the SPF calculations performed by IS-IS (the shortest path to each system and area)?

Question 21 Answer

`show clns neighbors`

Recall that IS-IS routers form adjacencies via CLNS.

Question 22 Answer

`show isis topology`

On a L1 router, only routers within the local area are listed. On a L1/L2 router, both local and remote routers are listed.

Question 23

What command gives a summary of the IS-IS process on the router?

IS-IS

Question 24

What configuration must be done on a router to begin IS-IS routing, and what are the commands to do so?

IS-IS

Question 23 Answer

```
show clns protocol
```

This command displays the router's system ID, its IS type, area ID, interfaces participating in IS-IS routing, routes being redistributed, the administrative distance for CLNS, and the type of metrics in use.

Question 24 Answer

- **Enable IS-IS routing**—router isis in global config mode
- **Assign the router a NET**—net [number] in router config mode
- **Enable IS-IS on the interfaces**—ip router isis in interface config mode

Question 25

You have an IS-IS router that is performing both L1 and L2 routing and has both L1 and L2 neighbors. How would you optimize the router's operation to conserve bandwidth and router resources?

IS-IS

Question 26

What is a device's OSI address called, and what is the particular type of OSI address used by a router called?

IS-IS

Question 25 Answer

Configure each interface as either L1 or L2 circuit type, depending on the type of adjacency needed out that interface. The command to do this is, at the interface configuration mode, **isis circuit-type [level-1 | level-1-2 | level-2-only]**. This prevents unnecessary hellos from being sent out interfaces, which uses bandwidth and router resources.

Question 26 Answer

An OSI address is called a Network Service Access Point, or NSAP. It is composed of an area address, a system ID, and the NSAP selector byte, or NSEL. When the NSEL is set to 00, the address is called a Network Entity Title, or NET. A router's NSEL is always 00, so the router's address is a NET.

Question 27

What is a SNPA, and how it is derived?

IS-IS

Question 28

A Level 1 (L1) router has traffic bound for a router in a different area. What does the L1 router do with the traffic?

IS-IS

Question 27 Answer

SNPA stands for Subnetwork Point of Attachment. It identifies a point at which a device connects to a network. It is roughly equivalent to a Layer 2 address in the non-CLNS world. The SNPA for a local-area network (LAN) connection is the MAC address of the interface. The SNPA for a wide-area network (WAN) interface is the virtual circuit identifier. For example, the data-link connection identifier (DLCI) on a Frame Relay connection. If the WAN interface is using High-Level Data Link Control (HDLC) encapsulation, the SNPA is simply *HDLC*. For example:

```
R2# show clns neighbor
System Id Interface SNPA           State  Holdtime Type Protocol
R1        Et0       0000.0c09.9fea Up     24       L1L2 IS-IS
R3        Se0       *HDLC*         Up     28       L1L2 IS-IS
```

Question 28 Answer

A Level 1 router has routes only to systems within its own area, and a default route for everything else. The default route points to a router doing Level 2 (L2) routing. Any traffic bound for a destination out of the local area is sent to the closest L1/L2 router. The SPF algorithm is used to determine the shortest paths to local area routers and L1/L2 routers.

Question 29

What two types of network topology are supported by IS-IS?

Question 29 Answer

Broadcast and point-to-point. Broadcast topology typically describes a LAN, but it might also be used with an NBMA network such as Frame Relay.

Section 6

BSCI

Migrating and Redistributing Routes Between Multiple IP Routing Protocols

One routing protocol might not be appropriate for your entire network over the entire life of the network. Network administrators often find themselves migrating from one protocol to another one or running multiple protocols in their network. This practice can lead to problems, and even break your routing, if not done properly. You need a thorough understanding of the issues involved to maintain a stable network. This section checks your knowledge of migrating from one routing protocol to another, redistributing between protocols, and controlling routing updates and route selection.

Question 1

When migrating from an older routing protocol to a new one, what are three typical changes that must be made?

Question 2

What is a potential problem when using secondary addresses with routing protocols?

Question 1 Answer

- Convert from an IP addressing plan that uses fixed-length subnet masks to one using variable-length subnet masks.

- Create a hierarchical IP addressing plan that supports summarization.

- Create a hierarchical network topology.

Question 2 Answer

By default, routing protocols source their updates from the primary IP address of the outgoing interface. If the router on the other end of the link has a primary address in a different subnet, the two routers might not form an adjacency or exchange updates. Be sure to use addresses in the same subnet as the primary address on neighboring routers.

Question 3

What commands would you use to configure interface s0/0 with a primary IP address of 172.16.3.1/30 and a secondary IP address of 192.168.12.2/30?

Question 4

Network migrations can either start at the core of the network and work out toward the edges, or start at the edges and work in toward the core. What are some advantages of starting at the core?

Question 3 Answer

```
interface s0/0
ip address 172.16.3.1 255.255.255.252
ip address 192.168.12.2 255.255.255.252 secondary
```

Question 4 Answer

Usually, fewer devices are at the core and there are more experienced network personnel in case problems arise. If you are migrating to protocols that require a backbone area, such as OSPF, the core must be configured before the edges.

Question 5

Network migrations can either start at the core of the network and work out toward the edges, or start at the edges and work in toward the core. What are some advantages of starting at the edge?

Question 6

How is the seed metric for a directly connected link usually decided?

Question 5 Answer

No matter how well you have tested your network design, unforeseen problems still possibly crop up. If the migration is begun at a network edge, these problems can be discovered and corrected without disturbing routing in the rest of the network.

Question 6 Answer

The seed metric is usually decided based on the interface being advertised—either bandwidth for OSPF or bandwidth and delay for EIGRP. For IS-IS, the metric begins at 10, and for RIP, it begins with a hop count of 0.

Question 7

What is the default seed metric for redistributed routes for each of the following protocols?

RIP, IGRP and EIGRP, OSPF, IS-IS

Question 8

What criteria are used to decide which routing protocol is the *edge* and which one is the *core*?

Question 7 Answer

- **RIP**—0, which is interpreted by RIP as infinity so the route is not advertised

- **IGRP and EIGRP**—0, which is also interpreted as infinity and the route is not advertised

- **OSPF**—20

- **IS-IS**—0, but IS-IS considers this a legal metric and advertises the route

Question 8 Answer

When you are migrating from one protocol to another, the new protocol is usually the core, and the old one is the edge protocol. If you are running multiple protocols continuously, the more advanced protocol is usually the core.

Question 9

Name three general ways to design your route redistribution.

Question 10

When redistributing routes into RIP, one optional value must be specified or the routes are not redistributed. What is this option?

Question 9 Answer

- Redistribute from the edge protocol to the core and send a default route back into the edge protocol.

- Redistribute from the edge protocol to the core and send the edge protocol some static routes about the core networks.

- Mutual redistribution between both the core and the edge protocols. If this is done, be sure to either filter or in some other way tune the redistributed routes to avoid problems.

Question 10 Answer

You must specify the seed metric or else RIP considers the route's metric to be infinity and does not redistribute the route. Do this either with the **default-metric** command or use the **metric** keyword as part of the redistribute command. The only exception to this rule is when redistributing static or connected routes, which are given a default metric of 1 by RIP.

Question 11

When redistributing into OSPF, which optional keyword allows non-classful networks (such as subnets) to be redistributed?

Question 12

When redistributing OSPF routes into another routing protocol, you have an option to specify the types of routes redistributed. What route types can you specify?

Question 11 Answer

The keyword **subnets**. Without the **subnets** keyword, only networks using the default classful subnet mask are redistributed.

Question 12 Answer

You can choose to redistribute only OSPF internal routes, external type 1 routes, or external type 2 routes. All route types are redistributed by default.

Question 13

When the default-metric command is given under a routing protocol's configuration, to what routes is that metric applied?

Question 14

What is the effect of the passive-interface command when given under EIGRP and OSPF?

Question 13 Answer

The **default-metric** is applied to all routes redistributed into that protocol. It can be overridden by the **metric** keyword in the **redistribute** command.

Question 14 Answer

The **passive-interface** command stops EIGRP and OSPF from sending hellos out the specified interface. Because no hellos are sent, no neighbor adjacencies are created out that interface. The network connected to the interface is still advertised out other interfaces, however.

Question 15

What does the passive-interface default command do when given under the routing process configuration mode?

Question 16

A route map has the following match statement. How does the router interpret this statement?

match condition1 condition2 condition3

Question 15 Answer

The **passive-interface default** command makes all router interfaces passive for that routing protocol. This is useful when you have a classful protocol that should run on only a few of the router's interfaces. To override this command for a specific interface, use the **no passive-interface** [*interface-type number*] command.

Question 16 Answer

The router applies a logical OR to match conditions on the same line. So the line in question would be interpreted as "match condition1 OR condition2 OR condition3."

Question 17

A route map has the following match statement. How does the router interpret this statement?

    match condition1
    match condition2
    match condition3

Question 18

What are some common uses for route maps?

Question 17 Answer

The router applies a logical AND to match conditions on separate lines. So the line in question would be interpreted as "match condition1 AND condition2 AND condition3."

Question 18 Answer

Route maps are often used for filtering during route redistribution, in policy-based routing, in Network Address Translation (NAT), and in setting BGP policies.

Question 19

You are redistributing routes from EIGRP AS 1 into OSPF process 1. What commands apply route map RED-2-OSPF to the redistribution?

Question 20

What is the command to apply an administrative distance of 150 to all routes matching access-list 15, no matter which neighboring router advertised those routes to us?

Question 19 Answer

```
router ospf 1
redistribute eigrp 1 route-map RED-2-OSPF
```

Question 20 Answer

```
distance 150 0.0.0.0 255.255.255.255 15
```

Question 21

The normal routing process chooses outbound interface based on _____, but policy-based routing causes the router to use _____ as the criteria for choosing an outbound interface.

Question 22

Each route map statement must contain either a permit or a deny. When using a route map for policy-based routing, what do *permit* and *deny* mean?

Question 21 Answer

The normal routing process chooses outbound interface based on the *destination network of the packet*, but policy-based routing causes the router to use *the source IP address of the packet, packet size, TOS value, or IP precedence value* as the criterion for choosing an outbound interface.

Question 22 Answer

In policy-based routing, if a source network matches the criteria specified in the match statement and the route-map statement is a permit, the traffic is policy routed. If it matches the criteria and the route-map statement is a deny, the traffic is not dropped; it is just routed normally. If the router reaches the end of the route map and no match has been found for the traffic, it is routed normally also.

Question 23

What are the commands to configure a route map called POLICY, which sends traffic matching access list 1 out interface serial0/0, if a route to the destination network already exists in the routing table?

Question 24

What are the commands to configure a route map called POLICY, which sends traffic matching access list 1 to the next-hop IP address of 172.30.1.1, if no route to the destination network already exists in the routing table?

Question 23 Answer

```
route-map POLICY permit 10
        match ip address 1
        set interface serial0/0
```

Question 24 Answer

```
route-map POLICY permit 10
        match ip address 1
        set ip default next-hop 172.30.1.1
```

Question 25

What commands tell the router to do policy-based routing on interface Ethernet 1/0, using route map POLICY?

ng multiple

Question 25 Answer

```
interface e1/0
ip policy route-map POLICY
```

Question 26 Answer

- If you use multiple vendors' equipment, then you can't use the Cisco proprietary EIGRP in the whole network. You might use EIGRP in the Cisco part of the network, and OSPF in the other part.

- Some applications or host systems might require the use of a specific protocol, such as RIP.

- Network administrators in some parts of your company might be more knowledgeable about a different protocol than the rest of the company, or company politics might require different protocols in different parts of the company.

Question 27

What are three issues that might cause problems when doing route redistribution?

Question 28

What is the default metric type for routes redistributed into OSPF, and what is the command to change this?

Question 27 Answer

- Route feedback, which can cause routing loops
- Suboptimal routing or path selection, caused by incompatible metrics between the two protocols
- Differences in routing information, caused by differences in convergence time between routing protocols

Question 28 Answer

The default metric type for routes redistributed into OSPF is E2. The metric for E2 routes stays the same as the route is advertised throughout the OSPF system. To change this, use the **metric-type 1** argument to the **redistribute** command line.

Question 29

You must specify a seed metric for all routes redistributed into EIGRP, except for what type of routes?

Migrating and
Redistributing
Routes

Question 29 Answer

When connected or static routes are redistributed into EIGRP, EIGRP calculates a seed metric based on interface values. IGRP routes that are automatically redistributed into EIGRP (IRGP and EIGRP processes having the same AS number running on the same router) also do not need a seed metric. All other routes must have a seed metric configured or they are not redistributed.

Section 7

Border Gateway Protocol (BGP)

BGP is an Exterior Gateway Protocol (EGP) that is a routing protocol used between autonomous systems. It is typically used within and between ISPs, although it can also be used between a company and its ISP, and between different parts of a large company. BGP is the routing protocol used in the Internet.

BGP is meant to be a stable and tunable protocol. It does few things dynamically, which makes it different from Interior Gateway Protocols (IGPs). Because so many configuration options for BGP exist, there are many ways to break it. It is important to understand the operation of BGP before configuring it or making changes to an existing configuration. This section tests you on your understanding of BGP operation and terminology and on configuring BGP for scalable operation.

Question 1

Define the term autonomous system as it is used with BGP.

Question 2

What is the range of possible autonomous system (AS) numbers, and what is the range of private AS numbers?

Question 1 Answer

An autonomous system is a group of networks under a common administration. Autonomous systems might run one or more IGPs internally and might be divided into several sections, but the rest of the world does not see that. To the rest of the world, an autonomous system is one single entity. BGP is used to route between autonomous systems.

Question 2 Answer

The range of AS numbers is 1–65,535. Of these, the range from 64,512 to 65,535 is set aside as private AS numbers. This is similar to private IP addresses; private AS numbers are not to be used on the Internet.

Question 3

A BGP router in AS 64888 receives updates with the following AS path attributes from an eBGP neighbor. What does the router do with each of the updates?

Network 172.20.3.0/24 AS Path 65000 64911 65101 64789

Network 172.21.1.0/24 AS Path 65000 65505 64888 64987

Border Gateway
Protocol (BGP)

Question 4

When should you NOT use BGP?

Border Gateway
Protocol (BGP)

Question 3 Answer

The update for network 172.20.3.0 would be accepted and checked for further attributes. The network for 172.21.1.0 would be rejected because the router's own AS number is contained in the update. The router presumes that accepting this update would cause a routing loop.

Question 4 Answer

You should not use BGP if you have only one connection to the Internet and default or static routes would give you all the information you need. BGP routes can consume a lot of bandwidth and router resources, so do not use BGP if you have a slow link to your ISP or if your router doesn't have enough memory or a fast processor. Also, do not use BGP unless you understand it well enough to control its operation properly.

Question 5

What databases do routers running BGP maintain, and what is contained in each?

Question 6

What are the four BGP message types, and what does each do?

Question 5 Answer

- **Neighbor database**—Lists each BGP neighbor and the state of their adjacency

- **Route database or Routing Information Base (RIB)**—Contains each network BGP knows about and all valid paths to that network

- **IP forwarding table (routing table)**—Lists the best path(s) to each destination network

Question 6 Answer

- **Open message**—Sent to establish an adjacency. Contains such information as AS number, holdtime, router ID, and password (if used).

- **Update**—Information about a path and the networks reachable via that path

- **Keepalive**—Used to maintain an adjacency, and acknowledge an open message. Keepalives are exchanged every 60 seconds by default.

- **Notification**—Sent when there is an error serious enough to bring down the BGP session between peers.

Question 7

Describe eBGP, and how eBGP peerings are established.

Question 8

Describe iBGP, and how iBGP peerings are established.

Question 7 Answer

External BGP, or eBGP, is simply BGP running between routers in two different autonomous systems. BGP assumes that external neighbors are directly connected; if they are not, you must configure BGP to look for that neighbor more than one hop away. The IP address of the eBGP neighbor must be reachable without using an IGP—either by being directly connected or by a static route—before BGP attempts to set up a peering.

Question 8 Answer

Internal BGP, or iBGP, is simply BGP running between two routers in the same autonomous system. BGP does not assume that iBGP neighbors are directly connected, so no special configuration is needed if they are several hops away. The IP address of the iBGP neighbor must be reachable, usually via a route advertised by an IGP. If there are multiple paths to an iBGP neighbor, peering is often done between loopback IP addresses rather than interface addresses.

Question 9

Describe the iBGP split-horizon rule.

Question 10

What commands are necessary to configure BGP on a router in AS 65000 with a router at IP address 192.168.1.1 as an iBGP neighbor and a router at IP address 10.10.10.10 as an eBGP neighbor in AS 65010?

Question 9 Answer

IBGP split-horizon says that any routes learned from an iBGP peer are never sent to other iBGP peers. BGP assumes that its iBGP peerings are fully meshed—that is, each router peers with every other BGP router in the AS. When a BGP router gets an update from an eBGP neighbor, it forwards that information to all its iBGP peers. If those iBGP peers then forward it to each other, a loop might be created within the AS.

Question 10 Answer

```
router bgp 65000
        neighbor 192.168.1.1 remote-as 65000
        neighbor 10.10.10.10 remote-as 65010
```

Question 11

When peering with a router's loopback address, what additional BGP configuration must be done?

Question 12

BGP expects its external neighbors to be directly connected. What additional configuration must be done if they are not directly connected?

Question 11 Answer

When peering with a loopback address, the router must be configured to use the loopback addresses the source IP address in its BGP messages. This is done with the command **neighbor [neighbor address] update-source [interface type number]**.

Question 12 Answer

If an external neighbor is not directly connected, BGP must be told to look more than one hop away for that neighbor. This is done with the command **neighbor [neighbor address] ebgp-multihop [number of hops]**. You might use this command if you are peering with an eBGP neighbor's loopback interface because you have multiple paths to that neighbor.

Question 13

Why would you use a peer group in BGP, and how is it configured?

Question 14

What is the function of the network command in BGP?

Question 13 Answer

If you want to apply the same outbound policy to many BGP neighbors, you would have to configure the policy over and over again for each neighbor. A quicker way to do it is to place those neighbors in the same peer group and configure the policy once for that peer group. The router then applies the policy to every member of the peer group. BGP generates only one update for the peer group, rather than multiple updates for each neighbor. You must first create the peer group and then place neighbors in it. The commands are as follows:

```
neighbor [peer group name] peer-group
neighbor [neighbor address] peer-group [peer group name]
```

Question 14 Answer

In an IGP, the **network** command activates the protocol on an interface, and thus only connected networks are used. This is not the case in BGP. In BGP, the **network** command tells the router to originate an advertisement for that network. The network does not have to be directly connected to the router, or even in the same AS. An exact match to the network—both prefix and subnet mask—must exist in the routing table before BGP originates an advertisement for that network.

Question 15

When is it safe to turn off synchronization in BGP, and how is this done?

Question 16

Describe the six BGP neighbor states.

Question 15 Answer

When all routers in the AS are running BGP, it is safe to turn off synchronization. If all routers are running BGP, all the routers learn of all routes, so no black holes exist. Note that you should then filter the routes advertised to your eBGP neighbors, unless you want to become a transit AS for them. The command to turn off synchronization is given under the BGP router configuration mode:

```
no synchronization
```

Question 16 Answer

- **Idle**—A neighbor has been configured, and the router is looking for that neighbor.

- **Connect**—The router is setting up a TCP session with the neighbor.

- **Open Sent**—The TCP session is established, and the routers are exchanging Open messages.

- **Open Confirm**—The router's Open message has been acknowledged.

- **Active**—The router has sent an Open message, but the other router has not responded.

- **Established**—BGP has established a BGP session between the two routers; they are peers. This is the state you want your BGP neighbors to be in.

Question 17

What command displays the BGP database, or RIB?

Question 18

What characteristics of BGP version 4 enable it to support classless interdomain routing (CIDR)?

Question 17 Answer

The command **show ip bgp** displays all the valid routes BGP knows about, the next hop for those routes, along with metric, local preference, weight, and AS path. It also signifies which path was chosen as the best route to each network.

Question 18 Answer

- BGPv4 updates contain subnet mask information.
- When a route is aggregated, the AS path attribute can list the AS numbers associated with the summarized routes to avoid loops.
- BGPv4 has the **aggregate-address** command that summarizes routes.
- BGP's atomic aggregate attribute tells other routers that this is a summary route, and the aggregator attribute tells the router ID and AS number of the router that did the summarization.

Question 19

How can you use the network statement to perform summarization?

Question 20

Define the following categories of BGP attributes:

- Well-known mandatory
- Well-known discretionary
- Optional transitive
- Optional nontransitive

Question 19 Answer

A BGP router can originate an advertisement about a summary network by using the **network** command. Recall that an exact match to the network must exist in the routing table. To create an exact match for a summary route, you can summarize the networks via your IGP, or use a static route pointing to Null0. Remember to use the **mask** keyword in the **network** command if a non-classful subnet mask is used.

Question 20 Answer

- **Well-known mandatory**—Must be understood and used by all BGP routers, and passed on to all BGP peers.

- **Well-known discretionary**—Must by understood by all BGP peers, might or might not be used, might be passed to some BGP peers.

- **Optional transitive**—Often a proprietary attribute, BGP routers are not required to implement it; passed on to BGP peers. If not understood, it is marked as partial.

- **Optional nontransitive**—Often a proprietary attribute, BGP routers are not required to implement it, and dropped if not understood.

Question 21

Describe the BGP AS-Path attribute and tell what type it is.

Question 22

Describe the BGP Next-Hop attribute and tell what type it is.

Question 21 Answer

AS-Path is a well-known, mandatory, transitive attribute. It is a list of all the autonomous systems that the update for this particular route has passed through. It is also BGP's main loop-prevention mechanism.

Question 22 Answer

The Next-Hop attribute is a well-known, mandatory, transitive attribute. It describes the IP address of the edge router in the next AS along the path to a destination network.

Question 23

How do you change the local preference for some routes advertised to you by an external BGP neighbor, but not for others?

Question 24

On Cisco BGP routers, the default MED value is 0. How do you set that to a value of 50 for all routes redistributed into BGP and advertised by your router to all its eBGP neighbors?

Question 23 Answer

You use a route map to do this. First, create an access list that permits the routes to be changed. Then, specify that access list in the route map's **match** statement. Use the **set** statement to change the local preference to the desired value. Remember to put an empty route map statement at the end, or no other routes are accepted. Last, apply the route map to the desired neighbor(s).

Question 24 Answer

Under the BGP router configuration mode, give the following command:

```
default-metric 50
```

Question 25

What are the benefits of receiving a default route from each of your ISPs, plus some more specific routes?

Question 26

How is a BGP router ID chosen?

Question 25 Answer

- Doesn't require a lot of bandwidth.

- Requires more router resources than just default routes, depending on the number of more specific routes accepted, but not as much as the full routing table.

- Can make better routing decision for paths to the more specific networks.

- Internal routers still have the default route for all other traffic out of the AS.

Question 26 Answer

BGP routers choose their router IDs in the same way as OSPF routers do. The highest IP address of a loopback interface is used as the router ID. If no loopback interfaces are on the router, the highest IP address of an active interface is used. The router ID can also be statically configured under the BGP routing process by using the **bgp router-id** command.

Question 27

How can you force a new BGP policy to be applied to a neighbor without tearing down the peering?

Question 28

What information is advertised by default in BGP when you summarize a range of networks, and how do you change this?

Question 27 Answer

You can use a "soft" reset. This doesn't destroy the peering, it just causes the router to either readvertise routes to that neighbor, or apply the policy to any information received from that neighbor (depending on whether it is an outbound or inbound policy). The command to do this is

```
clear ip bgp [* | ip address] soft [in | out]
```

Question 28 Answer

When you summarize a range of BGP networks, the default behavior is to advertise the summary as well as the more specific routes. The atomic aggregate attribute is set, but no additional AS path information is given. BGP automatically inserts a route to the summary, pointing to Null0, into the routing table.

To make the router suppress advertisement of the more specific routes, use the **summary-only** keyword at the end of the **aggregate-address** command. To make the router advertise a list of all the autonomous systems included in the summarized routes, use the **as-set** option.

Question 29

Describe the BGP weight attribute and tell what type it is.

Question 29 Answer

Weight is an optional nontransitive attribute, proprietary to Cisco. If a router has multiple eBGP neighbors, and thus multiple ways out of its AS, weight can be used to influence that router's path selection. Weight is assigned to routes advertised by neighbors, and the highest weight path is chosen. Weight has meaning for the local router only, so is not passed on to any peers.

BSCI Quick Reference Sheets

Advanced IP Addressing Issues

Scalable Network Design

A good network design is essential to a scalable network, so some basic design information is necessary. Networks can generally be broken into three functional layers:

- **Access**—Where end users connect to the network. Switches (which can connect to access layer routers) are the typical network device at this layer, with VLANs, firewall, and access lists providing security and scalability. Host addressing is usually Dynamic Host Configuration Protocol (DHCP).

- **Distribution**—Access layer switches and routers aggregate to this layer. Routers and multilayer switches route between VLANs and to services that are used by many segments of the network (such as e-mail servers). This layer controls access to the core.

- **Core**—This is the network backbone. It connects the different parts of the network. You generally find fast switches here, with as little in the way of security policies as possible. Core devices can be either fully meshed or in a hub-and-spoke with redundancy, as shown in the following figure.

These components can be arranged in your network either by function or by geography:

- **Functional design**—The network is divided up by department, division, or some other type of functional group. The distribution layer bounds each group and connects it to a common core.

- **Geographical design**—A much more common design. The network is divided by location. The distribution layer allows access to groups that need to communicate and connects to a common core.

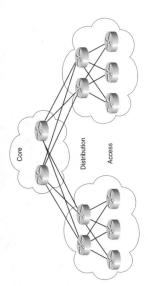

Hierarchical IP addressing is an IP addressing plan that purposefully allows points of summarization. This takes a network, breaks it into subnets by location, then further subnets those addresses by location. In the following figure, the access layer routers can summarize their networks to the distribution layer, who can then combine all the subnets into one summary to the core.

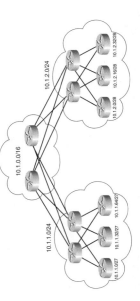

Scalable IP Addressing

A well-designed network along with a hierarchical IP addressing plan gives your network:

- **Scalability**—The network can grow to many users and many sites and still perform efficiently.

- **Predictability**—Traffic patterns are predictable and all routers choose the best paths.

- **Flexibility**—The impact of changes in the network are minimized, as the network has the ability to expand or contract.

Additionally, hierarchical IP addressing allows:

- Smaller routing tables because of summarization of networks
- More efficient use of IP addresses because addresses can be assigned contiguously

Variable-Length Subnet Masking

Variable-Length Subnet Masking (VLSM) involves using a subnet mask that gives you just the number of hosts needed. It requires the use of a classless routing protocol (one that has a field for subnet mask length in its updates.) In the previous figure, the networks on the right have a maximum of 14 hosts in each of them, while the networks on the left can have 30 hosts each. We have chosen the subnet mask based on the number of hosts in each network.

The formula to calculate the number of hosts allowed by a particular subnet mask is $2^n - 2$, where n is the number of host bits in the subnet. The formula to calculate the number of networks gained by subnetting is simply 2^n, where n is the number of network bits in addition to the classful bits. The following table shows some common subnet masks, with the number of hosts and subnets.

Subnets and Hosts

Original Network: 172.16.0.0, Subnet Mask 255.255.0.0 (/16)

Subnet Mask	Additional Subnets	Hosts
255.255.128.0 (/17)	2	32,766
255.255.192.0 (/18)	4	16,382
255.255.224.0 (/19)	8	8190
255.255.240.0 (/20)	16	4094
255.255.248.0 (/21)	32	2046
255.255.252.0 (/22)	64	1022
255.255.254.0 (/23)	128	510
255.255.255.0 (/24)	256	254
255.255.255.128 (/25)	512	126
255.255.255.192 (/26)	1,024	62

Original Network: 172.16.0.0, Subnet Mask 255.255.0.0 (/16)

Subnets and Hosts (Continued)

Subnet Mask	Additional Subnets	Hosts
255.255.255.224 (/27)	2,048	30
255.255.255.240 (/28)	4,096	14
255.255.255.248 (/29)	8,192	6
255.255.255.252 (/30)	16,384	2

Calculating VLSM IP Addresses

To plan an IP addresses scheme using VLSM, follow these general steps:

1. Begin by looking at the network that you use to create your subnets and determine how many bits you have to work with.

2. Look at all the segments that must be assigned IP addresses and determine the most number of hosts any network require.

3. Find the subnet mask for the largest subnet first. To figure out how many bits you must allow for hosts, add 2 to the maximum number of hosts (for network and broadcast addresses) and then round up to the nearest power of 2. Calculate how many bits equal that number.

4. Find the subnet mask for the number of host bits needed by the largest network. Or use the previous table to help you determine the necessary subnet mask.

5. Assign the subnets obtained by using this subnet mask as necessary to the largest subnets.

6. Determine the number of host bits needed for the next largest subnet(s). Take an unused subnet from above and subnet that further.

7. Continue subnetting the subnets for the smaller networks, until you have IP addresses for all networks.

Typically, point-to-point links are assigned a subnet mask of 255.255.255.252 (a 30 bit mask, also written as /30).

It is recommended that you assign hosts within a VLAN to the same subnet.

Remember that you have a finite number of bits to work with; the more subnets you need, the fewer hosts you can have per subnet, and vice versa.

Route Summarization

Summarization is, in a sense, the opposite of subnetting. When subnetting, you move the subnet mask boundary to the right, creating more subnets. When summarizing, you move the subnet mask boundary to the left, thus combining subnets. *Route summarization* is announcing one route that encompasses many networks. For example, if you were in a room with 20 members of the Smith family, you could either introduce all 20 of them individually or just summarize all 20 as "the Smith family." Which would use less of your brain's resources?

Summarization uses less router resources because you have fewer networks to keep in the routing table and to announce to your neighbors.

Calculating a Summary Address

1. The routes to be summarized must share the same high-order bits.
2. Routes can be summarized in powers of 2. If you move the subnet mask 1 bit to the left, that summarizes 2 networks. Moving it 3 bits to the left summarizes 8 networks, etc.
3. Organize the networks to be summarized numerically and write each in binary to determine what high-order bits they have in common.
4. Be careful about including routes in the summary that are not assigned to you. Don't over summarize.
5. A good hierarchical IP addressing design allows for maximum summarization.
6. You must use a classless routing protocol.
7. The router must base its routing decisions on the entire 32-bit IP address and a prefix length of up to 32 bits.

Summarization Example

You have networks 10.1.24.0, 10.1.25.0, 10.1.26.0, and 10.1.27.0. The third octet is where you can summarize, because it is the one that varies. Take a look at the third octet in binary:

```
24  --  00011000
25  --  00011001
26  --  00011010
27  --  00011011
```

Notice that the first six bits are always "000110" but the last two bits vary between 0 and 1. Because the last two bits include all possible combinations of 1 and 0, it is safe to summarize these four networks into one summary route. Configure the router to advertise "10.1.24.0 255.255.252.0".

The network portion of an IP address is referred to as the *prefix*.

Classless Interdomain Routing (CIDR)

CIDR is basically route summarization done on Internet routes. It was created to decrease the size of Internet routing tables, and make better use of existing IP addresses. Service providers are assigned a block of IP addresses that they can then further subnet and assign to customers. These addresses could be several contiguous networks, or just a subnet of a larger network. CIDR allows the assignment of address blocks regardless of the classful network boundary of the blocks. The service provider then advertises to the Internet the summary route for its entire block, instead of each customer's subnet.

IP Version 6

IP version 6 (IPv6) was created to help alleviate the shortage of IP addresses, and to introduce into IP addressing the same multiple levels of hierarchy as found in telephone numbers. Benefits of IPv6 include the following:

- Larger address space than IPv4—128 versus 32 bits.
- Simpler, more efficient header than IPv4—40 bytes long, 64-bit aligned.
- Autoconfiguration options for IPv6 hosts.
- IP mobility capability built in.
- Broadcasts are not used, just multicast and anycast.
- IPSec available on all IPv6 nodes.
- Cisco IOS has methods for easing transition to IPv6.

IPv6 Address Format

- Written in hexadecimal. Case insensitive.
- A series of eight 16-bit fields, separated by colons.
- The leading 0s in a field are optional (003c = 3c).
- Contiguous fields of all 0s can be written as "::" (two colons) once in an address.
- Allows multiple levels of aggregation.

Examples of IPv6 Addresses

```
1234:5678:90ab:cdef:1001:2202:2bad:babe

abcd::1001  (equals  abcd:0000:0000:0000:0000:0000:0000:1001)

a1:beef:3add:212::1  (equals  00a1:beef:3add:0212:0000:0000:0000:0001)

::  (equals all zeros)
```

- **Anycast**—A new type of address available in IPv6. The same IP address is assigned to multiple devices that have the same function, such as a web server. Devices send a message to the anycast address and routers route it to the closest device with that address.
- **Autoconfiguration**—When a host boots up it sends a Router Solicitation (RS). The router responds with a Router Advertisement containing a 64-bit network prefix and default gateway. The host then appends its MAC address to the prefix. This eliminates the need for DHCP or manual host addressing.

IPv6 Header

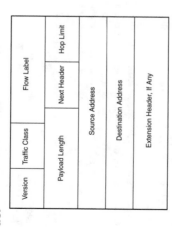

Version	Traffic Class	Flow Label	
Payload Length		Next Header	Hop Limit
Source Address			
Destination Address			
Extension Header, If Any			

- **Version**—4 bits—Contains the number 6 instead of 4.
- **Traffic Class**—8 bits—For setting quality of service options, similar to type of service (ToS) bits in IPv4.
- **Flow Label**—20 bits—Tags a flow to use with multilayer switching and for faster packet switching
- **Payload Length**—16 bits—The total length of the packet.
- **Next Header**—8 bits—Tells what header follows this one, in the data portion of the packet. Could be a Layer 4 header or an extension header.
- **Hop Limit**—8 bits—A Time-To-Live field. Each router decrements this value by 1, and the packet is dropped if it reaches 0.
- **Source and Destination Address**—128 bits each—These fields give the IP address of the source and destination device.
- **Extension Headers**—Size varies. Optional network layer information, usually read only by the destination device.

Transitioning to IPv6 from IPv4

- **Dual Stack method**—Run both versions on the routers interfaces.
- **Manual tunnel**—Use tunnels to connect areas of IPv6 separated by areas using IPv4. Tunnel endpoints must be dual stacked; tunnel is configured manually. Set up routing to go across the tunnel between the IPv6 networks.
- **6to4 tunnel**—Routers configure this automatically. Each 6 to 4 site is given a network address of 2002 concatenated with the hex equivalent of the IPv4 address of the edge router. IPv6 traffic is encapsulated in an IPv4 packet addressed to the other edge router. That router decapsulates the traffic and forwards it.
- **Routing IPv6**—IPv6 is supported in Enhanced Interior Gateway Routing Protocol (EIGRP), Open Shortest Path First (OSPF), Routing Information Protocol (RIP), Integrated Intermediate System-to-Intermediate System (IS-IS), and Border Gateway Protocol (BGP).

Network Address Translation (NAT)

NAT involves a network device swapping one IP address for another; it changes the source IP address of an outgoing packet and the destination IP address of an incoming one. This is done to hide IP addresses from the outside world and to enable multiple devices to use the same IP addresses.

NAT Terminology

- **Inside interface**—The router's interface that points to the inside of your company (E1/0 on R1).
- **Outside interface**—The router's interface that points to the rest of the world (S0/0 on R1).
- **Inside local IP address**—The actual IP address assigned to the host, usually a private address.
- **Inside global IP address**—What the inside local IP address has been translated to. This is what outside hosts use as the IP address for the inside host.
- **Outside global IP address**—The actual IP address of an outside host.
- **Outside local IP address**—What your network sees as the IP address of an outside host. This could be a translated address or the true address of the host.

Example: In the figure, PC1 has an address from the private addressing space. When it sends traffic through the Internet to PC2, R1 removes PC1's IP address (*inside local*) from the packet header and puts in a public address (*inside global*). PC2 replies to that public address. R1 then replaces the destination address with the original private address and sends it to PC1.

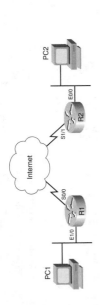

The address that PC1 has for PC2 is its outside local address. R2 might be doing NAT also, and PC2 might have a private (outside global) address that is never seen by PC1. NAT can be done in one of three ways:

- Always translate the same inside address to the same outside address.
- Pick an outside address from a pool of addresses when an inside address needs translating.
- Translate all inside addresses to the same outside address (called *overloading* the outside address).

NAT Configuration with Access Lists and Multiple Pools

Identify what traffic to translate with a standard or extended access list. Multiple access lists can be used if different traffic must be translated to different addresses. Standard access lists translate traffic based on source address; extended access lists can translate traffic based on source, destination, and other information. *Permit* traffic that should be translated.

Create the pools of outside addresses to use for translation. The command for this is as follows:

```
ip nat pool [pool name] [starting ip address] [ending ip address]
[prefix-length <prefix length>] netmask <subnet mask>]
```

Next, link this pool to the access list using the following command:

```
ip nat inside source list [ACL number] pool [pool name]
```

Lastly, specify which interfaces are inside and which are outside ones. The command, at the interface config mode, is

```
ip nat inside
```

or

```
ip nat outside
```

NAT with Route Maps

Test the actions of NAT with the **show ip nat translations** command. When doing NAT with just access lists, this command shows only the source addresses (*simple entries*). To see port and protocol information (*extended entries*) also, either use NAT with overloading or use a route map to specify traffic to be translated.

Route maps are described in detail in a later study sheet. Linking the access lists to a route map and using that to specify traffic to be translated give you an extended translation table.

NAT Translation Table Without Route Maps

Pro	Inside Global	Inside Local	Outside Local	Outside Global
---	63.1.1.1	10.1.1.1	---	---

NAT Translation Table with Route Maps

Pro	Inside Global	Inside Local	Outside Local	Outside Global
udp	63.1.1.1:2010	10.1.1.1:2010	82.3.1.2:69	82.3.1.2:69

Create access lists and address pools as before. Then, create route maps and refer to the access lists in the route maps. Next, link the route maps to the pools with the following command:

```
ip nat inside source route-map <route map name>  pool <pool name>
```

Understanding IP Routing

Static Routing

The easiest and most straightforward way to put a route into the routing table is to create a static route.

```
Router(config)# ip route {prefix} {mask} {next-hop} [distance] [permanent]
```

The next router along the path can be identified by an adjacent IP address or by a connecting point-to-point interface.

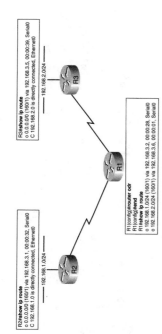

```
R3#show ip route
o 0.0.0.0/0 [160/1] via 192.168.3.5, 00:00:39, Serial0
C 192.168.2.0 is directly connected, Ethernet0
                    192.168.2.0/24

R2#show ip route
o 0.0.0.0/0 [160/1] via 192.168.3.1, 00:00:32, Serial0
C 192.168.1.0 is directly connected, Ethernet0
                    192.168.1.0/24

R1(config)#router odr
R1(config)#end
R1#show ip route
o 192.168.1.0/24 [160/1] via 192.168.3.2, 00:00:28, Serial0
o 192.168.2.0/24 [160/1] via 192.168.3.6, 00:00:01, Serial0
```

Static routes have a default administrative distance (AD), include a value for distance. A static route with a very high AD, so high that the route is not used as long as a route is learned from a routing protocol, is called a *floating static route*.

The **permanent** keyword causes the route to remain in the routing table, even if the next hop is lost.

Static routing does not adjust to network changes, static routing requires time to maintain in a growing network, and static routing doesn't scale well (each new branch office results in a new static route on all other routers).

Static routes don't communicate information to neighboring routers. An important point to remember about static routes is that for routers to communicate, the neighbor router needs a reciprocal route back.

Static routes are appropriate when

- There is a single exit path from a router.
- The bandwidth required to support a routing protocol is unacceptable.
- The memory and central processing unit (CPU) resources required to support a routing protocol are unacceptable.

The Default Route

The route to 0.0.0.0/0 is a special route—the default route. A *default route* is a path to "everywhere else." If several paths should be considered, the router chooses the path with the longest prefix match, so the default is also known as the "path of last resort." A typical branch office configuration, with serial0 leading back to HQ, might look like the following:

```
Router(config)# ip route 0.0.0.0 0.0.0.0 serial0
```

Dynamic Routing

Dynamic routing protocols automatically pick the best path of many and adjust to a new path as circumstances change, but they involve more advanced upkeep and overhead.
IP routing protocols include the following:

- RIP (v1 and v2)
- Interior Gateway Routing Protocol (IGRP)
- EIGRP
- OSPF
- IS-IS
- BGP

On Demand Routing

On Demand Routing (ODR) uses CDP information to build routing tables.
The Cisco Discovery Protocol (CDP) has the following characteristics:

- Runs automatically.
- Is globally disabled with the following command:
  ```
  Router(config)#no cdp run
  ```
- Is disabled on an interface with the following:
  ```
  Router(config-if)#no cdp enable
  ```
- Sends out updates every 60 seconds and holds updates for 180 seconds. The timer is changed using the following command:
  ```
  Router(config)#cdp timer seconds
  ```

ODR has the following characteristics:

- Is appropriate only for hub and spoke.
- Spokes send classless connected routes to hub router.
- Hub router sends default route to each spoke router.
- No spoke configuration is required (CDP must be running between each spoke and the hub).
- Enabling any routing protocol on spoke router disables ODR.

- Is enabled on hub with the command:

  Router(config)#**router odr**

- Has an AD of 160; the metric is always 1.

Classful IP Routing

Classful Routing

There are two classful IP routing protocols:

- RIPv1
- IGRP

Classful routing protocols do not include a subnet mask in routing updates. Therefore, the prefix length is assumed by the receiver to be either:

- The same as the receiving interface, if in the same classful network.
- Summarized to the classful mask, if in another classful network.

An example of RIP advertisements is shown to illustrate how subnet masks are assumed.

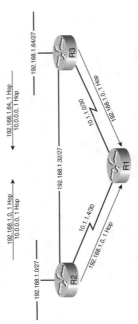

These assumptions lead to the two rules of classful network design:

- All subnets of a classful network must use the same mask.
- Each classful network must be contiguous.

An easy way to appreciate the issues with classful routing is to consider how the network in the following example functions when the interior link goes down. R1

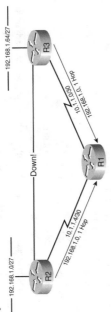

receives a route to 192.168.1.0 from R2 and R3 and, therefore, load balances over two paths to reach 192.168.1.65.

The problem is that when the interior link goes down, R1 does not receive information about the changed topology because of the classful summarization. R1 continues to load balance, and therefore, only half the traffic reaches 192.168.1.65.

The ip classless Command

Router(config)# **ip classless**

The ip classless command became a default in version 12.0 of the IOS. Without the command, a router operating classfully and needing to route traffic to another location within the same classful network checks the routing table for specific routing information and, if not found, drops the traffic. This makes sense because classful networks must be built with all subnets contiguous.

With ip classless, the router considers routes inside the classful network, and if no route is found, the router can resort to less specific routes including the default.

Classless IP Routing Protocols

Classless Routing

Classless IP routing protocols include RIPv2, BGP, EIGRP, OSPF, and IS-IS. Classless routing protocols include a subnet mask in routing updates, so they smoothly handle discontiguous subnets and situations of variable length subnet mask. Because of classless routing's ability to conserve address space and to handle any address space, classless routing is generally assumed to be taking place in modern IP networks.

Auto-Summary

Classless routing supports the use of arbitrary summary routes to reduce the routing table complexity. Summarization reduces the size and amount of routing protocol traffic and the amount of system resources used to maintain a routing protocol and hides (hopefully!) unimportant network details. Summarization is generally a good idea so RIPv2 and EIGRP attempt to automatically summarize at a logical place—the joining of classful networks. The problem is that this breaks discontiguous networks and ends up turned off in many current installations. The example shows the distribution of RIPv2 routes with automatic classful summarization in place. Notice that the subnet masks are included in each update, but that R1 still receives the same route to 192.168.1.0/24 from R2 and R3 and, therefore, load balances to reach an address in the Class C network. (All traffic eventually gets through, although not always along the shortest path.)

The following diagram illustrates the issue with summarization.

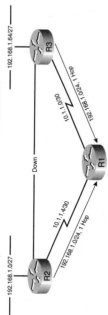

In this case, RIP is automatically summarizing at classful network boundaries. The link between R2 and R3 is broken, but each device still advertises the classfully complete network. The result is that R1 load balances to 192.168.1.65 over the perceived two equal-cost paths, resulting in 50 percent packet loss.

When automatic summarization is turned off, this issue is repaired because each specific route is communicated.

The advantages of classless routing protocols are as follows:

- Support for Variable-Length Subnet Masking (VLSM), which is more efficient of address space

- Support for classless interdomain routing (CIDR), or summaries to blocks of classful networks

No Auto-Summary

Automatic summarization is disabled under the routing process with the no auto-summary command:

```
Router(config-router)# no auto-summary
```

With auto-summary off, complete tables are now distributed. This means that R1 takes the shortest path to reach any destination.

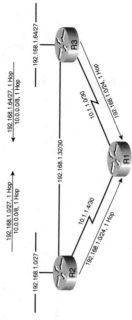

Comparing RIP and IGRP

IGRP

RIP was the original routing protocol, but was designed for a time when WAN links were commonly 56 K. By the late 1980s, it was recognized that a more advanced routing protocol was needed.

Interior Gateway Routing Protocol (IGRP) was not that protocol—OSPF was, but it wasn't coming fast enough. Cisco invented IGRP as an interim solution and carefully addressed the two largest problems with RIP:

- RIP puts out too much broadcast traffic.

- RIP assumes all links are the same speed.

Cisco addressed the issue of traffic volume by decreasing the frequency of routing updates—IGRP sends out a copy of it's routing table every 90 seconds instead of every 30 seconds like RIP. Unfortunately, the updates are broadcast just like RIP.

IGRP uses a complex metric that includes as variables the following:

- Bandwidth
- Delay
- Load (not used by default)
- Reliability (not used by default)

Maximum transmission unit (MTU) is tracked; this was meant to allow path MTU discovery, but it was never implemented. Hop count is also tracked, but strictly as a loop recognition technique.

IGRP is a Cisco proprietary classful IP routing protocol. By default, RIP and IGRP will be enabled on all interfaces that fall within the networks specified in the **network** command.

Unequal cost load balancing is a unique feature of IGRP and Enhanced IGRP (EIGRP). When unequal cost load balancing is active, the best metric to a route is multiplied by a whole-number variance. Any path lower than the product is load-balanced proportionally.

RIP Version 1

RIP v1 is a standard-based (RFC 1058) classful routing protocol that uses hop count as its metric. RIP broadcasts a copy of its route table every 30 seconds and, like all other IP routing protocols on a Cisco router, supports equal cost load balancing.

RIP Version 2

RIP v2 is a standards-based (RFC 1721, 1722, and 2453) classless routing protocol that uses hop count as its metric. Version 2 addresses several of the issues with Version 1:

- Version 2 is classless (VLSM).
- Version 2 supports route summarization and, by default, automatically summarizes at classful network boundaries. Automatic summarization can be disabled, and manual summarization configured.
- Version 2 uses multicasts instead of broadcasts
- Version 2 allows for authentication (plain text or MD5).

RIP is configured by entering the RIP router configuration mode and identifying the classful networks within which it should run. All interfaces on the router in the assigned networks run RIP.

```
Router(config)# router rip
Router(config-router)# network 192.168.1.0
```

By default, RIP sends version 1 and receives version 1 and 2 routes. To configure RIP to run only version 2 use the **version** command.

```
Router(config-router)# version 2
```

Configure specific interfaces to run either version 1 or 2 or both using the **ip rip send** or **ip rip receive** commands.

```
Router(config-router)# ip rip send version 2
Router(config-router)# ip rip receive version 2
```

Finally, configure a summary route out a particular interface using the **ip summary-address rip** command. Of course, automatic summarization is usually disabled also (**no auto-summary**). The following example advertises a default route out ethernet0 and a summary route 172.16.104.0/22 out serial0.

```
Router(config)# int e0
Router(config-if)# ip summary-address rip 0.0.0.0 0.0.0.0
Router(config)# int s0
Router(config-if)# ip summary-address rip 172.16.104.0 255.255.252.0
```

IP Routing Protocols

Administrative Distance

Cisco routers are capable of supporting several IP routing protocols concurrently. When identical prefixes are discovered from two or more separate protocols, administrative distance (AD) is used to discriminate between the paths. AD is really a poor choice of words—*trustworthiness* would be a better name. Routers use paths with the lower AD.

The following table lists the default values for various routing protocols. Of course, you have several ways to change AD for a routing protocol or for a specific route.

Information Source	AD
Connected	0
Static	1
External BGP	20
Internal EIGRP	90
IGRP	100
OSPF	110
IS-IS	115
RIP	120
ODR	160

Property	RIPv2	EIGRP	OSPF	IS-IS	BGP
Summarization	Auto and arbitrary	Auto and arbitrary	Arbitrary	Arbitrary	Auto and arbitrary
VLSM	Yes	Yes	Yes	Yes	Yes
Converge	Minutes	Seconds	Seconds	Seconds	Minutes
Timers: Update (hello/dead)	Update every 30 seconds	Triggered, (LAN 5/15, WAN 60/180)	Triggered, LSA refresh 30 minutes. (NBMA 30/120, LAN 10, 40)	Normal IS: Triggered (10/30), DIS 10 sec (3.3/10)	Triggered (60/180)

Information Source	AD
External EIGRP	170
Internal BGP	200
Unknown	255

Building the Routing Table

The router builds its routing table by ruling out invalid routes and carefully considering the remaining advertisements. The procedure is as follows:

- For each route received, verify the next hop. If invalid, discard the route.
- If more than one specific valid route is advertised by a routing protocol, choose the path with the lowest metric.
- If more than one specific valid route is advertised by different routing protocols, choose the path with the lowest AD.
- Routes are considered identical if they advertise the same prefix and mask, so 192.168.0.0/16 and 192.168.0.0/24 are separate paths and are entered into the routing table separately.

Comparing Routing Protocols

Generically, two things should always be considered in choosing a routing protocol: fast convergence speed and support for VLSM. EIGRP, OSPF, and IS-IS meet these criteria.

EIGRP is Cisco proprietary, but simple to configure and support. OSPF is standards based, but difficult to implement and support. IS-IS is an OSI network layer protocol that can carry IP information. It is fairly simple to configure and support, but not as full featured as OSPF.

The following table compares critical parts of all the routing protocols on the BSCI test.

Property	RIPv2	EIGRP	OSPF	IS-IS	BGP
Algorithm	Distance Vector	Advanced Distance Vector	Link State	Link State	Path vector

EIGRP

EIGRP Overview

EIGRP is a proprietary classless routing protocol that uses a complex metric that is based on bandwidth and delay. EIGRP addresses several issues with IGRP. The following are some features of EIGRP:

- Quick convergence.
- Support for VLSM.
- Is conservative of network bandwidth.
- Support for IP, AppleTalk, and IPX.
- Support for unequal-cost proportional load-balancing.
- Classless.
- Supports route summarization by default and automatically summarizes at classful network boundaries. Manual summarization can also be done with EIGRP.
- Uses multicasts (and unicasts where appropriate) instead of broadcasts.
- EIGRP supports authentication.

Database Structure

EIGRP uses three tables:

- The neighbor table is built from EIGRP hellos and used for reliable delivery.
- The topology table contains EIGRP routing information for best paths and loop-free alternatives.
- The routing table is used by EIGRP and other routing protocols for all best paths.

Route Selection

An EIGRP router receives advertisements from each neighbor that list the advertised distance and feasible distance to a route. *Advertised distance* is the metric from the neighbor to the network. *Feasible distance* is the metric from this router, through the neighbor, to the network.

The EIGRP path with the lowest feasible distance is called the successor path. Any EIGRP paths that have a lower advertised distance than the metric of the successor are guaranteed loop free and called feasible successors.

EIGRP Metric

The EIGRP metric is as follows:

$$Metric = 256(k1 \times \frac{10^7}{BW_{min}} + \frac{k2 \times BW_{min}}{256 - load} + k3 \times \sum Delays)(\frac{k5}{Reliability + k4})$$

The k values are constants. The defaults are k1 = 1, k2 = 0, k3 = 1, k4 = 0, and k5 = 0. If k5 = 0, the final part of the equation (k5 / [rel + k4]) is ignored. BW_{min} is the minimum bandwidth along the path—the choke point bandwidth. Delay values are associated with each interface. The sum of the delays (in 10s of microseconds) is used in the equation.

Taking the constants into account, the equation becomes this:

$$Metric = 256(\frac{10^7}{BW_{min}} + \sum Delays)$$

If default k values are used, this works out to be 256 (BW + cumulative delay). Bandwidth is the largest contributor to the metric. The delay value allows us to choose a more direct path when bandwidth is equivalent.

The EIGRP metric is 256 times the IGRP metric. The two automatically redistribute and algorithmically adjust metrics if they are configured on the same router for the same autonomous system.

EIGRP Messages

Packets

EIGRP uses five packet types:

- Hello—Identifies neighbors and serves as keepalive
- Update—Reliably sends route information
- Query—Reliably request specific route information
- Reply—Reliable response to query
- ACK—Acknowledgement

EIGRP is reliable, but not all traffic requires an ACK. Hellos and ACKs are not acknowledged.

When EIGRP first starts, it uses hellos to build a neighbor table. Neighbors are directly attached routers that agree on AS number and k values (timers don't have to agree). Subsequent traffic is sent with the expectation that each identified neighbor will respond.

If a reliable packet is not acknowledged, EIGRP periodically retransmits the packet to the non-responding neighbor as a unicast. EIGRP has a window size of one, so no other traffic is sent to this neighbor until it responds. After 16 retransmissions the neighbor is removed from the neighbor table.

Hellos also serve as keepalives. A neighbor is considered lost if no hello is received within three hello periods (called the hold time). The default timers are as follows:

- 5 seconds/15 seconds for multipoint circuits with bandwidth greater than T1 and for point-to-point media
- 60 seconds/180 seconds for other multipoint circuits with bandwidth less than or equal to T1

The neighbor table can be seen with the command **show ip eigrp neighbors**.

The process of route exchange between two EIGRP routers is as follows:

1. Router A sends out a hello.
2. Router B sends back a hello and an update. The update contains routing information.
3. Router A acknowledges the update.
4. Router A sends its update.
5. Router B acknowledges.

Hellos are used as keepalives from this point on. Additional route information is sent only if a route is lost or new route discovered.

The exchange process can be viewed using **debug ip eigrp packets**, and the update process can be seen using **debug ip eigrp**.

EIGRP DUAL

Diffusing Update Algorithm (DUAL)

DUAL is the algorithm used by EIGRP to choose best paths by looking at advertised distance (AD) and feasible distance (FD). Advertised distance is the metric from the neighbor to the destination. Feasible distance is the metric from this router, through the neighbor, to the destination. The path with the lowest metric is called the *successor* path. EIGRP paths with a lower advertised distance than the feasible distance of the successor path are guaranteed loop free and called *feasible successors*. If the successor path is lost, the router might start using the feasible successor immediately without fear of loops.

Feasible successors are not always available. If a successor path is lost and no backup path is identified, the router sends out queries on all interfaces trying to identify an alternate path.

Route Selection

An easy way to understand this is to consider a driving example. Located in Pittsburgh, you are told of three ways to New York:

- A direct path (435 miles)
- A path through Baltimore (AD: 224 miles, FD: 491 miles)
- A path through Chicago (AD: 851 miles, FD: 1319 miles)

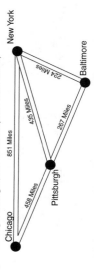

The direct path would be the successor path; it has the lowest metric.

The path through Baltimore would be a feasible successor—Baltimore is closer to New York (224 miles) than Pittsburgh (435 miles), so we're sure that going through Baltimore to New York doesn't involve looping back through Pittsburgh.

The path through Chicago would not be a feasible successor because Chicago (851 miles) is further away from New York than Pittsburgh (435 miles) and we can't say with certainty that traveling through Chicago to New York doesn't involve coming back through Pittsburgh.

Network Example

The following diagrams show EIGRP advertisements from the destination network to R3 and R5. R5 chooses R4 as the successor path because it is offering the lowest Feasible Distance. The Advertised Distance from R3 indicates that passing traffic through R3 will not loop, so R3 is a feasible successor.

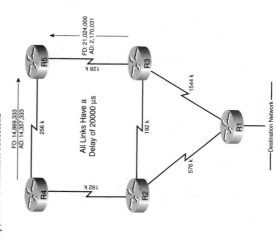

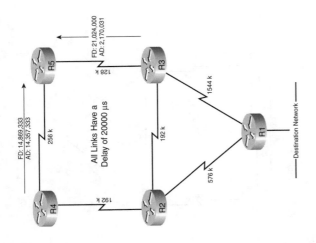

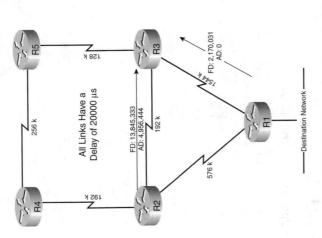

How does R3 choose its path? R1 will be the successor, but no feasible successor exists. If the direct path to R1 is lost then R3 has to query its neighbors to discover an alternative path. It waits to hear back from R2 and R5, but ultimately decides that R2 is the new successor.

Configuring EIGRP

Configuration

EIGRP is configured by entering router configuration mode and identifying the classful networks within which it should run. When setting up EIGRP, an autonomous system number must be used (7 is used in the example). Autonomous system numbers for EIGRP are not globally assigned, so most installations just make up numbers. Autonomous system numbers must agree for two routers to form a neighbor relationship and to exchange routes.

```
Router(config)# router eigrp 7
Router(config-router)# network 192.168.1.0
```

If a router has two interfaces—e0/0 (192.168.1.1/27) and e0/1 (192.168.1.33/27)—and needs to run only EIGRP on e0/0, the wildcard mask option can be used with the network command:

```
Router(config-router)# network 192.168.1.0 0.0.0.31
```

```
────── 192.168.1.0/27 ──────
```

Creating a Default Route

You can produce a default route in EIGRP in three ways:

- R1 can specify a default network:

```
R1(config)# ip default-network 10.0.0.0
```

R3 now sees a default network with a next hop of R1.

- Produce a summary route:

```
R1(config)# interface s0
R1(config-if)# ip summary-address eigrp 7 0.0.0.0 0.0.0.0
```

This passes a default route from R1 out its serial0 interface toward R3.

- Create a static default route and then include network 0.0.0.0 in EIGRP:

```
R1(config)# ip route 0.0.0.0 0.0.0.0 10.1.1.2
R1(config)# router eigrp 7
R1(config-router)# network 0.0.0.0
```

Troubleshooting EIGRP

The most straightforward way to troubleshoot EIGRP is to inspect the routing table—**show ip route**. To filter the routing table and show only the routes learned from EIGRP use **show ip route eigrp**.

show ip protocols is always the first place to check when investigating routing protocol issues. Use this command to verify autonomous system, timer values, identified networks, and EIGRP neighbors (routing information sources).

EIGRP specific issues can be investigated using **show ip eigrp topology**. This shows the EIGRP topology table and identifies successors and feasible successors.

Advanced EIGRP

Summarization

Just like RIPv2, EIGRP defaults to automatically summarizing at classful network boundaries. This is commonly disabled and arbitrary summarization is employed.

```
Router(config-router)# no auto-summary
```

Summaries can be produced manually on any interface. When a summary is produced, a matching route to null0 also becomes active as a loop prevention mechanism. Configure a summary route out a particular interface using the **ip summary-address eigrp** AS command. The following example uses EIGRP AS 7 and advertises a default route out ethernet0 and a summary route 172.16.104.0/22 out serial0.

```
Router(config)# int e0
Router(config-if)# ip summary-address eigrp 7 0.0.0.0 0.0.0.0
Router(config)# int s0
Router(config-if)# ip summary-address eigrp 7 172.16.104.0 255.255.252.0
```

Load Balancing

EIGRP, like most IP routing protocols on a Cisco router, automatically load balances over equal cost paths. What makes EIGRP unique is that it proportionally load balances over unequal cost paths. A variance is specified and load balancing is used for any path with a metric of less than the product of the variance and the best metric.

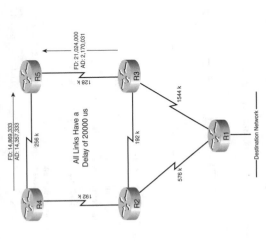

In this example, R5 uses the path through R4 since it offers the lowest metric (14,869,333). To set up unequal cost load balancing, assign a variance of 2, and now R5 uses all paths with a metric less than 29,738,666. This includes the path through R3.

```
R5(config-router)# variance 2
```

WAN Bandwidth

Other routing protocols burst to use all available link bandwidth. Because routing protocol traffic is treated as having a higher priority, this can sometimes lock out data traffic over WAN links. EIGRP is unique in offering a way to control this. By default, EIGRP limits itself to bursting to half the link bandwidth. This limit is configurable using the ip bandwidth-percent command. The following example assumes EIGRP AS 7 and limits EIGRP to a fourth of link bandwidth:

```
Router(config-if)# ip bandwidth-percent eigrp 7 25
```

The default value is acceptable in most cases. The real issue with WAN links is that the router assumes that each link has 1544 kbps bandwidth. If serial0 is attached to a 128 k fractional T1, EIGRP assumes it can burst to 768 k and could overwhelm the line. This is rectified by correctly identifying link bandwidth.

```
Router (config)# int serial 0
Router (config-if)# bandwidth 128
```

One situation suggests itself where all these techniques can be combined—Frame Relay.

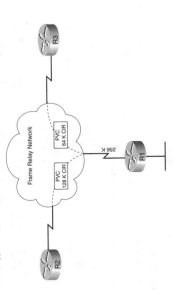

In this configuration, R1 has a 256 K connection to the Frame Relay network and two permanent virtual circuits (PVCs) with committed information rates (CIR) (minimum guaranteed bandwidth) of 128 K and 64 K. What value should be used for the interface bandwidth in this case? The usual suggestion is to use the CIR, but the two PVCs have different CIRs. Specifying a bandwidth of 128 on the main interface leads EIGRP to assume a bandwidth of 64 for each PVC, but causes the router to incorrectly report utilization through Simple Network Management Protocol (SNMP). We could use the bandwidth-percent command to allow a true bandwidth value while adjusting the burst rate to 64 for each PVC.

```
R1(config)# int serial 0
R1 (config-if)# bandwidth 256
R1 (config-if)# ip bandwidth-percent eigrp 7 25
```

A better solution is to use subinterfaces and identify bandwidth separately. In this case, s0.1 bursts to 64 k, and s0.2 bursts to 32 k.

```
R1(config)#int serial 0.1
R1(config-if)# bandwidth 128
R1(config)# int serial 0.2
R1(config-if)# bandwidth 10
R1(config-if)# ip bandwidth-percent eigrp 7 320
```

Notice that an arbitrarily low value has been used for the second PVC.

OSPF Overview

Dijkstra Algorithm

OSPF is an open standard classless routing protocol that converges quickly and uses cost as a metric (cost is by default automatically associated with bandwidth by Cisco IOS).

OSPF is a link-state routing protocol and uses Dijkstra's Shortest Path First (SPF) algorithm to determine best paths. The first responsibility of a link-state router is to create a database that reflects the structure of the network.

The router exchanges hellos with each neighbor, learning Router ID (RID) and cost.

The router then constructs a Link State Advertisement (LSA) with the RIDs and cost to each neighbor.

Each router in the routing domain shares its LSA with all other routers. Each router keeps the complete set of LSAs in a table—the Link State Database.

Each router runs the SPF algorithm to compute best paths.

Description of the SPF Algorithm

The following section is helpful for understanding the operation of the SPF algorithm, but it is not tested in this depth on the BSCI exam. The SPF algorithm uses four tables:

- **Link State Database**—All LSAs
- **Tentative**—A scratch pad table for the algorithm
- **Path**—The best OSPF path
- **Routing Table**—The best path given all sources

The SPF algorithm operates on each router in five steps:

Step 1 Place myself in path table with a cost of zero.

Step 2 For the new entry in the path table, look at its LSA in the Link State Database. Add the path cost to the node to the LSA cost. For each neighbor, if not already in the path or tentative table with a better cost, place in the tentative table.

Step 3 If the tentative table is empty, stop.

Step 4 Find the lowest cost entry in the tentative table and move to it to the path table.

Step 5 Go to Step 2.

For example, consider the following network.

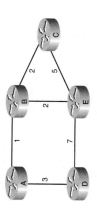

Router B builds an LSA that says, "My name is B, and I have a neighbor A with a cost of 1, neighbor C with a cost of 2, and neighbor E with a cost of 2."

The LSAs are distributed, and the Dijkstra algorithm is run.

Router B starts by placing itself at the root of the network with a cost of zero. B's LSA is added to the tent.

Topology	Path	Tent
B	B cost 0	A cost 1
		C cost 2
		E cost 2

The lowest cost entry in tent is A, so it is moved to the path and its LSA is incorporated in the tentative database. Because B is already in the path, an entry for B (via A) is not added to the tentative database.

Topology	Path	Tent
B	B cost 0	C cost 2
|	A cost 1	D via A cost 1 + 3 = 4
A		E cost 2

The lowest cost entry in tent is now C or E. Choosing C, it is moved to the path and its LSA is incorporated in the tentative database. Because E is already in the tentative database with a lower cost, the entry for E (via C) is not added to the tentative database.

Topology	Path	Tent
B /\ A C	B cost 0 A cost 1 C cost 2	D via A cost 1 + 3 = 4 E cost 2

The lowest cost entry in tent is now E. It is moved to the path and its LSA is incorporated in the tentative database. Because D is already in the tentative database with a lower cost, the entry for D (via E) is not added to the tentative database.

Topology	Path	Tent
B /\ A C E	B cost 0 A cost 1 C cost 2 E cost 2	D via A cost 1 + 3 = 4

The lowest cost entry in tent is now D. It is moved to the path and its LSA is incorporated in the tentative database. Because E and A are already in the path database with a lower cost, the tentative database is now empty.

Topology	Path	Tent
B /\ A C E | D	B cost 0 A cost 1 C cost 2 E cost 2 D cost 4	

The algorithm is now complete, and the best paths from B to any other location are now incorporated from the path database into the routing table.

Network Structure

OSPF routing domains are broken up into areas. The SPF algorithm runs within an area, and inter-area routes are passed between areas. A two-level hierarchy to OSPF areas exists—other areas are always attached directly to area 0 and only to area 0.

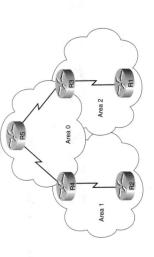

OSPF areas do the following:

- Minimize the number of routing table entries and the number of times the SPF algorithm is run.
- Contain LSA flooding to a reasonable area.
- Are recommended to contain 50–100 routers.

Router roles are defined as well.

An internal router has all interfaces in one area (R5, R2, R1).

An Area Border Router (ABR) has interfaces in two or more areas (R3, R4).

An Autonomous System Boundary Router (ASBR) has interfaces inside and outside the OSPF routing domain.

LSA Update

Each router maintains a database of the latest received LSAs. Each LSA is numbered with a sequence number, and a timer is run to age out old LSAs.

When a LSA is received, it's compared to the LS database. If it is new then it is added to the database and the SPF algorithm is run. If it is from a Router ID that is already in the database, then the sequence number is compared, and older LSAs are discarded. If it is a new LSA, it is incorporated in the database, and the SPF algorithm is run. If it is an older LSA, the newer LSA in memory is sent back to whoever sent the old one.

Configuring Single Area OSPF

Configuration

OSPF is configured by entering router configuration mode and identifying the range of interface addresses on which it should run and the areas they are in. When setting up OSPF, a process ID must be used (8 is used in the example), but the process ID does not have to agree on different OSPF devices for them to exchange information. The network statement uses a wildcard mask and can specify any range from a single address to all addresses.

```
Router(config)# router ospf 8
Router(config-router)# network 192.168.1.0 0.0.0.255 area 0
```

Troubleshooting OSPF

The first place OSPF issues are noticed is when inspecting the routing table—**show ip route**. To filter the routing table and only show the routes learned from OSPF use **show ip route ospf**.

show ip protocols should be used next. It offers a wealth of information for any routing protocol issue. Use this command to verify parameters, timer values, identified networks, and OSPF neighbors ("routing information sources").

Because wildcard masks sometimes incorrectly group interfaces to areas, another good place to check is **show ip ospf interface**. This shows the interfaces on which OSPF is running and their current correct assigned area.

show ip ospf shows the RID, timers, and counters. **show ip ospf neighbor** shows the OSPF neighbor table, identifies adjacency status, and reveals the designated router and backup designated router.

Router ID

The SPF algorithm is used to map the shortest path between a series of nodes. The issue is that an IP router is not identified by a single number—its interfaces are. For reasons of compatibility with the protocol a single address is used as the "name" of the router—the Router ID (RID).

By default, the Router ID is the highest loopback IP address. If no loopback addresses are configured, the RID is the highest IP address on an active interface when the OSPF process is started. The router ID is selected when OSPF starts and—for reasons of stability—is not changed until OSPF restarts. Of course, the OSPF process can be restarted by rebooting or by using the command **clear ip ospf process**. Either choice affects routing in your network for a period of time and should be used only with caution.

A loopback interface is a virtual interface. A loopback address is configured by creating an interface and assigning an IP address.

```
Router(config)# interface loopback0
Router(config-if)# ip address 10.0.0.1 255.255.255.255
```

The loopback address does not have to be included in the OSPF routing process, but it often is to provide a location to ping or trace to.

A way to short-circuit the RID selection is to assign it using the OSPF **router-id** command.

```
Router(config)# router ospf 8
Router(config-router)# router-id 10.0.0.1
```

Low-Level OSPF

Packets

OSPF uses five packet types:

- **Hello**—Identifies neighbors and serves as keepalive.
- **Link State Request (LSR)**—A request for an LSU. Contains the type of LSU requested and the ID of the router requesting it.
- **Database Description (DBD)**—A summary of the Link State Database, including the RID and sequence number of each LSA in the Link State Database.
- **Link State Update (LSU)**—Contains a full LSA (link state advertisement) entry. An LSA includes topology information, for example the RID of this router and the RID and cost to each neighbor. One LSU can contain multiple LSAs.
- **Link State Acknowledgment (LSAck)**—Acknowledges all other OSPF packets (except hellos).

All five packet types are directly placed into an IP packet (IP protocol 89) using a common OSPF header.

Neighborship

OSPF routers send out periodic multicast packets to introduce themselves to other routers on a link. They become neighbors when they hear their own router ID included in the hello of another router, thus proving bidirectional communication.

OSPF traffic is multicast to either of two addresses:

224.0.0.5—All SPF Routers

224.0.0.6—All SPF DRs

OSPF routers, if certain parameters agree, become neighbors when they see themselves in the "neighbors" field of an incoming hello. The following must match:

- Hello/dead timers
- Area ID
- Authentication type and password
- Common subnet
- Stub area flag

OSPF routers can be neighbors without being adjacent. Only adjacent neighbors exchange routing updates and synchronize their databases. On a point-to-point link, an adjacency is established between the two routers when they can communicate. On a multiaccess link, each router establishes an adjacency only with the DR and the backup DR (BDR).

Hellos also serve as keepalives. A neighbor is considered lost if no Hello is received within four Hello periods (called the dead time). The default timers are as follows:

- 10 seconds/40 seconds for LAN and point-to-point interfaces
- 30 seconds/120 seconds for nonbroadcast multiaccess (NBMA) interfaces

The neighbor table can be seen with **show ip ospf neighbors.**

The process of route exchange between two OSPF routers is as follows:

1. **Down state:** No hellos sent.
2. **Init state:** Router sends hello packets out all OSPF interfaces.
3. **Two-way state:** Router receives a hello from another router that contains its own router ID in the neighbor list.
4. **Exstart state:** Routers determine who will start the exchange process.
5. **Exchange state:** Routers exchange DBDs listing the LSAs in their LS database by RID and sequence number.
6. **Loading state:** Each router compares the DBD received to the contents of its LS database. It then sends a Link State Request for missing or outdated LSAs. Each router responds to its neighbor's LSR with a Link State Update. Each LSU is acknowledged.
7. **Full state:** The LS database has been synchronized with the adjacent neighbor.

Sequence Numbers

OSPF sequence numbers are 32 bits. The first legal sequence number is 0x80000001. Larger numbers are more recent.

Normally, the sequence number changes only under two conditions:

- The LSA changes because a route is added or deleted.
- The LSA ages out (LSAs are updated every half hour, even if nothing changes).

The command **show ip ospf database** shows the age (in seconds) and sequence number for each RID.

Troubleshooting

The neighbor initialization process can be viewed using **debug ip ospf adjacencies.** All OSPF traffic can be seen from **debug ip ospf packet.**

OSPF Network Types

Expectations of Dijkstra's SPF Algorithm

The SPF algorithm builds a directed graph—paths made up of a series of points connected by direct links. One of the consequences of this "directed graph" approach is that the algorithm has no way to handle a multiaccess network. The solution used is to elect one router to represent the entire segment—a designated router (DR).

Designated Routers

Point-to-point links fit the SPF model perfectly and don't need any special modeling method. On a point-to-point link, no DR is elected and all traffic is multicast to 224.0.0.5.

On a multiaccess link one of the routers is elected as a designated router (DR) and another as a backup DR (BDR). All other routers on that link become adjacent only to the DR and BDR, not to each other (they stop at the *two-way state*). The DR is responsible for creating and flooding a network LSA (type 2) advertising the multiaccess link. Non-DR (DROTHER) routers communicate with the DRs using IP address 224.0.0.6. The DRs use IP address 224.0.0.5 to pass information to other routers.

The DR and BDR are elected as follows:

- A starting router listens for OSPF hellos. If none are heard within the dead time, it declares itself the DR.
- If one or more other routers are heard, the router with the highest OSPF priority is elected DR, and the election process starts again for BDR. Priority of zero removes a router from the election.
- If two or more routers have the same OSPF priority, the router with the highest RID is elected DR, and the election process starts again for BDR.

- Broadcast—Default mode for LANs. Uses DRs and automatic neighbor discovery. Proprietary when used on WAN interface.
- Point-to-point (P2P)—Proprietary mode that discovers neighbors and doesn't use DR.

Mode	RFC or Cisco	DR	Adjacencies	Neighbor Discovery	Timers Hello/Dead	Topo
NBMA	RFC	Yes	2n–3	Manual	30/120	Full
P2MP	RFC	No	n(n–1)/2	Automatic	30/120	Any
P2MPNB	Cisco	No	n(n–1)/2	Manual	30/120	Any
Broadcast	Cisco	Yes	2n–3	Automatic	10/40	Full
P2P	Cisco	No	1	Automatic	10/40	P2P

The interface type is selected—assuming the default is unsatisfactory—using the command ip ospf network:

```
Router(config-if)# ip ospf network point-to-multipoint
```

When using the NBMA or P2MP non-broadcast mode, neighbors must be manually defined under the routing process:

```
Router(config-router)# neighbor 172.16.0.1
```

- DR election does not take place again unless the DR or BDR are lost. Because of this, the DR is sometimes the first device started with a non-zero priority.

As mentioned, the best way to specify a router to be the DR is to use the OSPF priority. The default priority is one. A priority of zero means that a router does not act as DR or BDR—it can be only a DROTHER. Priority can be set with the ip ospf priority command in interface configuration mode.

```
Router(config)# int ethernet 0
Router(config-if)# ip ospf priority 2
```

Nonbroadcast Multiaccess Networks

Routing protocols assume that multiaccess links support broadcast and have full connectivity (from any device to any device). In terms of OSPF, this means the following:

- All Frame Relay or ATM maps should include the broadcast attribute.
- DR and BDR should have full VC connectivity to all other devices.
- Hub-and-spoke environments should either have the DR as the hub or be configured using point-to-point subinterfaces.
- Partial mesh environments should be configured using point-to-point subinterfaces, especially when no single device has full connectivity to all other devices. If there is a subset of the topology with full connectivity, then that subset can use a multipoint subinterface.
- Full mesh environments can be configured on the main interface, but often logical interfaces are used to take advantage of the other benefits of subinterfaces.

OSPF supports five network types:

- NBMA—Default for multipoint serial interfaces. RFC-compliant mode that uses DRs and requires manual neighbor configuration.
- Point-to-multipoint (P2MP)—Doesn't use DRs so adjacencies increase logarithmically with routers. Resilient RFC compliant mode that automatically discovers neighbors.
- Point-to-multipoint nonbroadcast (P2MNB)—Proprietary mode that is used on Layer 2 facilities where dynamic neighbor discovery is not supported. Requires manual neighbor configuration.

OSPF Advertisements and Cost

LSA Types

OSPF advertises many different things in different ways. The type of advertisement establishes context for its contents.

Type	Description	Routing Table Symbol
1	Intra-area LSA of a router	O
2	Intra-area LSA of DR	O
3	Inter-area route passed by ABR	O IA
4	Inter-area route to an ASBR	O IA
5	External type 2 route from ASBR. Metric doesn't accrue in OSPF (default).	O E2
5	External type 1 route from ASBR. Metric accumulates in OSPF.	O E1
6	Multicast (not used by Cisco)	N/A
7	Not-so-stubby area (NSSA) external route passed through stubby area	O N2 O N1

Cost

By default, Cisco assigns a cost to each interface that is inversely proportional to 100 Mbps.

$$Cost = \frac{100\ Mbps}{Bandwidth}$$

The default formula doesn't differentiate between fast ethernet and gigabit ethernet, for example. In such cases, the cost formula can be adjusted using the auto-cost command. Values for bandwidth (in Kb) up to 4,294,967 are permitted (1 Gb is shown in the example).

```
Router(config-router)# auto-cost reference-bandwidth 1000000
```

The cost can also be manually assigned under interface configuration mode. Cost is a 16-bit number, so can be any value up to 65,535.

```
Router(config-router)# ip ospf cost 27
```

OSPF Summarization

OSPF Benefits of Summarization

All routing protocols benefit from summarization, but OSPF especially benefits because it is already sensitive to the memory and CPU speed of the routers. Summarization prevents topology changes from being passed outside an area and thus saves routers in other areas from having to run the SPF algorithm. OSPF can produce summaries within a classful network (VLSM) or summaries of blocks of classful networks (CIDR).

Creating a Summary

Inter-area summarizations are created on the ABR under the router process using the area range command. The following command advertises 172.16.0.0/12 from area zero.

```
Router(config-router)# area 0 range 172.16.0.0 255.240.0.0
```

Summarizing external routes is done on an ASBR with the summary-address command under the routing process. The following example summarizes a range of external routes to 192.168.0.0/16 and injects a single route into OSPF.

```
Router(config-router)# summary-address 192.168.0.0 255.255.0.0
```

Creating a Default Route

The default route is a special type of summarization—it summarizes everything. This provides the ultimate benefit of summarization by reducing the routing information to a minimum. Several different ways to use the router IOS to place a default route into OSPF.

The best-known way to produce an OSPF default is to use the default-information command:

```
Router(config-router)# default-information originate [always]
```

This command, without the keyword **always**, readvertises a default learned from another source into OSPF. If the **always** keyword is present, OSPF advertises a default even if one does not already exist.

A default summary can also be produced using the **summary-address** command or the **area range** command (to just produce a default into an area). Reducing routing information in non-backbone areas is a common requirement because these routers are the most vulnerable, in terms of processor and speed, and the links that connect them have the least bandwidth. A specific concern is that an area will be overwhelmed by external routing information.

Making an area a **stub** area forces its ABR to drop all external (type 5) routes and replaces them with a default route. In some cases an area can be made totally stubby (**stub no-summary**), in which case all inter-area and external routes are replaced by a default.

```
Router(config-router)# area 7 stub [no-summary]
```

Stub areas are attractive because of their low overhead. They do have some limitations, including the following:

- Stub areas can't include a virtual link.
- Stub areas can't include an ASBR.
- Stubbiness must be configured on all routers in the area.

A third kind of stubby area is a not-so-stubby area (NSSA). NSSA is like a stub or totally stub area, but allows an ASBR within the area. External routes are advertised as type 7 routes and sent to the ABR, which converts them to traditional type 5 external routes. The NSSA area allows the network to adapt to your company's physical topology and has advantages in terms of filtering and summarization of external routes. An NSSA area is identified with the **area nssa** command:

```
Router(config-router)# area 7 nssa [no-summary]
```

IS-IS

Intermediate System-to-Intermediate System (IS-IS) is a link state routing protocol that is part of the OSI family of protocols. Integrated IS-IS can carry IP network information, but does not use IP as its transport protocol. It uses CLNS and CLNP to deliver its

updates. IS-IS is a classless interior gateway protocol that uses router resources efficiently, and scales to very large networks, such as large Internet service providers (ISPs).

IS-IS Acronyms

Term	Acronym	Description
Intermediate System	IS	The OSI name for a router.
End system	ES	A host, such as a computer.
Connectionless Network Services	CNLS	An OSI data delivery service that provides best-effort delivery.
Connectionless Network Protocol	CLNP	The OSI protocol used to provide the connectionless services.
End system hello	ESH	Sent by hosts to routers
Intermediate System hello	ISH	Sent by routers to hosts
IS to IS hello	IIH	Hellos exchanged between routers. Seperate level 1 and level 2 IIHs exist
Type Length Value	TLV	Fields in the IS-IS updates that contain IP subnet, authentication, and end system information
Network Service Access Point	NSAP	The address of a CLNS device. Addresses are assigned per device, not per interface as with IP.

Term	Acronym	Description
Network Entity Title	NET	A router's NSAP. The last byte of a NET is always zero.
NSAP Selector	NSEL	The last byte of a NSAP address. Identifies the process on the device, such as routing.
Link State PDU	LSP	A routing update.
Subnetwork Point of Attachment	SNPA	Layer 2 identification for a router's interface, such as MAC address or DLCI.
Circuit ID		Identifies a physical interface on the router.
Link State Database	LSDB	
Sequence Number Protocol Data Unit	SNP	An IS-IS packet that is sequenced and must be acknowledged. The sequence number helps a router maintain the most recent link state information.
Complete Sequence Number PDU	CSNP	A summary of a router's complete Link State Database.
Partial Sequence Number PDU	PSNP	Used to acknowledge receipt of a CSNP and to request more information about a network contained in a CSNP.
Partial route calculation	PRC	Used to determine end system and IP subnet reachability.

Types of IS-IS Routers

An IS-IS network is divided into areas. Within an area, routers can be one of three types:

- **Level 1 (L1) router**—Routes to networks only within the local area (intra-area routing). Uses a default route to the nearest Level 2 router for traffic bound outside the area. Routing is based on System ID. Keeps one LSDB for the local area. (R1, R2, and R5 in this figure.)

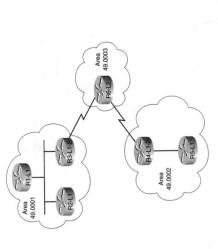

- **Level 2 (L2) router**—Routes to networks in other areas (interarea routing). The routing is based on area ID. Keeps one LSDB for routing to other areas. (R6 in this figure.)
- **Level 1-2 (L1-2) router**—Acts as a gateway into and out of an area. Does Level 1 routing within the area and Level 2 routing between areas. Keeps two LSDB, one for the local area and one for interarea routing. (R3 and R4 in this figure.)

The IS-IS backbone is not a specific area, as in OSPF, but an unbroken chain of routers doing Level 2 routing. R3, R6, and R4 are the backbone in this figure.

NSAP Address Structure

Area ID—1 to 13 bytes long	System ID—Must be exactly 6 bytes long	NSEL—1 byte

In Cisco implementation of integrated IS-IS, NSAP addresses have three parts. A router always has a NSEL of 00. An area ID that begins with 49 designates private area addressing. MAC addresses or IP addresses padded with 0s are often used as system IDs.

Adjacency Formation in IS-IS

IS-IS routers form adjacencies based on the level of IS routing they are doing and their area number. This is a CLNS adjacency and can be formed even if IP addresses don't match.

- Level 1 routers form adjacencies only with L1 and L1-2 devices in their own area. (In the previous figure, R1 with R2 and R3.)
- Level 2 routers form adjacencies only with Level 2 capable devices (either L2 or L1-2 routers). These can be in the local area or in other areas. (In the previous figure, R6 with R3 and R4
- Level 1-2 routers form Level 1 adjacencies with L1 routers in their own area, and Level 2 adjacencies with routers in other areas. (In the previous figure, R4 has a L1 adjacency with R5 and a L2 adjacency with R6.)

IS-IS in a Broadcast, Multiaccess Network

On a network such as Ethernet, IS-IS routers elect a Designated Intermediate System (DIS). The DIS is elected based on priority, with MAC address as the tiebreaker. Routers form adjacencies with all routers on the LAN as well as the DIS. The DIS creates a *pseudonode* to represent the network and sends out an advertisement to represent the LAN. All routers advertise only an adjacency to the pseudonode. If the DIS fails, another is elected; no backup DIS exists. The DIS sends Hellos every 3.3 seconds; other routers send them every 10 seconds. The DIS also multicasts a CSNP every 10 seconds.

IS-IS on a Point-to-Point Link

No DIS exists on a point-to-point link. When an adjacency is first formed over the link, the routers exchange CSNPs. If one of the routers needs more information about a specific network, it sends a PSNP requesting that. After the initial exchange, LSPs are sent to describe link changes, and they are acknowledged with PSNPs.

IS-IS Configuration Tasks

- Enable IS-IS on the router.
- Configure each router's NET.
- Enable IS-IS on the router's interfaces.

Basic IS-IS Commands

Command	Description
router isis	Enables IS-IS on the router
net	Assigns the router's NSAP address
ip router isis	Enables IS-IS on an interface
is-type	Sets the IS level for the whole router
isis circuit-type	Sets the IS level for an interface
isis metric	Changes the metric for an interface
summary-address	Summarizes IP networks for IS-IS
show isis topology	Displays the topology database and least cost paths
show clns route	Displays the L2 routing table
show isis route	Displays the L1 routing table—requires CLNS routing enabled
show clns protocol	Displays the router's IS type, system ID, area ID, interfaces running IS-IS, and any redistribution
show clns neighbors	Displays the adjacent neighbors and their IS level
show clns interface	Displays IS-IS details for each interface, such as circuit type, metric, and priority
show ip protocols	Displays the integrated IS-IS settings

Tuning IS-IS

You need to do three basic types of tuning to IS-IS routers:

- Set the IS level.
- Set the circuit type on L1-2 routers.
- Summarize addresses.

Setting the IS Level

Cisco routers are L1-2 by default. If the router is completely an internal area router, set the IS level to L1. If the router routes only to other areas and has no internal area interfaces, set the IS level to L2. If the router has both internal and external area interfaces, leave the IS level at L1-2.

Setting the Circuit Type

On L1-2 routers, all interfaces send out both L1 and L2 hellos, trying to establish both types of adjacencies. This can waste bandwidth. If only an L1 router is attached to an interface, then change the circuit type for that interface to L1, so that only L1 hellos are sent. If there is only a L2 router attached to an interface, change the circuit type for that interface to L2.

Summarizing Addresses

Although IS-IS does CLNS routing, it can summarize the IP addresses that it carries. Summarized routes can be designated as Level 1, Level 2, or Level 1-2 routes. The default is Level 2.

Optimizing Routing

Migrating IP Addressing

Most networks operate more efficiently when using a modern routing protocol. When migrating to a new routing protocol, you might also need to change IP address schemes. You often change IP addressing when moving from a FLSM protocol to a VLSM one, or to create route summary points within the network. Here are some areas to consider when planning this:

- Host addresses—Change or add DHCP.
- NAT—Translate the new addresses.

- DNS servers—If server have new addresses, new DNS mappings made need to be configured.
- Access lists and firewalls—Update traffic filters to work for the new addresses.
- Routing—Update routers to route for the new networks.
- Secondary addressing—You might need to have both old and new addresses on the router interfaces during transition.
- Timing of the transition—Who gets converted when. Considers the day of the week and time of day.
- Transition strategy—Which parts of the network are changed first, second, etc. How to avoid disrupting user traffic during the transition.

Migrating Routing Protocols

The steps in migrating to a new routing protocol are as follows:

Step 1	Decide on a timeline for the migration.
Step 2	Identify boundary routers that are to run both protocols.
Step 3	Decide which protocol is to be the core and which is to be the edge protocol.
Step 4	Decide where and in what direction to redistribute routes.
Step 5	Test the plan in a lab.
Step 6	Back up all device configurations before changing them.

Route redistribution can cause problems because of route feedback, incompatible metrics, and inconsistent convergence times. The safest way to run multiple protocols is to redistribute the edge protocol into the core, and send a default route or use static routing back to the edge. The next best way is to redistribute both ways and filter to avoid route feedback distance, or change the administrative distance of redistributed routes.

Each protocol has some unique characteristics when redistributing, as shown in the following table.

Route Redistribution Characteristics

RIP	Metric must be set except when redistributing static or connected routes, which have a metric of 1.
OSPF	Default metric is 20. Can specify the metric type; the default is E2. Must use **subnets** keyword or only classful networks are redistributed.
EIGRP	Metric must be set, except when redistributing static or connected routes, which get their metric from the interface. Metric value is "bandwidth, delay, reliability, load, MTU." Redistributed routes have a higher administrative distance than internal ones.
IS-IS	Default metric is 0. Can specify route level; default is L2. Can choose to redistribute only external or internal routes into IS-IS from OSPF and into OSPF from IS-IS.
Static/Connected	Only routes that are in the routing table and learned via the specified protocol are redistributed. To include local networks, you must redistribute connected interfaces. You can also redistribute static routes into a dynamic protocol.

Seed Metric

Redistribution involves configuring a routing protocol to advertise routes learned by another routing process. Protocols use incompatible metrics, so the redistributed routes must be assigned a new metric compatible with the new protocol. Normally, metrics are based on an interface value, such as bandwidth, but no interface for a redistributed route exists. A route's original metric is called its *seed metric*.

Set the metric for all redistributed routes with the **default-metric** [*metric*] command. To set the metric for specific routes, either use the **metric** keyword when redistributing or use the **route-map** keyword to link a route map to the redistribution.

Configuring Route Redistribution

You can redistribute between protocols that use the same protocol stack, e.g., IP protocols cannot advertise IPX routes. Configuring redistribution is simple; issue this command under the routing process that is to receive the new routes:

redistribute [*route source*]

Tools for Controlling/Preventing Routing Updates

- Passive interface
- Default and/or static routes
- Distribute list
- Route map
- Change administrative distance

Passive Interface

Passive interface prevents RIP and IGRP from sending updates out an interface. It prevents other routing protocols from sending hellos out of an interface; thus, they don't discover neighbors or form an adjacency out that interface. RIP, IGRP, and older versions of EIGRP require a classful network in the **network** statement. To avoid running the protocol all interfaces within that network, use the **passive-interface** command and specify an interface that doesn't run the protocol. To turn off the protocol on all interfaces, use **passive-interface default**, then **no passive-interface** for the ones that should run the protocol.

Distribute Lists

A distribute list allows you to filter routing updates through an access list. Configure an access list and then link that access list to the routing process with the **distribute-list** command.

The **distribute-list** command has two options:

- **distribute-list** [ACL] **in**—Filters updates as they come in an interface. For OSPF, this controls routes placed in the routing table but not the database. For other protocols, this controls the routes the protocol knows about.
- **distribute-list** [ACL] **out**—Filters updates going out of an interface and also updates being redistributed in from another protocol.

Route Maps

Route maps *match* conditions, and then *set* options for traffic that matches. Each statement has a sequence number, statements are read from the lowest number to highest, and the router stops reading when it gets a match. The sequence number can be used to insert or delete statements. Here are some uses for route maps:

- **Filtering redistributed routes**—Use the **route-map** keyword in the **redistribute** command.

- **NAT**—To specify the private addresses to be translated.

- **Policy-based routing**—To specify which traffic should be policy routed, based on very granular controls.

- **BGP policy**—To control routing updates and to manipulation path attributes.

Route Map Syntax

Route maps are created with the command:

route-map [*name*] **permit** | **deny** [*sequence no.*]

Each statement in a route map begins this same way, with the same route map name but different sequence numbers, and with *match* and/or *set* conditions below it. *Permit* means that any traffic matching the *match* conditions is used. *Deny* means that any traffic matching the *match* conditions is not used.

Match and Set Conditions

Each route map statement can have from none to multiple **match** and **set** lines. If no match line exists, the statement matches anything, similar to a "permit any" in an access list. If there is no **set** line, the matching traffic is either permitted or denied, with no other conditions being set.

Multiple **match** conditions on the same line use a logical OR. For example, the router interprets **match a b c** as "match a or b or c." Multiple **match** conditions on different lines use a logical AND. For example, the router interprets the following as "match a and b and c":

```
match a
match b
match c
```

In route redistribution, here are some common things to match:

- **ip address**—Refers the router to an access list that permits or denies networks.

- **ip next-hop**—Refers the router to an access list that permits or denies next-hop IP addresses.

- **ip route-source**—Refers the router to an access list that permits or denies advertising router IP addresses.

- **metric**—Permits or denies routes with the specified metric from being redistributed.

- **route-type**—Permits or denies redistribution of the route type listed, such as internal or external.

- **tag**—Routes can be labeled (tagged) with a number, and route maps can look for that number.

In route redistribution, some common things to set are

- **metric**—Sets the metric for redistributed routes

- **metric-type**—Sets the type, such as E1 for OSPF

- **tag**—Tags a route with a number that can be matched on later by other route maps

- **level**—For IS-IS, sets the IS level for this route

Route Map Example

```
route-map Demo permit 10
match ip address 23
set metric 550
route-map Demo permit 20
```

Manipulating Administrative Distance

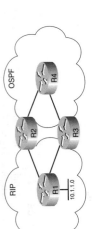

When a router receives routes to the same destination network from more than one routing process, it decides which to put in the routing table by looking at the administrative distance (AD) value assigned to the routing process. The route with the lowest AD is chosen. AD can be changed for all routes of a process, or only for specific routes within a process. The command is as follows:

distance {*admin distance*} [*address mask*] [*ACL*]

Using the **address/mask** keywords in the command changes the AD of routes learned from the neighbor with that IP address. Specifying an access list number or name changes the AD only on networks permitted in the ACL. EIGRP and BGP have different AD values for internal and external routes, so you have to list those separately when using the command with those protocols.

In the previous figure, look at the path to the 10.1.1.0 network. Redistribute RIP into OSPF on R2. These routes inherit OSPF's AD when they are advertised to R4. R4 then advertises them to R3 as OSPF routes. We have route feedback. R3 now knows about the 10.1.1.0 network from two routing processes: RIP, with an AD of 120, and OSPF, with an AD of 110. The path for RIP is through R1, the shortest path. The path for OSPF is through R4 and R2, then to R1—a much longer path. But the router puts the OSPF path in the routing table, based on AD.

To prevent this, increase the AD of the redistributed RIP routes when OSPF advertises them. Note—this doesn't change all OSPF routes, just the ones learned from RIP. The commands, given on R2, are

```
access-list 10 permit 10.1.1.0
router ospf 1
  redistribute rip subnets
  distance 125 0.0.0.0 255.255.255.255 10
```

Now R3 hears about the 10.1.1.0 network from RIP with an AD of 120, and from OSPF with an AD of 125. The RIP route is, therefore, put into the routing table.

Policy-Based Routing

Routers normally route traffic based on destination network. Policy-based routing (PBR) overrides this and causes them to choose a path based on the following:

• Port number of the application used
• Protocol number
• Packet size

PBR lets you load share based on characteristics of the traffic, rather than bandwidth of the links, and you also can set quality of service (QoS) values. It is applied to packets as they enter the router, and is configured by using route maps.

PBR Basics

1. Configure a route map to match traffic against either a standard or extended access list, or packet length.
2. If traffic matches the conditions and the route map statement is a *permit*, policy route the traffic.

3. If traffic matches the conditions and the route map statement is a *deny*, do normal routing.
4. If all the statements in the route map have been checked and no match exists, route the traffic normally (based on destination).

Configuring PBR

You can set the following options in the route map:

• **ip next-hop**—The IP address of the next hop router. The router checks the routing table to make sure this next hop is reachable.
• **interface**—The outbound interface for the traffic. An explicit route must already be in the routing table for the destination network, but this statement overrides it.
• **ip default next-hop**—The IP address of a next hop router to send traffic if there is no explicit route for the destination network in the routing table.
• **default interface**—The outbound interface for traffic for which there is no explicit route in the routing table.
• **ip tos**—Sets the type of service bits in the IP header; used for QoS purposes.
• **ip precedence**—Sets the precedence value in the IP header; used for QoS purposes.

The policy must be applied to the incoming interface with the command **ip policy route-map** *<route map name>*. Verify the policy with the following commands:

• show ip policy
• ping
• traceroute
• show route-map *<name>*
• debug ip policy

BGP

BGP Basics

• BGP stands for Border Gateway Protocol.
• BGP uses the concept of autonomous systems. An autonomous system is a group of networks under a common administration.
• Autonomous systems run Interior Gateway Protocols (IGPs) within the system. They run an Exterior Gateway Protocols (EGP) between them.
• BGP version 4 is the only EGP currently in use.

- BGP neighbors are called *peers* and must be statically configured.
- Uses TCP port 179.
- BGP is a path-vector protocol. Its route to a network consists of a list of autonomous systems on the path to that network.
- BGP's loop prevention mechanism is autonomous system number. When an update about a network leaves an autonomous system, that autonomous system's number is prepended to the list of autonomous systems that have handled that update. When an autonomous system receives an update, it examines the autonomous system list. If it finds its own autonomous number in that list, the update is discarded.

Example: In the following figure, BGP routers in AS100 see network 10.1.1.0 as having an autonomous system path of 200 300 400.

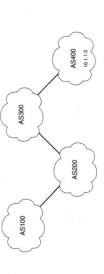

BGP Databases

- **Neighbor database**—List of all configured BGP neighbors. To view, type **show ip bgp summary**.
- **BGP database, or RIB (Routing Information Base)**—List of networks known by BGP, along with their paths and attributes. To view, type **"show ip bgp"**.
- **Routing table**—List of the paths to each network used by the router, and the next hop for each network. To view, type **show ip route**.

BGP Message Types

- **Open message**—After a neighbor is configured, BGP sends an open message to try to establish a peering with that neighbor. Includes information such as autonomous system number, router ID, and hold time.
- **Update message**—Message used to transfer routing information between peers.
- **Keepalive message**—BGP peers exchange keepalive messages every 60 seconds by default. These keep the peering session active.

- **Notification message**—If a problem occurs that causes the BGP peer to be ended, a notification message is sent to the BGP neighbor, and the connection is closed.

Internal and External BGP

Internal BGP (iBGP) is a BGP peering between routers in the same autonomous system. External BGP (eBGP) is a BGP peering between routers in different autonomous systems. BGP treats updates from internal peers differently than updates from external peers. In this figure, routers A and B are eBGP peers. Routers B, C and D are iBGP peers.

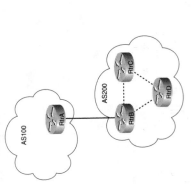

BGP Split Horizon Rule

Routes learned from iBGP neighbors are not forwarded to other iBGP neighbors. BGP assumes that all internal BGP routers are fully meshed, so if one internal router has gotten an update from an iBGP peer, all internal routers should have received it. Without BGP split horizon, routing loops and black holes could be introduced within an autonomous system.

For example, in the previous figure, if RtrB receives an update from RtrA, it forwards the update to RtrC and RtrD. But C and D do not send it back to B, or to each other.

iBGP Next Hop

When a BGP router receives an update from an eBGP neighbor, it must pass that update to its iBGP neighbors without changing the next-hop attribute. The next-hop IP address is the IP address of an edge router belonging to the next-hop autonomous

Basic BGP Commands

Command	Description
router bgp [AS number]	Starts the BGP routing process on the router.
neighbor [ip address] remote-as [AS number]	Sets up a peering between BGP routers.
neighbor [peer group name] peer-group	Creates a peer group, which you can then put neighbors in.
neighbor [ip address] peer-group [peer group name]	Assigns a neighbor to a peer group.
neighbor [ip address] next-hop-self	Configures a router to advertise its connected interface as the next hop for all routes to this neighbor.
neighbor [ip address] update-source loopback 0	Configures a router to use the IP address of its loopback 0 interface as the source for its advertisements to this neighbor.
no synchronization	Turns off BGP synchronization.
network [prefix> [mask [subnet mask]]	Initiates the advertisement of a network in BGP.
no auto-summary	Turns off automatic summarization of routes to the classful network boundary.

system. Therefore, iBGP routers must have a route to the network connecting their autonomous system to that edge router. For example, in the figure below, RtrA sends an update to RtrB, listing a next hop of 10.2.2.1—it's serial interface. When RtrB forwards that update to RtrC, the next-hop IP address will still be 10.2.2.1. RtrC needs to have a route to the 10.2.2.0 network to have a valid next hop.

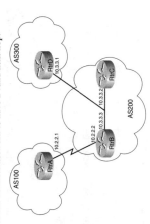

BGP Next Hop on a Multiaccess Network

On a multiaccess network, BGP can adjust the next-hop attribute to avoid an extra hop. In the previous figure, RtrC and RtrD are eBGP peers, and RtrC is an iBGP peer with RtrB. When C sends an update to D about network 10.2.2.0, it normally gives its interface IP address as the next hop for D to use. But since B, C, and D are all on the same multiaccess network, it adds an extra hop for D to send traffic to C, and C to send it on to B. So RtrC advertises a next hop of 10.3.3.3 (RtrB's interface) for the 10.2.2.0 network. To change this behavior, use the neighbor [ip address] next-hop-self command.

BGP Synchronization Rule

When a BGP router receives information about a network from an iBGP neighbor, it does not use that information until a matching route is learned via an IGP or static route. It also does not advertise that route to an eBGP neighbor. In the preceding figure, if RtrB advertises a route to RtrC, C does not submit it to the routing table or advertise it to RtrD unless it also learns the route from some other IGP source. It is usually safe to turn off synchronization when all routers in the autonomous system are running BGP. To turn it off, use the command no synchronization under BGP router config mode.

The BGP network Command

In most IGPs, the **network** command starts the routing process on an interface. In BGP, the command tells the router to originate an advertisement for that network. The network does not have to be connected to the router; it just has to be in the routing table. In theory, it could even be a network in a different autonomous system (not usually recommended). When advertising a network, BGP assumes you are using the default classful subnet mask. If you want to advertise a subnet, you must use the optional keyword **mask** and specify the subnet mask to use.

BGP Peering

BGP assumes that external neighbors are directly connected and that they are peering with the IP address of the directly connected interface of their neighbor. If not, you must tell BGP to look more than one hop away for its neighbor, with the **neighbor** [*ip address*] **ebgp-multihop** [*no. of hops*] command. You might use this command if you are peering with loopback interface IP addresses. BGP assumes that internal neighbors might not be directly connected, so this command is not needed with iBGP.

BGP Peering States

- **Idle**—No peering; router is looking for neighbor. **Idle (admin)** means that the neighbor relationship has been administratively shut down.
- **Connect**—TCP handshake completed.
- **OpenSent**—An open message was sent to try to establish the peering (also called **Active** state).
- **OpenConfirm**—Router has received a reply to the open message.
- **Established**—Routers have a BGP peering session. This is the desired state.

Summarizing BGP Routes

You can perform route summarization in BGP in several ways:

- Leave auto-summarization on and allow the router to advertise the default classful route.
- Use the **network** command along with a static route pointing to Null0. In the following figure, AS200 has the entire 10.2.0.0 subnet. First, configure a static route for the summary, pointing to Null0 (remember that a route must be in the routing table before BGP originates an advertisement for that network):

```
ip route 10.2.0.0 255.255.0.0 null0
```

Then, put a network statement for the summary network into BGP:

```
network 10.2.0.0 mask 255.255.0.0
```

- Use the **aggregate-address** command—the preferred method. At least one more specific network of the summarized routes must be in the BGP table, either from the **network** command, or via an advertisement from another router.

In the following figure, RtrB uses the following command to summarize its subnets:

```
aggregate-address 10.2.0.0 255.255.0.0
```

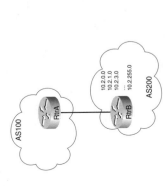

BGP advertises the summary route and the more specific routes. To suppress advertisement of the specific routes, add the summary-only keyword to the preceding command. If the routes come from other autonomous systems, you should add the as-set keyword. This tells BGP to advertise a list of the autonomous system numbers associated with the specific routes. BGP's default is to advertise the route with only the autonomous system number of the summarizing router. The aggregate-address command causes BGP to automatically create a route for the summary, pointing to Null0, to prevent loop formation.

BGP Attributes

BGP chooses a route to network based on the attributes of its path. Four categories of attributes exist:

- **Well-known mandatory**—Must be recognized by all BGP routers, present in all BGP updates, and passed on to other BGP routers. Example: autonomous system path, origin, next hop.
- **Well-known discretionary**—Must be recognized by all BGP routers and passed on to other BGP routers, but need not be present in an update. Example: Local preference.
- **Optional transitive**—Might or might not be recognized by a BGP router, but is passed on to other BGP routers. If not recognized, it is marked as partial. Example: aggregator, community.
- **Optional nontransitive**—Might or might not be recognized by a BGP router and is not passed on to other routers. Example: Multi-Exit Discriminator (MED), originator ID.

Autonomous system path	An ordered list of all the autonomous systems through which this update has passed.
Origin	How BGP learned of this network. i = by **network** command, e = from EGP, ? = redistributed from other source.
Next hop	The IP address of the next-hop router.
Local preference	A value telling iBGP peers which path to select for traffic leaving the AS.
Weight	Cisco proprietary, to tell a router which of multiple local paths to select for traffic leaving the AS. Only has local significance.
Multi-Exit Discriminator (MED)	Suggests to a neighbor autonomous system which of multiple paths to select for traffic bound for your autonomous system.

Applying BGP Policies

These attributes are usually manipulated using route maps. You can set a default local preference by using the command **bgp default local-preference** and a default MED for redistributed routes with the **default-metric** command under the BGP routing process.

But by using route maps, you can change attributes for certain neighbors only, or for certain routes only.

When attributes are changed, you must tell BGP to apply the changes. Either clear the BGP session (**clear ip bgp ***) or do a soft reset (**clear ip bgp * soft in | out**).

BGP Path Selection Criteria

BGP tries to narrow its path selection down to one best path; it does not load balance by default. To do so, it examines the path attributes in the following order:

1. Is the route synchronized (if iBGP) with a valid next hop and no autonomous system loops?
2. Choose the route with the highest weight.
3. If weight is not set, choose the route with the highest local preference.
4. Choose a route that was originated locally over one that was advertised to you.
5. Choose the path with the shortest autonomous system path.
6. Choose the path with the lowest origin code (i is lowest, e is next, ? is last).
7. Choose the route with the lowest MED, if the same autonomous system advertises the possible routes.
8. Choose an eBGP route over an iBGP route.
9. Choose the route through the nearest IGP neighbor.
10. Choose the oldest route.
11. Choose a path through the neighbor with the lowest router ID.

To enable BGP to load balance over more than one path, you must enter the command **maximum-paths** [*no. of paths*]. BGP can load balance over a maximum of 6 paths.

Multihoming

Multihoming means connecting to more than one ISP at the same time.

Multihoming is done for redundancy and backup in case one ISP fails—and for better performance—if one ISP provides a better path to often used networks. Three ways exist to receive routes from each ISP:

- Default routes from each provider. Low use of bandwidth and router resources, IGP metric determines path chosen for routes outside the autonomous system.
- Default routes plus some more specific routes. Medium use of bandwidth and router resources. Can manipulate path for specific routes, IGP metric chooses path for default routes.
- All routes from all providers. Highest use of bandwidth and router resources. Typically done only by ISPs. Path selection can be controlled via BGP policy routing tools.

Part II

BCMSN

Section 1
Implementing Switching in the Network

Section 2
Configuring VLANS and VTP

Section 3
Implementing and Tuning Spanning Tree Protocol

Section 4
Enhancing Spanning Tree Protocol

Section 5
Multilayer Switching

Section 6
Improving Network Availability

Section 7
Cisco AVVID Services and Applications

Section 8
Implementing QoS

BCMSN Quick Reference Sheets

Section 1

Implementing Switching in the Network

Campus network stability and scalability are the results of applying good design principles. Stable and scalable networks—the kind that let you see family and take vacations—should support low-latency throughput, redundancy, and fast failover. One possible design model is the Cisco Enterprise Composite Model.

This section reviews the older Hierarchical Design Model and the newer Enterprise Composite Model. It also reviews the role the Composite Model plays in switch selection.

Finally, this section compares the management of CatOS and IOS based switches. CatOS is the older Cisco OS for switches, commonly known as "set-based" OS because all the commands start with **set, show,** or **clear.** CatOS has become deprecated as newer switches take advantage of the Layer 3 capabilities of the IOS. Understanding how the operating systems compare and the upgrade process are currently major concerns for network operators.

BCMSN

Question 1

What is the Cisco AVVID network architecture?

Question 2

What is the Cisco Enterprise Composite Model?

Question 2 Answer

The Cisco Architecture for Voice, Video, and Integrated Data is a strategy for building standards-based enterprise networks to support next-generation multimedia applications.

Question 3 Answer

The Enterprise Composite Model divides the network into three sections that each contains access, distribution, and core functions:

- **Enterprise campus**—Traditional hierarchical network
- **Enterprise edge**—Elements that provide Internet connectivity
- **Service provider edge**—Upstream connection points

Question 3

How does the campus portion of the Enterprise Composite Model break down?

Question 4

How does the edge portion of the Enterprise Composite Model break down?

Question 4 Answer

The Enterprise Composite Model describes the campus as including four parts:

- **Campus Infrastructure**—The traditional three layer network
- **Network Management**—Monitoring, logging, and provisioning of network resources
- **Server Farm**—Centrally located enterprise servers
- **Edge Distribution**—Point of contact between the Campus and Edge

Question 5 Answer

Cisco proposes four operation areas to be included in the edge area:

- **Internet Connectivity**
- **Remote access/virtual private network (VPN)**—Trusted access from outside the firewall
- **Wide-area network (WAN)**—Wide-area connectivity behind the firewall
- **E-commerce**—Services required when marketing and selling products and services online

Question 5

What impact do Layer 2 switches have on collision domains and broadcasts domains?

Question 6

What is multilayer switching (MLS)?

Question 6 Answer

Each Layer 2 switch port is a separate collision domain, reducing the opportunities for collisions. Switches also support full duplex, which is a communication method where collisions are not possible.

Layer 2 switches are able to group ports into VLANs, with each VLAN being a separate broadcast domain.

Question 7 Answer

MLS is capable of the following:

- Layer 2 switching (based on MAC)
- Layer 3 switching (routing by IP)
- Layer 4 switching (policy control by TCP or UDP ports)

Question 7

Compare and contrast Fast Ethernet and 10 Mbps Ethernet, in terms of the data link layer logic and format.

Question 8

What is a collapsed backbone?

Question 8 Answer

Ethernet and Fast Ethernet:

- Both use CSMA/CD for half-duplex connections.
- Both support full duplex.
- Both use the same MAC addresses and frame formats.

Fast Ethernet:

- Uses a new physical layer
- Increases speed by a factor of 10

Question 9 Answer

When a small campus design requires only two distribution switches, the switches are interconnected instead of connected through a separate core device.

Question 9

How is a small campus design principally differentiated from a medium-sized design (according to the Cisco design model)?

Question 10

According to the Cisco Enterprise Composite Model, what would be the design of the Server Farm module?

Question 10 Answer

Small campuses typically use a collapsed backbone.

Question 11 Answer

- Servers would connect to server access layer switches (Layer 2 switches).

- The server access switches would be redundantly interconnected through server distribution switches (Layer 3 switches).

- The server distribution switches would redundantly connect into the campus backbone.

Question 11

How are switches used at the enterprise edge?

Question 12

Compare the two operating systems run by various Cisco switches.

Question 12 Answer

To redundantly interconnect the e-commerce, Internet connectivity, remote access/VPN, and WAN modules

Question 13 Answer

CatOS supports only Layer 2 functions and is found on 4000 (Sup. I or II), 5000, and 6000 series switches. It uses **set, clear,** and **show** commands.

IOS (Native mode) supports Layer 2 and 3 functions and is found on switches such as the 2950, 3550, 4000 (Sup. III or IV), and 6000 series. It uses the same command syntax as routers.

The 6500 also supports a hybrid mode that uses CatOS for Layer 2 and IOS for Layer 3.

Question 13

What are some ways to mitigate the overhead caused by debugging?

Question 14

What command prepends date and time to debugging messages?

Question 14 Answer

- Debugging from a console port creates a processor interrupt for each character. Debugging from a Telnet session creates less overhead.
- Be as specific as possible with debugging commands.
- Debug events rather than packets.
- Use an ACL to limit debug output.
- Never use **debug all**.
- Remove debug commands when done using **undebug all**.
- Debug at off-peak times.

Question 15 Answer

```
IOS(config)# service timestamps debug datetime msec
```

Question 15

What command shows current processor utilization?

Question 16

What five steps are required to switch from CatOS to native IOS?

Question 16 Answer

```
IOS# show processes
```

Question 17 Answer

Step 1   Back up configuration.

Step 2   Boot to ROMMON.

Step 3   Boot native image.

Step 4   Make changes to always boot native IOS.

Step 5   Reload configuration.

Question 17

AVVID can be described as composing three main elements. Name them.

Question 18

From an IOS switch, what command backs up the running configuration to nonvolatile RAM (NVRAM)? To a TFTP server?

Question 18 Answer

AVVID includes the following:

- **Network infrastructure**
- **Intelligent network services**—Provides manageable and secure tools for network applications (multicast, security, quality of service [QoS], etc.)
- **Network solutions**—Applications that take advantage of the network structure and services; Voice over IP (VoIP), for example.

Question 19 Answer

```
copy running-config startup-config
copy running-config tftp
```

Section 2

Configuring VLANs and VTP

BCMSN

A virtual local-area network (VLAN) is a way to segment a network at OSI Layer 2. The use of VLANs creates separate ports on a switch into separate Layer 3 broadcast domains. Traffic for multiple VLANs can be passed between switches via trunk links. Switches exchange information about VLANs using VLAN Trunking Protocol (VTP).

Question 1

What are the two ways that VLANs can be associated with switch ports, and how do they differ?

Question 2

How can the use of VLANs increase security within your campus network?

Question 1 Answer

Ports can be assigned to VLANs either statically or dynamically. Dynamic VLAN assignment requires a VLAN Membership Policy Server (VMPS), which keeps a database of MAC addresses to VLAN assignment. When a user logs in, the VMPS assigns their port to the appropriate VLAN for as long as that user is connected. Static VLAN assignment is done by an administrator and does not change unless the switch configuration is changed.

Question 2 Answer

In a network without VLANs, all devices can reach all other devices without going through a router. When using VLANs, a device in one VLAN cannot reach a device in a different VLAN without a router. This protects servers from general access and allows access to be controlled by the security features of routers.

Question 3

Explain the two methods of designing VLANs.

Question 4

What are two methods of encapsulating frames over a trunk link?

Question 3 Answer

VLANs can be designed as either local VLANs or end-to-end VLANs. Local VLANs are created based on geographical location of the users, such as a floor of a building. About 20 percent of the traffic is local to the VLAN, and 80 percent goes outside the VLAN. End-to-end VLANs are based on user functions and security policies and can span the entire switched network. About 80 percent of traffic stays within the VLAN, and 20 percent goes outside it.

Question 4 Answer

Cisco proprietary Inter-Switch Link (ISL) and the IEEE's 802.1Q protocol

Question 5

How does Inter-Switch Link (ISL) identify VLANs?

Question 6

How does 802.1Q identify VLANs?

Question 5 Answer

ISL adds a 26-byte header and a 4-byte footer to the frame. In the header is a 10-bit VLAN identification field. This identifies the VLAN of the device that originated the message. The trailer is a FCS field that contains a cyclic redundancy check (CRC) value for the new frame. The original frame is not touched; it is just encapsulated within the ISL header and footer. The ISL header also has a field that tells the switch if the traffic is bound for it, such as with BPDUs or CDP frames. This field allows ISL to perform PVST across the switched network.

Question 6 Answer

The 802.1Q protocol inserts a 4-byte tag into the original frame, after the source and destination MAC address fields. This tag contains a 12-bit field that identifies the VLAN of the device that originated the frame. Since the original frame was modified, a new FCS is calculated.

Question 7

What are the three VTP modes for a switch?

Question 8

What steps regarding VTP should be taken when introducing a new switch into an existing network?

Question 7 Answer

Server—Can create, delete, and rename VLANs. Initiates a VTP advertisement when there is a change to synchronize its database with other switches and forwards any VTP advertisement it receives.

Transparent—Can create, delete, and rename VLANs. Does not initiate a VTP advertisement, but forwards any VTP advertisement it receives. Does not synchronize its database with other switches.

Client—Cannot change the VLAN structure. Can initiate VTP messages and forward VTP advertisements. Synchronizes its database with other switches.

Question 8 Answer

Step 1	Delete any existing VLANs.
Step 2	Reset the VTP revision number to 0 by power-cycling the switch.
Step 3	Configure VTP settings, such as domain name, before configuring trunk links.
Step 4	Enable any desired trunk links.

Question 9

How do you verify a switch's VTP settings?

Question 10

What are the types of VTP advertisements, and when are they used?

Question 9 Answer

Use the command **show vtp status**.

Question 10 Answer

- **Advert-request**—Used to request VLAN information.
- **Summary-advert**—Sent when VLAN topology changes, and also every 5 minutes. Contains the VTP revision number.
- **Subset-advert**—Contains detailed information about VLANs, such as their number and name. Sent in response to an Advert-request.

Question 11

What commands are necessary to create a VLAN number 15, named MYVLAN, in VLAN database mode?

Question 12

What are the commands to configure a switch interface as an 802.1Q trunk link in "auto" DTP mode?

Question 11 Answer

From privilege EXEC mode, type

```
vlan database
 vlan 15
  name MYVLAN
```

Question 12 Answer

At the interface configuration mode, type

```
switchport trunk encapsulation dot1q
switchport mode dynamic auto
switchport trunk native vlan [vlan #] (if not default of 1)
```

Question 13

Suppose you want a switch trunk to carry all VLANs except VLANs 5–10. What are the commands to configure this?

Question 14

What are the DTP modes for a trunk link?

Question 13 Answer

At the interface configuration mode for the trunk port, type

```
switchport trunk allowed vlan remove 5-10
```

Question 14 Answer

- **Desirable**—The switch contacts the other end and actively tries to create a trunk. The link becomes a trunk if the other side is set to trunk, desirable, or auto. This is the default setting.

- **Auto**—The switch waits to be contacted about trunking. The link becomes a trunk if the other side is set to trunk or desirable.

- **Trunk**—The interface attempts to negotiate trunk status using DTP and becomes a trunk if the other side is set to trunk, desirable, or auto.

- **Nonnegotiate**—The interface becomes a trunk and does not generate DTP messages. You must configure the other side for the link to become a trunk.

Question 15

How does the Cisco 3550 route between VLANs?

Question 16

How do you configure an interface for dynamic VLAN assignment?

Question 15 Answer

The 3550 uses switch virtual interfaces (SVIs) as the router interfaces that exchange traffic between VLANs.

Question 16 Answer

At the global configuration mode, tell the switch the IP address of the primary and any secondary VMPS servers:

```
vmps server <ip address> primary
vmps server <ip address> (for secondary servers)
```

At the interface configuration mode, type

```
switchport mode access
switchport access vlan dynamic
```

Question 17

Why does 802.1Q trunking require the configuring of a native VLAN?

Question 18

What happens if you statically assign a switch port to a VLAN and that VLAN gets deleted?

Question 17 Answer

Frames from the trunk interface's native VLAN are sent as regular traffic; they are not tagged with the 802.1Q field. Thus, the native VLAN must match on both sides of the trunk link.

Question 18 Answer

All ports that belong to a deleted VLAN become inactive until they are either assigned to another VLAN or the original VLAN is recreated.

Question 19

What features are available with VTP version 2 that are not in VTP version 1?

Question 20

List four things to check when troubleshooting VTP between two switches.

Question 19 Answer

VTP version 2 supports

- Token Ring VLANs
- Unrecognized TLVs (Type Length Value)
- Transparent switches pass along messages from both versions of VTP
- Consistency checks

Question 20 Answer

- Are the switches connected by a trunk link?
- Are the switches in the same VTP domain?
- Is one of the switches in transparent mode?
- If using passwords, do both switches have the same password?

Question 21

Is a VLAN a broadcast domain or a collision domain?

Question 22

Describe how VLAN information is maintained as a frame travels from a PC, through a switch, across a trunk to another switch, and then out to another PC.

Question 21 Answer

A VLAN is a broadcast domain. Devices within a VLAN hear broadcasts only from other devices in that VLAN.

Question 22 Answer

When the frame comes into the switch, the switch adds a tag that associates it with the VLAN of the port it came in on. As the frame exits the trunk port, the internal tag is removed and the ISL encapsulation or 802.1Q tag is added to the frame. When the switch on the other end of the trunk receives the frame, it removes the trunking information and reassociates the frame with its VLAN. The original frame is then sent out the access port to the destination PC.

Question 23

What commands are necessary to assign a switch interface to VLAN 15?

Question 24

What are the commands necessary to create a VLAN number 15, named MYVLAN, in global configuration mode?

Question 23 Answer

From the interface configuration mode, type

```
switchport mode access
switchport access vlan 15
```

Question 24 Answer

From the global configuration prompt, type

```
(config)# vlan 15
(config-vlan)# name MYVLAN
```

Section 3

Implementing and Tuning Spanning Tree Protocol

Spanning Tree Protocol (STP) was created to prevent problems that develop in a redundant switched network. It executes a spanning-tree algorithm that works by choosing one reference point in the network. Then, each switch selects one path back to the root and puts all others in a standby, or blocked, state. Spanning tree is enabled by default on all Cisco switches and has a default configuration. You might want to make some changes, however, to optimize spanning-tree operation for your particular network.

Question 1

What is the criterion for spanning-tree root bridge election?

Question 2

A Cisco switch has the MAC address of 0100-0c23-4567 and is using the default priority value. What is the switch's Bridge ID (BID) for VLAN 1?

Question 1 Answer

The spanning-tree root bridge is selected by comparing Bridge IDs. Bridge ID consists of a priority value concatenated with one of the switch's management MAC addresses. The switch with the lowest Bridge ID is elected.

Question 2 Answer

80-00-01-00-0c-23-45-67. The default priority for Cisco switches is 32,768 (8000 in hex). This is combined with the switch MAC address to create the spanning-tree Bridge ID for VLAN 1.

Question 3

What are the five spanning-tree port states and their default timers?

Question 4

What are the three spanning-tree timers and their default values?

Question 3 Answer

- **Blocking**—20 sec (or MaxAge timer)
- **Listening**—15 sec (or FwdDelay timer)
- **Learning**—15 sec (or FwdDelay timer)
- **Forwarding**—As long as necessary
- **Disabled**—Administratively shut

Question 4 Answer

- **Hello**—How often a switch sends BPDU hellos to connected switches. Default value—2 sec.

- **Forward Delay**—How long a port listens to BPDUs and learns MAC addresses before beginning to forward traffic. Default value—15 sec.

- **Maximum Age**—How long a newly activated port is in the blocking mode before starting to listen to BPDUs. Also used for deciding when the root bridge has failed, and for fast aging out of MAC entries when there is an election.

Question 5

How many instances of spanning tree are carried by a 802.1Q trunk?

Question 6

What command configures a switch to be the root for VLAN 15?

Question 5 Answer

The 802.1Q standard specified a common spanning tree across all VLANs. However, Cisco switches connected by 802.1Q trunks maintain a separate spanning tree for each VLAN allowed on the trunk.

Question 6 Answer

spanning-tree vlan 15 root primary

Question 7

What is the recommended way of changing the spanning-tree timers?

Question 8

How would you verify the spanning-tree settings, such as priority, for a particular switch port?

Question 7 Answer

Cisco recommends changing the spanning-tree timers by changing the diameter setting on the spanning-tree root command, rather than changing them manually. The command is **spanning-tree vlan [*vlan #*] root primary I secondary diameter [*# of switches*]**

Question 8 Answer

Use the command **show spanning-tree interface [*port #*]**.

Question 9

What are two ways to use spanning-tree settings to load share in a switched network?

Question 10

What three problems can be caused by loops in your switched network?

Question 9 Answer

You can manipulate the port priority settings on parallel trunk links so that one link carries traffic for a range of VLANs and blocks for others, and the other trunk carries the VLANs that were blocked on the first link.

You can manipulate path costs on a per-VLAN basis to accomplish the same result.

Question 10 Answer

Switching loops can cause broadcast storms, multiple copies of the same frame, and rapidly changing MAC address table entries.

Question 11

What command disables spanning tree on a specific VLAN?

Question 12

How is the spanning-tree designated switch selected?

Question 11 Answer

At global configuration mode, type

```
no spanning-tree vlan [vlan #]
```

Question 12 Answer

One switch is designated to send traffic to each Ethernet segment. That switch is chosen by comparing the path cost to the root of the ports connected to that segment. The switch that has the port with the lowest interface path cost is the designated switch for that segment. In case of a tie, the bridge with the lowest BID is selected.

Question 13

What information is contained in a Bridge Protocol Data Unit (BPDU)?

Question 14

How does a port behave when it is in the spanning-tree learning state?

Question 13 Answer

A BPDU contains the following information:

- Protocol ID
- Protocol version
- BPDU message type
- Flags
- The Bridge ID of the root bridge
- The local switch's path cost to the root
- The local switch's Bridge ID
- Port ID
- Message age
- Timer information: forward delay, max-age, and hello
- Transmitting interface

Question 14 Answer

Learning—The switch discards frames inbound to and outbound from this port. It does learn MAC addresses and receive BPDUs from this port.

Question 15

How does a port behave when it is in the spanning-tree forwarding state?

Question 16

What do you have to do to enable PVST+ (per-VLAN spanning tree plus) on an 802.1Q trunk link?

Question 15 Answer

Forwarding—This port fully participates in data exchange. It receives and forwards frames, learns MAC addresses, and receives BPDUs on this port.

Question 16 Answer

Nothing. PVST+ is enabled by default on Cisco 802.1Q trunks links.

Question 17

How can you influence the selection of the spanning-tree root port on a switch?

Question 18

Although it is recommended that you change the switch priority by using the spanning-tree root command, what is the command if you want to change the switch priority manually?

Question 17 Answer

You can "rig" the election of the root port by changing port costs. Recall that the port with the lowest cost path to the root is selected as the root port. You can either give the desired interface a lower cost or raise the cost of the undesirable interfaces.

Question 18 Answer

At the global configuration mode, type

```
spanning-tree vlan [vlan #] priority [priority]
```

Question 19

What MAC address does a switch use in the spanning-tree BID for each VLAN?

Question 20

What is one command that displays the spanning-tree timers for all VLANs?

Question 19 Answer

Switches have a pool of MAC addresses. The first address is assigned to VLAN 1, the second to VLAN 2, etc.

Question 20 Answer

At the privileged exec prompt, type

```
show spanning-tree bridge
```

Question 21

How is the spanning-tree root port selected?

Question 22

What are the advantages and disadvantages of a common, or mono, Spanning Tree?

Question 21 Answer

Each switch needs one port to use for communicating with the root bridge. This port is selected by lowest path cost. Path cost is based on the speed of the link at each interface and is the cumulative cost of the entire path to the root. In the event of a tie, the port with the lowest sender BID is selected. If there is still a tie, then lowest local Port ID determines root port.

Question 22 Answer

An advantage of CST is that only one set of BPDUs is being sent out, thus saving on bandwidth. Also, only one set of STP devices must be tracked, which saves processing time on the switch.

Disadvantages include the fact that the spanning tree might be very large, with many switches involved in an election when topology changes. This can cause longer network convergence times. Additionally, because all traffic flows toward the root, sharing a root might cause some traffic to take suboptimal paths.

Section 4

Enhancing Spanning Tree Protocol

Bridges and switches perform three functions: They associate MAC addresses with ports, make forwarding and filtering decisions, and avoid loops. The last function, avoiding loops, is critical because Ethernet Frame headers do not include a field that can detect loop formation. When loops form, new traffic continues to join the loop until all available bandwidth is consumed.

The Spanning Tree Protocol (STP) recognizes looping conditions and disables forwarding on some ports so that loops do not form. STP is dynamic because it recognizes when conditions change and when ports must be reopened.

STP's slowness has been its only criticism. The traditional response to this criticism has been that loops are so bad that slow is better than a broadcast storm. New technologies, however, have rendered this a moot point. Cisco Systems has offered abilities such as PortFast, which speeds up STP, for quite a while. The IEEE has also recently offered its own set of extensions that achieve similar results, such as 802.1w (Rapid STP).

This chapter tests your knowledge of Spanning Tree, the proprietary and standards-based updates, and related functions. This material is not only critically important for the test, but also for the foundation of a well-developed campus network.

Question 1

When would you configure a switch port for Port Fast?

Question 2

How does configuring Port Fast on a switch interface change its function?

Question 1 Answer

Configure a switch port for Port Fast only when it is an access port. Do not connect a switch or bridge to a port in Port Fast mode.

Question 2 Answer

An interface in Port Fast mode immediately transitions from blocking to forwarding, without going through the listening and learning states. This allows an end station to connect to the network right away, without the 30 seconds used by spanning tree (an access port would not go through 20 seconds of blocking anyway). As a precaution, if the port receives a BPDU, it goes to the blocking state.

Question 3

What is spanning-tree Root Guard, and when is it used?

Question 4

What is the command to configure Uplink Fast on a 2950 or 3550 switch?

Question 3 Answer

Root Guard prevents switches outside your control from being selected as root of your network. If an interface configured for Root Guard is selected as the root port, the interface is put into blocked mode. Use this only on interfaces that should never become a root port.

Question 4 Answer

At global configuration mode, type

```
spanning-tree uplinkfast
```

When Uplink Fast is enabled, the switch priority is changed to 49152 for all VLANS and the port cost of all ports is increased by 3000. This is to reduce the chance of the switch becoming the root bridge or the designated bridge. (Note: Priority and port cost values are changed only if they are at their default values to begin with.)

Question 5

What is the command to configure Root Guard on a 3550 switch?

Question 6

What is BPDU Guard and when it is used?

Question 5 Answer

At the interface configuration mode, type

```
spanning-tree guard root
```

Question 6 Answer

BPDU Guard helps prevent loops that might develop if an unauthorized switch is connected to the network via an access port. When BPDU Guard is running on a switch, if an interface configured for Port Fast receives a BPDU, that port is shut down. The interface is placed in ErrDisable state and must be manually re-enabled.

Question 7

What is the purpose of Rapid Spanning Tree Protocol (RSTP)?

Question 8

What are the three 802.1w Rapid Spanning Tree port states?

Question 7 Answer

RSTP provides faster convergence when a switch or switch port fails. It selects ports as a backup to the root and the designated port. If the original port fails, the alternate port becomes active through the exchange of a handshake with the switch port on the other end of the link. Because it is a standards-based protocol, it is not Cisco proprietary.

Question 8 Answer

Discarding, Learning, Forwarding

Question 9

How do the Rapid Spanning Tree port states compare with the 802.1D spanning-tree port states?

Question 10

What is the main difference between the way 802.1D BPDUs and 802.1w BPDUs are generated?

Question 9 Answer

RSTP Port State	STP Port State
Discarding	Disabled
Discarding	Blocking
Discarding	Listening
Learning	Learning
Forwarding	Forwarding

Question 10 Answer

With 802.1D STP, a non-root bridge generated BPDUs only when it received one in its root port. With 802.1w, every switch sends a BPDU every hello timer interval.

Question 11

What is the main purpose of Multiple Spanning Tree (MST)?

Question 12

List the three parameters that must be configured on a switch using MST.

Question 11 Answer

The main purpose of MST is to conserve switch resources by reducing the number of spanning-tree instances to fit the physical topology.

Question 12 Answer

- An MST region name
- An MST configuration revision number
- A mapping of VLAN to spanning-tree instance

Question 13

What command verifies the MST configuration of a switch?

Question 14

What is the purpose of EtherChannel?

Question 13 Answer

At the privileged exec prompt, type

```
show spanning-tree mst
```

Question 14 Answer

EtherChannel groups multiple switch ports into one logical link, thus forming a faster connection and enabling load balancing over the links.

Question 15

What commands configure Layer 3 EtherChannel #2, assign it an IP address, and place ports 2/1–2/4 in the channel?

Question 16

What commands configure Layer 2 EtherChannel #3 and place ports 3/1–3/2 in the channel?

Question 15 Answer

Beginning at global configuration mode, create the logical port-channel interface:

```
interface port-channel 2
     no switchport
     ip address [address] [mask]
```

Then, assign the physical interfaces to the EtherChannel bundle:

```
interface range fastethernet 2/1 - 2/4
     no ip address
     channel-group 2 mode desirable
```

Question 16 Answer

Beginning at global configuration mode:

```
interface range fastethernet 3/1 - 3/2
     channel-group 3 mode desirable
```

Question 17

What command displays the Port Channel actions on EtherChannel #2 and lets you verify which ports are in this bundle?

Question 18

What two protocols dynamically form EtherChannels?

Question 17 Answer

At the privileged exec prompt, type

```
show etherchannel 2 port-channel
```

Question 18 Answer

Port Aggregation Protocol (PAgP) and Link Aggregation Control Protocol (LACP)

Question 19

What are the three PAgP EtherChannel modes for an interface?

Question 20

What are the four LACP EtherChannel modes for an interface?

Question 19 Answer

- **On**—The port channels, without using PAgP negotiation. The port on the other side must also be set to On.

- **Auto**—Responds to PAgP messages, but does not initiate them. Port channels if the port on the other end is set to Desirable.

- **Desirable**—Port actively negotiates channeling status with the interface on the other end of the link. Port channels if other side is Auto or Desirable.

Question 20 Answer

- **On**—The link aggregation is forced to be formed, and no negotiation is taking place. (We neither send the LACP packet nor process the incoming LACP packet.) This is similar to the *on* state for PAgP.

- **Off**—The link aggregation is not formed. We do not send or understand the LACP packet. This is similar to the *off* state of PAgP.

- **Active**—Port actively negotiates channeling with the port on the other end of the link. Channel forms if the other side is Passive or Active.

- **Passive**—Responds to LACP messages, but does not initiate them. Channel forms if the other end is set to Active.

Question 21

Your company administrator wants to configure one EtherChannel to load balance based on the MAC address and another to load balance based on the IP address. How would you configure this?

Question 22

How does Unidirectional Loop Detection (UDLD) work?

Question 21 Answer

The command to tell the switch how to load balance over EtherChannels is given at the global configuration mode and thus affects all EtherChannels. So, you must use the same load-balancing technique on all channels.

Question 22 Answer

When UDLD is enabled on a link, the switch sends periodic UDLD echo probes to its neighbor. The neighbor then echoes these packets back. If no reply is received, but the link is physically up, the switch determines that the link is unidirectional and shuts down the interface.

Question 23

What command configures an interface for Port Fast?

Question 24

How does a RSTP switch react when it receives a BPDU with the Topology Change (TC) bit set?

Question 23 Answer

At the interface configuration mode, type

```
spanning-tree portfast
```

Question 24 Answer

- It ages out the MAC addresses learned from all ports except the one that received the TC BPDU.

- It starts the Topology Change timer and sets the TC bit on all BPDUs out its designated ports and its root port until the timer expires.

Question 25

Which interface characteristics must match on both side of the link in order for an EtherChannel to form?

Question 25 Answer

- **Speed**—All ports must be set at the same speed.
- **Duplex**—All ports must be the same duplex.
- **SPAN**—No port can be set as a SPAN port.
- **VLANs**—All ports must be in the same VLAN, or be trunks. Trunk ports must carry the same VLANs.
- All ports in the EtherChannel must be enabled.

Section 5

Multilayer Switching

Multilayer switching (MLS) combines the low latency of traditional switching operations with the Layer 3 and 4 capabilities of a router. MLS devices can move traffic at wire speeds while routing traffic between interfaces and support routing protocols and policy functions.

This section covers the theory and configuration of MLS operations, building to Cisco Express Forwarding (CEF). The final part of this section covers inter-VLAN routing as it is supported by an MLS switch.

Question 1

What is Cisco Express Forwarding (CEF)?

Question 2

In what order does an MLS switch handle the following *routing* operations?

Output VLAN ACL processing

Destination IP lookup

Input routing access control list (ACL) processing

Input VLAN ACL processing

Output queuing

Receive traffic

Quality of service (QoS) decisions

Send traffic

Output routing ACL processing

Question 1 Answer

CEF is a topology-based switching method that prebuilds a Forwarding Information Base (FIB)—as compared to fast switching, which stores forwarding information on demand.

Question 2 Answer

1 Receive traffic

2 Input VLAN ACL processing

3 Input routing ACL processing

4 Destination IP lookup

5 Output routing ACL processing

6 Output VLAN ACL processing

7 QoS decisions

8 Output queuing

9 Send traffic

Question 3

In what order does a Layer 2 switch handle the following operations?

Input ACL

Look up destination MAC in CAM

Output queuing

Output ACL

QoS decisions

Receive traffic

Transmit traffic

Question 4

In what order does an MLS switch handle the following *switching* operations?

QoS decisions

Input VLAN ACL processing

Send traffic

Output queuing

Receive traffic

Output VLAN ACL processing

Question 3 Answer

1 Receive traffic

2 Input ACL

3 Look up destination MAC in CAM

4 Output ACL

5 QoS decisions

6 Output queuing

7 Transmit traffic

Question 4 Answer

1 Receive traffic

2 Input VLAN ACL processing

3 Output VLAN ACL processing

4 QoS decisions

5 Output queuing

6 Send traffic

Question 5

What portion of the frame and packet headers are rewritten by an intermediate router?

Question 6

What is a TCAM table?

Question 5 Answer

Frame: Source and destination MAC.

Packet: TTL is decremented.

Packet: IP Header checksum.

Frame: FCS recomputed.

Question 6 Answer

Ternary Content Addressable Memory (TCAM) is a special piece of memory that is designed to quickly look up and match patterns. Each bit can be 0, 1, or X; thus, it is called ternary.

Question 7

Where does a Layer 2 switch store destination MAC addresses?

Question 8

What is NetFlow?

Question 7 Answer

A Layer 2 switch stores destination MAC addresses in the CAM table.

Question 8 Answer

NetFlow-based switching uses software to route the first packet in flow and cache the result. Subsequent packets are then forwarded much faster according to the hardware cache.

NetFlow switching also provides administrators with a wealth of detailed information about traffic on their data network.

Question 9

What is an ASIC?

Question 10

When using CEF, what kinds of traffic are software (process) switched?

Question 9 Answer

An application-specific intergrated circuit (ASIC) is a specialized chip, one of which forwards traffic from each port on the switch.

Question 10 Answer

Some examples of process-switched traffic on a CEF switch include the following:

- Packets that are sourced by the L3 switch
- Encrypted packets and those forwarded over a tunnel interface
- Debugged traffic
- Packets that go through Network Address Translation (NAT)

Question 11

How is CEF enabled and disabled on a 3550, 4000, or 6500?

Question 12

What command is necessary to associate an IOS switch port with a VLAN?

Question 11 Answer

3550—Enable CEF with the command **ip route-cache cef**.

4000—CEF is on by default. Disable with the interface command **no ip cef**.

6500 with feature card—CEF cannot be disabled.

Question 12 Answer

```
interface fastethernet0/1
switchport access VLAN 7
```

Question 13

What is the difference between an SVI and a routed port on a Layer 3 switch?

Question 14

How is a routed port configured on a Layer 3 switch?

Question 13 Answer

An SVI is a virtual port that is associated with a VLAN.

A routed port is a physical port that acts like a port on a router.

Question 14 Answer

```
interface f0/1
no switchport
```

Question 15

What commands are necessary to configure inter-VLAN routing on a Layer 3 switch?

Question 16

How is a router-on-a-stick configured to route between VLAN 1 and VLAN 7 on an 802.1q trunk?

Question 15 Answer

```
L3Sw(config)# ip routing
L3Sw(config)# interface vlan 7
L3Sw(config-if)# ip address 10.0.7.1 255.255.255.0
L3Sw(config-if)# interface vlan 8
L3sw(config-if)# ip address 10.0.8.1 255.255.255.0
```

Question 16 Answer

```
interface fastethernet0/0
      ip address 10.0.1.1 255.255.255.0
      encapsulation dot1q 1 native
interface fastethernet0/0.7
      encapsulation dot1q 7
      ip address 10.0.7.1 255.255.255.0
```

Question 17

What command displays the CEF FIB?

Question 18

What command displays the CEF adjacency table?

Question 17 Answer

```
show ip cef <type>slot/port
```

Question 18 Answer

```
show adjacency <type>slot/port
```

Question 19

How is an SVI created?

Question 19 Answer

```
interface vlan7
```

Section 6

Improving Network Availability

This section covers options for ensuring that network resources are continuously available. This is achieved by selecting and configuring hardware that supports the availability requirements and by using technologies such as Hot Standby Router Protocol (HSRP) and Virtual Router Redundancy Protocol (VRRP) to guarantee router redundancy.

Question 1

What are two methods of hardware redundancy?

Question 2

How is a redundant campus topology achieved?

Question 1 Answer

Redundant modules within a device

Redundant devices

Question 2 Answer

Each access layer device attaches to two upstream distribution layer devices. Each distribution device has a connection to two upstream core layer devices. Any campus link can therefore be lost (with the exception of the client link) without losing connectivity.

Question 3

What is RPR+?

Question 4

If two supervisor cards are placed in a Catalyst 6500, which is the redundant card?

Question 3 Answer

Route Processor Redundancy Plus (RPR+) allows a redundant supervisor card to assert itself within a minute of losing the primary supervisor. RPR+ is faster than RPR because it keeps the redundant Supervisor up and the configuration synchronized between the two.

Question 4 Answer

The first card to boot is the primary, and the second is the spare.

Question 5

An administrator wants to remove a supervisor card from a 6500 but realizes it is the active card. What command changes the active supervisor?

Question 6

A Catalyst 6500 has two power supplies. Each power supply provides enough electricity to run the switch. What steps are necessary to configure the second as a redundant unit?

Question 5 Answer

```
redundancy force-switchover
```

Question 6 Answer

```
L3Sw# power redundancy-mode redundant
```
(This is the default.)

Question 7

PCs are typically set up with a single default gateway. What are some technologies that allow a PC to take advantage of a redundant gateway?

Question 8

How does Proxy ARP allow a PC to take advantage of a redundant gateway?

Question 7 Answer

Proxy ARP

ICMP Router Discovery Protocol (IRDP)

Routing protocols

Hot Standby Router Protocol (HSRP)

Virtual Redundant Router Protocol (VRRP)

Question 8 Answer

The PC ARPs for all destinations. A router with a route to the destination replies to the ARP with its own MAC address.

Question 9

What is the disadvantage of using IRDP as a method of recognizing redundant gateways?

Question 10

What are the responsibilities of the HSRP active router?

Question 9 Answer

Each IRDP router picks and advertises a hello frequency (usually 10 minutes) and a lifetime value (usually 30 minutes). It can take a long time to timeout an IRDP router.

Question 10 Answer

The HSRP active router

- Forwards traffic sent through the virtual router.

- Replies to traffic sent to the virtual router, such as ARPs or Telnet requests.

- Tranmits HSRP hellos to assert itself as the active router and to advertise its health.

Question 11

How is the HSRP active router chosen?

Question 12

List and describe the six HSRP states.

Question 11 Answer

If PREEMPT is configured, it is the router with the highest priority (default is 100).

If PREEMPT is not configured, it is the first router to boot.

Question 12 Answer

1 **Initial state**—Starting point.

2 **Learn state**—Router has not received a hello from the active router, and does not yet know the virtual IP address.

3 **Listen state**—Router is not active or standby.

4 **Speak state**—Sending hellos and participating in elections. Router does not progress past speak unless it is the standby or active router.

5 **Standby state**—Waiting for active router failure.

6 **Active state**—Actively serving as the virtual router.

Question 13

What commands are required to configure a Layer 3 switch to participate in HSRP on VLAN 27 with a priority of 135? The virtual router should have a MAC address of 0000.0C07.AC21 and an IP address of 192.168.0.254. The router should become the active router as soon as it starts unless there is a router with a higher priority.

Question 14

The active router has a priority of 100 when a second router with a priority of 150 in HSRP group 1 starts. Which router is the active router? What command changes this?

Question 13 Answer

```
interface vlan27
    standby 33 ip 192.168.0.254
    standby 33 priority 135
    standby 33 preempt
```

Question 14 Answer

If PREEMPT is not configured on the second router, the active router does not change.

If PREEMPT is configured on the second router, it takes over as the new active router.

```
standby 1 ip preempt
```

Question 15

Two routers connect to the Internet and are configured as HSRP peers. The active router has a priority of 125, and the standby router uses the default priority of 100. If the active router fails, the standby automatically takes its place.

One day, you notice that the T1 on s0 of the active router is down. Because the active router is still functioning, HSRP does not transition traffic to the router with the good circuit. What configuration change can be made to allow this to happen automatically?

Improving Network Availability

Question 16

What is the advantage of using VRRP as a method of recognizing redundant gateways?

Improving Network Availability

Question 15 Answer

```
standby 1 track s0 26
```

The active router's priority is decremented by 26 (125 to 99) if s0 goes down.

Question 16 Answer

The Virtual Router Redundancy Protocol (VRRP) backup router can recognize a loss of the master router in seconds and assert itself. The client barely sees a slow down in its traffic. VRRP is an open standard.

Question 17

What is the advantage of using GLBP as a method of recognizing redundant gateways?

Question 18

What is SRM and how is it different from HSRP?

Question 17 Answer

Gateway Load Balancing Protocol (GLBP) is similar to HSRP or VRRP in that it allows for physically redundant gateways. HSRP and VRRP have idle backups though. GLBP allows for automatic selection and use of all routers in the standby group.

Question 18 Answer

Single Router Mode (SRM) uses two MSFCs to achieve redundancy; however, the standby is booted and synchronized but does not actually appear on the network unless the primary fails.

Question 19

What is SLB?

Improving Network Availability

Question 20

What configuration commands are required to use the uplink port on the standby Supervisor card?

Improving Network Availability

Question 19 Answer

Server Load Balancing (SLB) makes a set of servers appear as a single virtual server to clients. Requests are distributed to all active servers—meaning that maintenance work can be done on a single server without affecting the availability of the virtual server.

Question 20 Answer

None—The redundant uplink is always available.

Question 21

What is the MAC address of the HSRP virtual router?

Question 21 Answer

The HSRP virtual router uses a MAC address of 0000.0C07.ACxx, where xx is the group number in hex. Group one uses 0000.0C07.AC01.

Section 7

Cisco AVVID Services and Applications

AVVID stands for Architecture for Voice, Video, and Integrated Data. In the past, companies might have had separate networks for voice, video, and data. But these are now converging and being run over the same network. The result is that voice, video, and mission-critical data are contending for bandwidth with general network data. For a converged network to run effectively requires good design and appropriate quality of service (QoS) configuration.

Catalyst switches are a key component of an efficient AVVID network. They have the performance and speed to reliably handle large amounts of data and the intelligence to enforce QoS policies.

Question 1

What are two problems that cause packet loss in a campus network?

Cisco AVVID Services and Applications

Question 2

What are some features of the 2950 and 3550 switches that enable them to support Cisco AVVID?

Cisco AVVID Services and Applications

Question 1 Answer

Jitter (variable delay) causes buffer over- and underruns. Congestion at the interface can be caused by traffic from a fast port being switched to exit out a slower port, which causes the transmit buffer to be overrun.

Question 2 Answer

- They support multiple VLANs on each access port by using voice VLANs. This enables the IP phones to belong to a separate VLAN from the computers.

- They can classify, mark, and police traffic, as well as provide differentiated queuing to different classes of traffic.

- They can be configured to trust the QoS markings provided by the IP phones or other devices.

Question 3

What are the network requirements for Voice over IP (VoIP) traffic?

Question 4

What is an IP multicast?

Question 3 Answer

- Maximum delay of 150—200 ms (one-way)
- No more than 1 percent packet loss
- Maximum average jitter of 30 ms
- Bandwidth of 21—106 kbps per call, plus about 150 bps per phone for control traffic

Question 4 Answer

An IP multicast is a message addressed to a group IP address, in the range of 224.0.0.0–239.255.255.255.

Question 5

What range of multicast IP addresses is reserved for network protocols?

Question 6

Describe a multicast source-based tree.

Question 5 Answer

The range of IP address 224.0.0.0 to 224.0.0.255 is reserved for network protocol use. 224.0.0.1 is the all-hosts group and 224.0.0.2 is the all-routers group.

Question 6 Answer

A multicast source-based tree has a multicast server at its root and one path to each segment of the network branching out from the root. A separate source tree is formed for each multicast server. The tree is identified by the notation (S,G) where S is the server IP address and G is the group IP address.

Question 7

How does Reverse Path Forwarding (RPF) create a loop-free distribution tree?

Question 8

List four situations when PIM dense mode is appropriate.

Question 7 Answer

- When a router receives a multicast packet, it looks up the source address in the routing table.

- The router notes the interface out of which it would send traffic to reach that source address. If the packet arrived in this interface, the router forwards it on.

- If the packet arrived on any other interface, the router drops it.

Question 8 Answer

- Multicast servers and receivers are near each other.

- There are just a few servers and many receivers.

- You have a high volume of multicast traffic.

- The multicast stream is fairly constant.

Question 9

List two situations where PIM sparse mode is appropriate.

Question 10

Complete this sentence:

IGMP messages are exchanged between _____ and _____, whereas CGMP messages are exchanged between _____ and _____.

Question 9 Answer

1 Pockets of users are widely dispersed around the network.

2 Multicast traffic is intermittent.

Question 10 Answer

IGMP messages are exchanges between *routers* and *hosts*, whereas CGMP messages are exchanged between *routers* and *switches*.

Question 11

What is the main difference between IGMP v1 and IGMP v2?

Question 12

What is the main difference between IGMP v2 and IGMP v3?

Question 11 Answer

The main difference between IGMP v1 and IGMP v2 is that host using IGMP v2 can send an explicit leave message when they leave a multicast group. IGMP v1 hosts leave silently.

Question 12 Answer

Hosts using IGMP v3 can tell the router from which sources they accept multicasts, whereas hosts using IGMP v2 accept multicasts from any source by default.

Question 13

What are three ways to control multicast traffic in a switch?

Question 14

List two ways for a router to learn of its rendezvous point (RP).

Question 13 Answer

- Create VLANs to bound the multicast group. Every host that wants to receive the multicast must belong to this VLAN.

- Use IGMP snooping to read IGMP reports and queries.

- Use CGMP to let the router tell the switch of hosts belonging to multicast groups.

Question 14 Answer

- You can configure a router with the IP address of the RP with the command **ip pim rp-address**

- The router can dynamically discover its RP, using auto-RP.

Question 15

What are the command(s) to configure a router as an auto-RP mapping agent?

Question 16

What are the commands to configure a router as a possible rendezvous point when using auto-RP? Assume you are using interface Lo2 as the source address, using a scope of 4, and specifying your multicast groups in access list 24.

Question 15 Answer

At the global configuration mode, type

```
ip pim send-rp-discovery scope [ttl]
```

Question 16 Answer

At the global configuration mode, type

```
ip pim send-rp-announce lo2 scope 4 group-list 24
```

Question 17

What are some differences between PIM v1 and PIM v2?

Question 18

When planning bandwidth requirements for a converged network (voice, video, and data), what is the maximum amount of bandwidth you should use?

Question 17 Answer

- PIM v1 is Cisco proprietary, whereas PIM v2 is standards-based.

- Both versions can dynamically map RPs to multicast groups. PIM v1 uses an auto-RP mapping agent; PIM v2 uses a bootstrap router (BSR).

- PIM v1 uses a Time-To-Live value to bound its announcements; PIM v2 uses a configured domain border.

- In PIM v2, sparse and dense mode are group properties, not interface properties.

Question 18 Answer

Do not plan to use more than 75 percent of a link's bandwidth. The other 25 percent is needed for router and overhead traffic.

Question 19

What feature of Catalyst switches allows IP phones to be dynamically placed in their own VLAN, separate from data hosts?

Question 20

Describe a multicast shared tree.

Question 19 Answer

Auxiliary VLANs, also called voice VLANs

Question 20 Answer

With a shared tree, each multicast group has one root, regardless of the number of servers. This root is called the rendezvous point (RP). Servers and clients register with the RP. Servers send multicast traffic to the RP, which forwards it to the clients. The tree is identified by (*,G) where * means all servers, and G is the multicast group IP address.

Question 21

How does PIM sparse mode distribute its multicast information?

Question 22

What does a switch do with a multicast by default?

Question 21 Answer

PIM sparse mode does not assume that any routers want to receive the multicast, but instead waits to hear an explicit message from them, joining the group. Then it adds branches to the tree to reach the hosts behind those routers. PIM sparse mode uses rendezvous points (RPs) to connect hosts and servers initially. Then once the source server is learned, there is a switchover to a source tree.

Question 22 Answer

Switches flood multicasts by default, sending a copy out every port.

Section 8

Implementing QoS

By default, networks offer only a best-effort delivery of data. When congestion occurs, all traffic has an equal chance of being delayed or dropped. However, most networks have applications that are sensitive to delay or data loss. For example, ERP applications, such as Oracle and PeopleSoft, tend to require low bandwidth and are highly sensitive to data loss. Voice traffic also requires low bandwidth, but is more sensitive to delay than data loss. Videoconferencing requires high levels of bandwidth and is sensitive to both data loss and delay.

Quality of service (QoS) mechanisms let us categorize network traffic according to its importance and give preferential treatment to the more important applications. You can even guarantee voice traffic a certain amount of bandwidth throughout the entire network, if needed. However, this comes at the expense of lower priority traffic. It is important to understand your network and the results of different QoS tools before implementing QoS.

Question 1

When implementing QoS at Layer 2 in Cisco switches, what bits in a frame are used to determine the type of service needed?

Question 2

What CoS is normally given to voice traffic?

Question 1 Answer

The 3 priority bits (the 802.1p bits) in the 802.1Q trunking header, or 3 of the 4 priority bits in the ISL trunking header, are set to specify the class of service (CoS) needed.

Question 2 Answer

A CoS value of 5 is normally given to voice traffic. This is the equivalent of IP Precedence 5 for critical traffic.

Question 3

Which two CoS values are reserved and cannot be assigned to traffic?

Question 4

Which CoS value is typically used for normal data traffic?

Question 3 Answer

CoS values 6 and 7, the highest priority values, are reserved. These correspond to IP Precedence values 6 (Internet) and 7 (Network).

Question 4 Answer

Normal data traffic is typically assigned a CoS value of 0, which corresponds to IP Precedence value 0 (Routine).

Question 5

How many queues are available by default on a Cisco 3550 when QoS is enabled? What CoS values are mapped to those queues?

Question 6

What are the default QoS settings on a Cisco 3550 switch?

Question 5 Answer

By default, each interface on a 3550 has four queues available. Each queue has the same default weight:

- **Queue 1**—CoS values 0 and 1
- **Queue 2**—CoS values 2 and 3
- **Queue 3**—CoS values 4 and 5
- **Queue 4**—CoS values 6 and 7

Question 6 Answer

By default, QoS is disabled. All frames are sent to output Queue 1 and are sent best-effort delivery. When the queue is full, frames are dropped. The existing CoS setting of any incoming frames is not trusted and is reset to 0.

Question 7

How are Layer 3 packets marked for class of service?

Question 8

By default, which CoS/IP Precedence values are mapped to which DSCP settings by the 3550 and 2950?

Question 7 Answer

The IP header contains an 8-bit Type of Service field. You can use this field in two ways:

- Use the upper 3 bits in this field to set the IP Precedence, which is compatible with the CoS bits in the trunking header on the switch.

- Use the upper 6 bits to set the DiffServe Code Point (DSCP) value. The upper 3 bits are backward compatible to IP Precedence and denote a priority value. The next 2 bits designate a drop probability for the packet. The sixth bit is 0 (unused).

Question 8 Answer

CoS Values	DSCP Settings
0	0
1	8
2	16
3	24
4	32
5	40
6	48
7	56

Question 9

If a frame comes into a switch interface already marked with a CoS value, what does the switch do with it by default?

Question 10

By default, which DSCP values are mapped to which CoS settings by the 3550 switch?

Question 9 Answer

By default, the switch does not trust the existing CoS marking and overwrites it.

Question 10 Answer

DSCP Values	CoS Settings
0–7	0
8–15	1
16–23	2
24–31	3
32–39	4
40–47	5
48–55	6
56–63	7

Question 11

What commands would you use to tell a specific 2950 or 3550 switch port to trust the CoS values on frames it receives, and to tag any unmarked frames with the CoS value corresponding to IP Precedence "priority"?

Implementing
QoS

Question 12

What are the steps to classify and mark traffic at an interface on a 2950 or 3550 switch using ACLs?

Implementing
QoS

Question 11 Answer

At the interface/port configuration mode, type

```
mls qos trust cos
mls qos 1
```

Question 12 Answer

Step 1 Create an access list permitting the traffic that should belong to a specific class. Each class has its own access list.

Step 2 Create a class map that has a match statement for the ACL(s) that specify traffic belonging to that class.

Step 3 Create a policy map that calls each class map and sets a policy for each (e.g., sets the DSCP value).

Step 4 Link the policy map to the appropriate interfaces with the **service-policy** command.

Question 13

What are the two types of bandwidth policing that can be configured on the switch?

Question 14

When doing QoS bandwidth policing, what happens to traffic that exceeds the specified bandwidth?

Question 13 Answer

Individual and aggregate. The 3550 switch can police bandwidth use either for each individual class of traffic (individual), or it can limit bandwidth use for all traffic (aggregate).

Question 14 Answer

Policed traffic that exceeds the specified rate can be dropped, or it can be marked with a lower DSCP value and then sent.

Question 15

Describe the Expedite queue on the 3550 and how it is enabled on the switch.

Question 16

At what point in the network should QoS marking (IP Precedence, DSCP, CoS) be done?

Question 15 Answer

The Expedite queue is a strict priority queue. It is serviced ahead of the other queues until it is empty. This queue is configured at interface configuration mode with the command **priority-queue out**. The fourth queue on each interface is used for the Expedite queue.

Question 16 Answer

Cisco recommends marking traffic for quality of service as close to the source as possible. If the source is an IP telephone, the phone can mark its traffic. If not, the access layer switch can do the marking. All network devices along the path should then be configured to trust the marking and provide a level of service based on it.

Question 17

The Catalyst 2950 switch has four output queues at each interface. Traffic can be scheduled to leave these queues in two different ways. What are they and how do they work?

Question 18

What command(s) are needed to configure strict priority queuing on a 2950 switch?

Question 17 Answer

- Weighted Round Robin (WRR) transmits some packets from each queue in a round robin fashion. The number of packets transmitted depends on the weight of the queue.

- Strict priority queues are assigned a priority value from 0 to 7 (7 is the highest priority). Packets from lower priority queues are not transmitted until the high priority queue is empty.

Question 18 Answer

At the interface configuration mode, type

```
no wrr-queue bandwidth
wrr-queue cos-map <queue no.> <cos range>
```

Question 19

What QoS mechanisms are appropriate for use at the access layer?

Question 20

What QoS mechanisms are appropriate for use at the distribution layer?

Question 19 Answer

At the access layer, classify and mark the traffic, and perhaps do policing. If the traffic is already classified by a trusted end station, configure the switch to trust the markings.

Question 20 Answer

At the distribution layer, configure the switch to trust the priority marking it receives from the access layer switches. If the markings are from an untrusted source, configure the switch to override them. You might then want to modify the switch's default per-hop behavior based on these values. If using WRED, you might change the DSCP-to-threshold mappings. You might also change the DSCP-to-CoS mappings to put traffic in different egress queues. Lastly, you typically change the relative weights of the queues on the egress interface.

Question 21

What are the 7 IP Precedence values and their meaning?

Question 22

How does the 3550 switch divide outbound bandwidth among the four egress queues?

Question 21 Answer

Precedence	Name
7	Network
6	Internet
5	Critical
4	Flash-override
3	Flash
2	Immediate
1	Priority
0	Routine

Question 22 Answer

The switch uses Weighted Round Robin (WRR) to service the four queues, unless one is configured as the expedite queue then the expedite queue is serviced ahead of other queues.

BCMSN Quick Reference Sheets

The Evolving Network Model

The Hierarchical Design Model

Cisco Systems has used the three-level *Hierarchical Design Model* for years. This older model provided a high-level idea of how a reliable network could be conceived, but was largely conceptual because it didn't provide specific guidance.

The layers break up a network in the following way:

- **Access layer**—End stations attach to VLANs.
  - —Clients attach to switch ports
  - —VLAN assigned/broadcast domains established
  - —Built using low-cost ports
  - —Simple quality of service (QoS) policies applied
- **Distribution layer**—Intermediate devices route and apply policies.
  - —VLANs terminated; routing is done between them
  - —Policies applied, such as
    - route selection
      - access lists
        - QoS
- **Core layer**—Backbone provides high-speed path between distribution elements.
  - —Distribution devices interconnected
  - —High speed (there's plenty of traffic)
  - —No policies (tough enough to keep up)

Later versions of this model showed redundant distribution and core devices and connections to make the model more fault tolerant. A set of distribution devices and their accompanying access layer switches were called a switch block.

Problems with the Hierarchical Design Model

This early model was a good starting point, but it failed to address key issues, such as

- Where do wireless devices fit in?
- How should Internet access and security be provisioned?
- How should remote access, such as dialup or virtual private network (VPN), be accounted for?
- Where should workgroup and enterprise services be located?

Enterprise Composite Network Model

The Cisco newer model, the enterprise composite model, is significantly more complex and attempts to address the major shortcoming of the hierarchical model by expanding the older version and making specific recommendations about how and where certain network functions should be implemented. This model is based on the principles described in the Cisco Architecture for Voice, Video, and Integrated Data (AVVID).

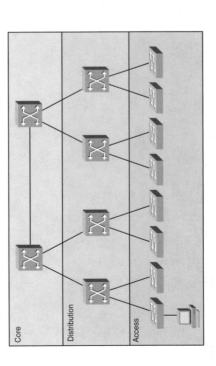

This simple drawing illustrates how the three-layer model might have been built out. A distribution Layer 3 switch would be used for each building on campus, tying together the access-switches on the floors. The core switches would link the various buildings together.

The enterprise composite model is broken up into three large sections:

- Enterprise campus
- Enterprise edge
- Service provider edge—The different public networks that are attached

The first section, the enterprise campus, looks like the old hierarchical model with some added details. It features six sections:

1. Campus backbone—Like the old "core"
2. Building distribution
3. Building access
4. Management
5. Edge distribution—A distribution layer out to the WAN
6. Server farm—For enterprise services

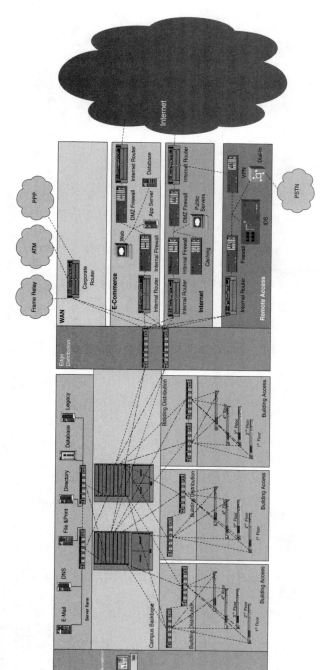

The enterprise edge details the connections from the campus to the wide area and includes the following:

1. E-commerce
2. Internet connectivity
3. Remote access—Dial and VPN
4. Wide-area network (WAN)—Internal links

The service provider edge is just a list of the public networks that facilitate wide-area connectivity:

1. Internet service provider (ISP)
2. Public Switched Telephone Network (PSTN)—Dialup
3. Frame Relay, Asynchronous Transfer Mode (ATM), and Point-to-Point Protocol (PPP)—Private connectivity

Multilayer Switching

Comparing Devices

Layer 2 switches
- MAC address learning
- Hardware-based bridge
- Forwarding/filtering based on MAC address
- Spanning tree to avoid loops
- Wire speed, low latency
- Scalable

Routers
- Understand network structure
- Forward along best path based on Layer 3 address
- Can apply policies to traffic
- Security
- Quality of service
- Routing
- Lower speed, higher latency

Layer 3 Switches
- Hardware-based routing
- Provide flow accounting
- Understand network structure
- Forward along best path
- Can apply policies to traffic
- Security
- Quality of service
- Routing
- Wire speed, low latency

Comparing Ethernet Versions

All versions of Ethernet have features in common:

- Same frame definition and field values
- Same MAC address structure

Ethernet
- 10 Mbps using Manchester encoding, half or full duplex
- Links extend 100 m, typically on CAT-5 cable
- Not typically deployed today

Fast Ethernet
- 100 Mbps using 4B5B encoding, half or full duplex
- Links extend 100 m on CAT-5 or CAT-6 cable
- Used for client attachment today

Gigabit Ethernet
- 1000 Mbps (1 Gbps) using 8B10B encoding, full duplex
- 1000Base-T supports 100 m links using CAT-5 or CAT-6 cable
- 1000Base-SX supports 550 m links using multimode fiber
- 1000Base-LX supports 10 km links using single-mode fiber
- Used to aggregate traffic to distribution or core switches today

10Gigabit Ethernet
- 10,000 Mbps (10Gbps), full duplex only
- Supports multimode (less than 300 m) and single-mode fiber (up to 40 km)
- Not common today; sometimes used to aggregate traffic in backbone

Long Range Ethernet
- 5–15 Mbps
- Links use very high data rate digital subscriber line (VDSL) modulation to extend 500 feet on CAT-1/2/3
- Used to provide broadband in multi-unit dwellings (apartments, office buildings, hotels)

Metro Ethernet

- Uses "dark fiber" or service provider
- Ethernet principles extended into metropolitan-area network (MAN)

Switching Roles in the Enterprise Composite Model

- Building Access—Typically Layer 2 switches
- Building Distribution—Typically Layer 3 switches
- Campus Backbone—Layer 2 switches if no Layer 3 capabilities required
- Server Farm—Usually Layer 3 switches at access and distribution

Catalyst Switch Basics

CatOS Versus IOS

CatOS

- Layer 2 switching
- Can use MSFC with IOS for Layer 3 (multilayer switching/functionality)
- Found on Catalyst 4000 and 6500 (optional)

IOS

- Layer 2 and 3 switching
- Ports can be "routed" or "switched"
- Found on Catalyst 2950 (Layer 2 only), 3550, 4000, and 6500 (optional)

Saving Catalyst Files

- Trivial File Transfer Protocol (TFTP)
  —To copy IOS to TFTP: **copy flash tftp**
  —To copy IOS from TFTP: **copy tftp flash**
  —Verify Flash contents: **show flash**
  —To save current configuration to NVRAM: **copy run start**
  —To save current configuration to TFTP: **copy run tftp**

IOS Troubleshooting

Show

- Provides snapshots of device performance
- Low overhead
- Information organized

Debug

- Provides real-time display of device performance
- High overhead
- Uses **show** processes to see processor utilization
- Information not organized
- Uses **service timestamps debug datetime msec** to see event times
- Focuses debugging to minimize impact

VLAN Implementation

What Is a VLAN?

A VLAN is a logical LAN or a logical subnet. It defines a broadcast domain. A physical subnet is a group of devices sharing the same physical wire. A logical subnet is a group of switch ports assigned to the same VLAN, regardless of their physical location in a switched network.

Two types of VLANs are

- **End-to-end VLAN**—Hosts in the VLAN reside on several different switches and are scattered throughout the network. Used when hosts are assigned to VLANs based on functions or workgroups, rather than physical location. VLANs should not extend past the Building Distribution submodule.

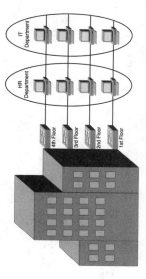

- **Geographic (local) VLAN**—Hosts are assigned to VLANs based on their location, such as a floor in a building. A router accomplishes sharing of resources between VLANs. This type is typically found in the Building Access submodule.

To use dynamic VLAN assignment, the commands are similar. At interface configuration mode, type

```
switchport mode access
switchport access vlan dynamic
```

If using dynamic, you must also enter the IP address of the VMPS server at global configuration mode:

```
vmps server ip address
```

Verifying VLAN Configuration

To see a list of all the VLANs and the ports assigned to them, use the command **show vlan**. To narrow down the information displayed, you can use these keywords after the command: **brief**, **id**, *vlan-number*, or **name** *vlan-name*.

```
ASW# show vlan brief
VLAN Name                             Status    Ports
---- -------------------------------  --------  ------------------------------
1    default                          active    Fa0/1, Fa0/2, Fa0/3,
                                                Fa0/10,Fa0/11,Fa0/12
20   VLAN0020                         active    Fa0/5,Fa0/6,Fa0/7
21   VLAN0021                         active    Fa0/8,Fa0/9
1002 fddi-default                     active
1003 trcrf-default                    active
1004 fddinet-default                  active
1005 trbrf-default                    active
```

Other verification commands include the following:

- **show running-config interface** *interface no.*—Use to verify the VLAN membership of the port:

```
ASW# show run interface fa0/5
Building configuration...
Current configuration 64 bytes
interface FastEthernet 0/5
switchport access vlan 20
switchport mode access
```

- **show mac address-table interface** *interface no.* **vlan** *vlan no.*—Use to view MAC addresses learned through that port for the specified VLAN:

```
ASW# show mac address-table interface fa0/1
         Mac Address Table
-------------------------------------------
Vlan    Mac Address      Type        Ports
----    -----------      ----        -----
1       0030.b656.7c3d   DYNAMIC     Fa0/1
Total Mac Addresses for this criterion: 1
```

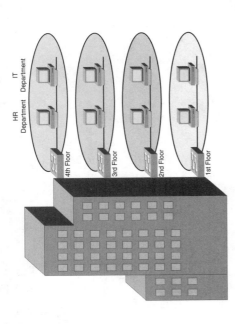

HR Department   IT Department

4th Floor
3rd Floor
2nd Floor
1st Floor

VLAN membership can be assigned either statically by port, or dynamically by MAC address using a VLAN Membership Policy Server (VMPS).

Creating a VLAN in Global Config Mode

```
(config)#vlan 12
(config-vlan)#name MYVLAN
```

Creating a VLAN in Database Mode

```
#vlan database
(vlan)#vlan 12 name MYVLAN
```

Delete a VLAN by using the same command with no in front of it. You do not need to include the name when deleting.

Assigning Ports to VLANs

When statically assigning ports to VLANs, first make it an access port and then assign the port to a VLAN. At the interface configuration prompt, type

```
switchport mode access
switchport access vlan 12
```

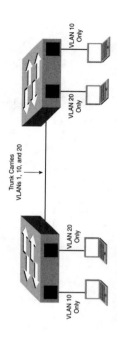

Two methods of identifying VLANs over trunk links are

- **ISL (Inter-Switch Link)**—Cisco proprietary; encapsulates the original frame in a header that contains VLAN information. Is protocol-independent; can identify Cisco Discovery Protocol (CDP) and bridge protocol data unit (BPDU) frames.
- **802.1Q**—Standards-based; tags the frames (inserts a field into the original frame immediately after the source MAC address field); supports Ethernet and Token Ring networks.

When a frame comes into a switch port, the frame is tagged internally within the switch with the VLAN number of the port. When it reaches the outgoing port, that internal tag is removed. If the exit port is a trunk port, then its VLAN is identified either in the ISL encapsulation or the 802.1Q tag. The switch on the other end of the trunk removes the ISL or 802.1Q information, checks the VLAN of the frame, and adds the internal tag. If the exit port is a user port, then the original frame is sent out unchanged, making the use of VLANs transparent to the user.

If a non-trunking port receives an ISL-encapsulated frame, the frame is dropped. Also, if the ISL header and footer cause the MTU size to be exceeded, it might be counted as an error.

If a non-trunking port receives an 802.1Q frame, the source and destination MAC addresses are read, the tag field is ignored, and the frame is switched normally at Layer 2.

Configuring a Trunk Link

Ports can become trunk ports either by static configuration or dynamic negotiation using Dynamic Trunking Protocol (DTP). A switch port can be in one of five DTP modes:

- **Access**—The port is a user port and cannot be a trunk.
- **Trunk**—The port is a trunk and negotiates trunking with the port on the other end of the link.

- **show interfaces** *interface no.* **switchport**—Use to see detailed information about the port configuration, such as entries in the Administrative Mode and Access Mode VLAN fields:

```
ASW# show interfaces fa0/1 switchport
Name: Fa0/1
Switchport: Enabled
Administrative Mode: dynamic desirable
Operational Mode: static access
Administrative Trunking Encapsulation: negotiate
Operational Trunking Encapsulation: native
Negotiation of Trunking: On
Access Mode VLAN: 1 (default)
Trunking Native Mode VLAN: 1 (default)
Trunking VLANs Enabled: ALL
Pruning VLANs Enabled: 2-1001
Protected: false
Unknown unicast blocked: false
Unknown multicast blocked: false
Broadcast Suppression Level: 100
Multicast Suppression Level: 100
Unicast Suppression Level: 100
```

Troubleshooting VLAN Issues

The three steps in troubleshooting VLAN problems are

1. **Check the physical connectivity**—Make sure the cable is good and the network adapter and switch port are both good. Check the port's link LED.

2. **Check the switch configuration**—If you see frame check sequence (FCS) errors or late collisions, suspect a duplex mismatch. Also check configured speed on both ends of the link. Increasing collisions might mean an overloaded link, such as with a broadcast storm.

3. **Check the VLAN configuration**—If two hosts can't communicate, make sure they are both in the same VLAN. If a host can't connect to a switch, make sure the host and the switch are in the same VLAN.

VLAN Trunking

A *trunk* is a link that carries traffic for more than one VLAN. Trunks multiplex traffic from multiple VLANs. Trunks connect switches and allow ports on multiple switches to be assigned to the same VLAN.

- **Nonnegotiate**—When this keyword is added, the port is a trunk and does not do DTP negotiation with the other side of the link.
- **Dynamic Desirable**—Actively negotiates trunking with the other side of the link. Becomes a trunk if the port on the other switch is set to **trunk**, **dynamic desirable**, or **dynamic auto** mode.
- **Dynamic Auto**—Passively waits to be contacted by the other switch. Becomes a trunk if the other end is set to **trunk** or **dynamic desirable** mode.

Configure a port for trunking at the interface configuration mode:

`switchport mode {dynamic {auto | desirable} | trunk}`

If dynamic mode is used, DTP negotiates trunking state and encapsulation. If trunk mode is used, you must specify encapsulation:

`switchport trunk encapsulation {isl | dot1q | negotiate}`

Native VLAN with 802.1Q

If you are using 802.1Q, you must specify a native VLAN for the trunk link with this command:

`switchport trunk native vlan vlan no.`

Frames from the native VLAN are sent over the trunk link untagged. It is the VLAN the port would be in if it were not a trunk and must match on both sides of the trunk link. VLAN 1 is the default native VLAN for all ports.

VLAN Mapping

ISL trunking recognizes only VLANs numbered 1–1001, but 802.1Q can use VLANs 0–4094. If you are using both ISL and 802.1Q in your network and have VLANs numbered above 1001, you have to map the 802.1Q VLANs to ISL numbers. Some rules about mapping VLANs are as follows:

- You can configure only eight mappings.
- Mappings are local to the switch—The same mappings must be configured on all switches in the network.
- You can map only to Ethernet ISL VLANs.
- The 802.1Q VLANs with the same number as mapped ISL VLANs are blocked. (For example, you map 802.1Q VLAN 1500 to ISL VLAN 150, and then 802.1Q VLAN 150 is blocked on that switch.)
- Don't map the 802.1Q native VLAN.

VLANs Allowed on the Trunk

By default, a trunk carries traffic for all VLANs. You can change that behavior for a particular trunk link by giving the following command at the interface config mode:

`switchport trunk allowed vlan vlans`

Make sure that both sides of a trunk link allow the same VLANs.

Verifying a Trunk Link

You can use two commands to verify your trunk configuration:

`show running-config`
`show interfaces [interface no.] switchport | trunk`

Using the **trunk** keyword with the **show interfaces** command gives information about the trunk link:

```
ASW# show interfaces fastethernet 0/1 trunk
Port      Mode        Encapsulation   Status      Native vlan
Fa0/1     desirable   n-802.1q        trunking    1
Port      Vlans allowed on trunk
Fa0/1     1-150
<further output omitted>
```

802.1Q Tunnels

Tunneling is a way to send 802.1Q-tagged frames across a foreign network (such as a service provider's network) and still preserve the original 802.1Q tag. The service provider (SP) configures its end of the trunk link as a tunnel port and assigns a VLAN to carry your traffic within its network. The SP switch then adds a second 802.1Q tag to each frame that came in the tunnel port. Other switches in the SP network see only this second tag, and don't read the original tag. When the frame exits the SP network, the extra tag is removed, leaving the original 802.1Q tag to be read by the receiving switch in your network.

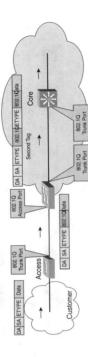

Layer 2 Protocol Tunneling

If a service provider separates sections of your network, you can use Layer 2 protocol tunneling to tunnel CDP, Spanning Tree Protocol (STP), and VLAN Trunking Protocol (VTP) frames across the SP's cloud. This is called Generic Bridge PDU Tunneling (GBPT). Frames from the previously mentioned control protocols are encapsulated as they enter the SP's network on a tunnel port, and de-encapsulated when they exit that network.

Troubleshooting Trunking

- Both sides of the link in the correct trunking mode?
- Same trunk encapsulation on both sides?
- If 802.1Q, same native VLAN on both sides?

VLAN Trunking Protocol

VLAN Trunking Protocol (VTP) runs over trunk links and synchronizes the VLAN databases of all switches in the VTP domain. A VTP domain is an administrative group. All switches within that group must have the same VTP domain name configured, or they will not synchronize databases.

VTP works by using configuration revision numbers and VTP advertisements:

- All switches send out VTP advertisements every five minutes or when a change to the VLAN database happens (a VLAN is created, deleted, or renamed.)
- VTP advertisements contain a configuration revision number. This number is increased by 1 for every VLAN change.
- When a switch receives a VTP advertisement, it compares the configuration revision number against the one in its VLAN database.
- If the new number is higher, the switch overwrites its database with the new VLAN information and forwards the information to its neighbor switches.
- If the number is the same, the switch ignores the advertisement.
- If the new number is lower, the switch replies with the more up-to-date information contained in its own database.

VTP Switch Roles

A VTP switch can be

- A **server**—The default. Servers can create, delete, and rename VLANs. They originate both periodic and triggered VTP advertisements and synchronize their databases with other switches in the domain.
- A **client**—Clients cannot make VLAN changes. They originate periodic VTP advertisements and synchronize their databases with other switches in the domain.

- **Transparent**—Can create, delete, and rename VLANs, but its VLANs are local only. Does not originate advertisements; does not synchronize its database with any other switches. It forwards VTP advertisements out its trunk links, however.

VTP Pruning

Recall that, by default, switches flood broadcasts, multicasts, and unknown unicasts across trunk links. Suppose a host in VLAN 10 on Switch B sends a broadcast. Hosts in VLAN 10 on Switch C need to see that broadcast, but Switch A has no ports in VLAN 10, so it just drops the broadcast traffic.

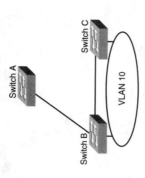

Enabling VTP Pruning causes the switch to keep track of VLAN port assignments in its downstream switches. The switch then sends only flooded traffic on trunks toward switches that have ports assigned to the VLAN originating the traffic. It prunes flooded traffic from all other trunks. VTP Pruning increases the available bandwidth by preventing unnecessary traffic on trunk links.

Two versions of VTP exist—Version 1 and Version 2. To use Version 2, all switches in the domain must be capable of using it. Configure one server for Version 2, and the information is propagated through VTP. Version 2 has the following added features:

- It supports Token Ring VLANs.
- Transparent switches pass along messages from both versions of VTP.
- Consistency checks are performed only when changes are configured through the command-line interface (CLI) or Simple Network Management Protocol (SNMP).

Configuring VTP

VTP configuration is done at the global config mode. To configure the switch's VTP mode, type

vtp {server | client | transparent}

To configure the VTP domain name, type

vtp domain *name*

To configure a VTP password (all switches in the domain must use the same password), type

vtp password *password*

To configure the switch to use VTP Version 2, type

vtp v2-mode

To enable pruning, type

vtp pruning

To specify which VLANs are to be pruned, type

switchport trunk pruning vlan {add | except | none | remove} *vlan-list*
[*,vlan[,vlan[,,,]]*]

Verifying and Monitoring VTP

To get basic information about the VTP configuration, use **show vtp status**.
The following example shows the default settings:

```
ASW# show vtp status
VTP Version                     : 1
Configuration Revision          : 0
Maximum VLANs supported locally : 1005
Number of existing VLANs        : 5
VTP Operating Mode              : Server
VTP Domain Name                 :
VTP Pruning Mode                : Disabled
VTP V2 Mode                     : Disabled
VTP Traps Generation            : Disabled
MD5 digest                      :
```

Troubleshooting VTP

Here are some common items to check when troubleshooting problems with VTP:

- Make sure you are trunking between the switches. VTP is sent only over trunk links.
- Make sure the domain name matches on both switches (name is case sensitive).
- If the switch is not updating its database, make sure it is not in transparent mode.
- If using passwords, make sure they all match. To remove a password, use **no vtp password**.

Adding a New Switch to a VTP Domain

Adding a new switch in client mode does not prevent it from propagating its incorrect VLAN information. A server synchronizes to a client if the client has the higher configuration revision number. You must reset the revision number back to 0 on the new switch. The easiest way to do this is to change the domain name. Then, change it back to the correct one and attach the switch to the network.

Understanding the Spanning Tree Protocol

Switches either forward or filter Layer 2 frames. The way they make the forwarding/filtering decision can lead to loops in a network with redundant links. Spanning tree is a protocol that detects potential loops and breaks them.

A Layer 2 switch is functionally the same thing as a transparent bridge. Transparent bridges

- Learn MAC addresses by looking at the source address of incoming frames. They build a table mapping MAC address to port number.
- Forward broadcasts and multicasts out all ports except the on they came in on. (This is called *flooding*.)
- Forward unknown unicasts out all ports except the one they came in on. An unknown unicast is a message bound for a unicast MAC address that is not in the switch's table of addresses and ports.
- Do not make any changes to the frames as they forward them.

Spanning Tree Protocol (STP) works by selecting a root bridge, then selecting one loop-free path from the root bridge to every other switch. (STP uses the term *bridge* because it was written before there were switches.) Consider the following switched network.

Spanning tree must select:

- One root bridge
- One root port per non-root bridge
- One designated port per network segment

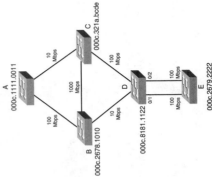

Spanning Tree Election Criteria

1. Lowest Root Bridge ID (BID)
2. Lowest path cost to the root
3. Lowest sender Bridge ID
4. Lowest sender Port ID (PID)

Bridge ID = Bridge priority : Bridge MAC address

Bridge priority = A 2-byte value, 0–65,535 (0–FFFF hex).

Default priority is 32,768 (8000 hex)

Port ID = Port priority : port number

Port Priority = A 6-bit value, 0–63, default is 32

Path cost—Cumulative value of the cost of each link between the bridge and the root.
An old way of calculating cost and a new way of calculating cost exists:

Link Speed	Old Cost	New Cost
10 Mbps	100	100
100 Mbps	10	19
1 Gbps	1	4
10 Gbps	1	2

The STP Election

Root Bridge Election

Looking at the example, first select the root bridge. Assume each switch is using the default priority.

- Switch A BID = 80-00-00-0c-11-11-00-11
- Switch B BID = 80-00-00-0c-26-78-10-10
- Switch C BID = 80-00-00-0c-32-1a-bc-de
- Switch D BID = 80-00-00-0c-81-81-11-22
- Switch E BID = 80-00-00-0c-26-79-22-22

Switch A has the lowest BID, so it is elected the root. Each non-root switch must now elect a root port.

Root Port Election

- **Switch B**—Uses the connected link to A, path cost of 19 (link speed of 100 Mbps).
- **Switch C**—The connected link has a path cost of 100 (link speed of 10 Mbps), the link through B has a path cost of 38 (two 100 Mbps links), and so that port is chosen.
- **Switch D**—The link through B has a path cost of 119, the path cost through C to A is 119, the path through C then B is 57, so that port is chosen.
- **Switch E**—The lowest path cost is the same for both ports (76—through D to C to B to A). Next, check sender BID. Sender for both ports is D, so that doesn't break the tie. Next, check sender Port ID. Assuming default port priority, the PID for 0/1 is lower than the PID for 0/2, so the port on the left is the root port.

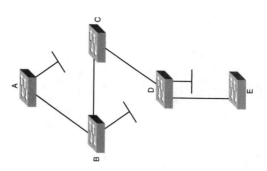

Designated Port Election

- The root bridge is the designated bridge for every segment connected to it (A–B and A–C in our example).
- **Segment B–D**—B has the lowest path cost to root (19 versus 119), so it is designated for this segment.
- **Segment C–D**—C has the lowest path cost to the root (100 versus 119), so it is designated for this segment.
- **Segment B–C**—B has the lowest path cost to the root (19 versus 100), so it is designated for this segment.
- **Both segments D–E**—D has the lowest path cost to the root (57 versus 76), so it is designated for both segments.

Now the looped topology has been turned into a tree, with A at the root. Notice that no more redundant links exist.

Bridge Protocol Data Units

Switches exchange Bridge Protocol Data Units (BPDUs). Two types of BPDUs exist: configuration and topology change.

Configuration BPDUs are sent every two seconds from the root towards downstream switches. They are used during an election, maintain connectivity between switches, and send timer information from the root.

Topology Change (TCN) BPDUs are sent towards the root when

- There is a link failure.
- A port starts forwarding, and there is already a designated port.
- The switch receives a TCN from a neighbor.

When a switch receives a TCN BPDU, it acknowledges that with a configuration BPDU that has the Topology Change Acknowledgment bit set.

When the root bridge receives a TCN, it starts sending configuration BPDUs with the Topology Change bit set for a period of time equal to Max Age plus Forward Delay. Switches that receive this change their MAC table Aging Time to the Forward Delay time, causing MAC addresses to age out faster. The topology change also causes a new election of the root bridge, root ports, and designated ports.

BPDU Fields

Some of the fields in the BPDU include the following:

- Root Bridge ID
- Sender's Root Path Cost
- Sender's Bridge ID
- Sender's Port ID
- Message Age
- Hello time—2 sec by default
- Forward Delay—15 sec by default
- Max Age—20 sec by default

Spanning Tree Port States

When a port is first activated, it transitions through the following stages:

Port State	Timer	Actions
Blocking	Max Age (20 sec)	Discards frames, does not learn MAC addresses, does receive BPDUs
Listening	Forward Delay (15 sec)	Discards frames, does not learn MAC addresses, receives BPDUs to determine its role in the network
Learning	Forward Delay (15 sec)	Discards frames, does learn MAC addresses, does receive and transmit BPDUs
Forwarding		Accepts frames, learns MAC addresses, receives and transmits BPDUs

Designing for Spanning Tree

To optimize data flow in the network, design and configure switches for the following STP roles:

- Primary and secondary root bridges (set priority values)
- Designated and root ports (set port priorities/path cost)
- Enable STP enhancements such as Root Guard

Spanning Tree and PVST

With PVST (per-VLAN spanning tree), a different instance of STP exists for each VLAN. To derive the VLAN BID, the switch picks a different MAC address from its base pool for each VLAN. Each VLAN has its own root bridge, root port, etc. You can configure these so that data flow is optimized, and traffic load is balanced among the switches. Spanning tree is enabled by default on every VLAN.

Configuring Spanning Tree

To change the STP priority value, type
Switch(config)# **spanning-tree vlan** *vlan no.* **priority** *value*

To configure a switch as root without manually changing priority values, type
Switch(config)# **spanning-tree vlan** *vlan no.* **root {primary | secondary}**

To change the STP port cost for an access port, type
Switch(config-if)# **spanning-tree cost** *value*

To change the STP port cost for a VLAN on a trunk port, type
Switch(config-if)# **spanning-tree vlan** *vlan no.* **cost** *value*

To display the STP information for a particular VLAN, type
Switch# **show spanning-tree vlan** *vlan no.*

To display the STP information for an interface, type

Switch # **show spanning-tree interface** *interface no.* **[detail]**

To verify STP timers, type

#**show spanning-tree bridge brief**

Spanning Tree Enhancements

Cisco has some proprietary enhancements to spanning tree that help speed up network convergence. They include the following:

- Port Fast
- Uplink Fast
- Backbone Fast

Port Fast

Port Fast is for access (user) ports only. It causes the port to bypass the STP listening and learning states, and transition directly to forwarding. If a BPDU is received, Port Fast is abandoned, the port placed in blocking, and the switch runs through the entire Spanning Tree procedure.

(config-if)# **spanning-tree portfast**

Uplink Fast

Uplink Fast is for speeding convergence when a direct link to an upstream switch fails. The switch identifies backup ports for the root port (these are called an *uplink group*). If the root port fails, one of the ports in the uplink group is unblocked and transitions immediately to forwarding—bypassing the listening and learning stages. It should be used in wiring closet switches with at least one blocked port:

(config)# **spanning-tree uplinkfast**

Backbone Fast

Backbone Fast is used for speeding convergence when a link fails that is not directly connected to the switch. It helps the switch detect indirect failures. If a switch running Backbone Fast receives an inferior BPDU from its designated bridge, it knows a link on the path to the root has failed. (An inferior BPDU is one that lists the same switch for root bridge and designated bridge.)

The switch then tries to find an alternate path to the root by sending a Root Link Query (RLQ) protocol data unit (PDU) out all alternate ports. The root then responds

with a RLQ response, and the port receiving this response can transition to forwarding. Alternate ports are determined in this way:

- If the inferior BPDU was received on a blocked port, the root port and any other blocked ports are considered alternates.
- If the inferior BPDU was received on the root port, all blocked ports are considered alternates.
- If the inferior BPDU was received on the root port and there are no blocked ports, the switch assumes it has lost connectivity with the root and advertises itself as root.

Configure this command on all switches in the network:

(config)#**spanning-tree backbonefast**

Rapid Spanning Tree Protocol

Rapid Spanning Tree Protocol (RSTP)—802.1w—is a standards-based, non-proprietary way of speeding STP convergence. Switch ports exchange an explicit handshake when they transition to forwarding. RSTP describes different port states than regular STP, as shown in the following table.

STP Port State	Equivalent RSTP Port State
Disabled	Discarding
Blocking	Discarding
Listening	Discarding
Learning	Learning
Forwarding	Forwarding

RSTP Port Roles

RSTP also defines different spanning-tree roles for ports:

- **Root port**—The best path to the root (same as STP)
- **Designated port**—Same role as with STP
- **Alternate port**—A backup to the root port
- **Backup port**—A backup to the designated port
- **Disabled port**—One not used in the spanning tree
- **Edge port**—One connected only to an end user

BPDU Differences in RSTP

In regular STP, BPDUs are originated by the root and relayed by each switch. In RSTP, each switch originates BPDUs, whether or not it receives a BPDU on its root port. All 8 bits of the BPDU type field are used by RSTP. The TC and TC Ack bits are still used; the other 6 bits specify the port's role and its RSTP state and are used in the port hand-shake. The RSTP BPDU is set to Type 2, Version 2. PVST is done by Rapid per-VLAN spanning tree plus (PVST+) on Catalyst switches.

RSTP Fast Convergence

- RSTP uses a mechanism similar to Backbone Fast—When an inferior BPDU is received, the switch accepts it. If the switch has another path to the root, it uses that and informs its downstream switch of the alternate path.

- Edge ports work the same as Port Fast ports—They automatically transition directly to forwarding.

- Link type—If you connect two switches through a point-to-point link and the local port becomes a designated port, it exchanges a handshake with the other port to quickly transition to forwarding. Full-duplex links are assumed to be point-to-point; half-duplex links are assumed to be shared.

- Also, backup and alternate ports can transition to forwarding when no BPDUs are received from a neighbor switch (similar to Uplink Fast).

If an RSTP switch detects a topology change, it sets a TC timer to twice the hello time and sets the TC bit on all BPDUs sent out its designated and root ports until the timer expires. It also clears the MAC addresses learned on these ports.
If an RSTP switch receives a TC BPDU, it clears the MAC addresses on that port and sets the TC bit on all BPDUs sent out its designated and root ports until the TC timer expires.

Multiple Spanning Tree (MST)

With MST, you can group VLANs and run just one instance of spanning tree for a group of VLANs. This cuts down on the number of BPDUs in your network. Switches in the same MST Region share the same configuration and VLAN mappings. Configure MST with these commands:

```
(config)# spanning-tree mode mst
(config)# spanning-tree mst configuration
(config-mst)# name region_name
(config-mst)# revision number
(config-mst)# instance number vlan vlan range
(config-mst)# end
```

To be compatible with 802.1Q trunking, which has one Common Spanning Tree (CST) for all VLANs, MST runs one instance of an Internal Spanning Tree (IST). The IST appears as one bridge to a CST area and is MST instance number 0. The original MST spanning trees (called M-Trees) are active only within the region—they combine at the edge of the CST area to form one.

EtherChannel

EtherChannel is a way of combining several physical links between switches into one logical connection. Normally, spanning tree would block redundant links. EtherChannel gets around that and allows load balancing across those links. Load balancing is done based on such things as source or destination MAC address or IP address. At global config mode, type

```
port-channel load-balance type
```

A logical interface—the Port Channel interface—is created. Configuration can be applied both to the logical and physical interfaces.
Here are some guidelines for EtherChannel:

- Interfaces in the channel do not have to be physically next to each other or on the same module.

- All ports must be the same speed and duplex.

- All ports in the EtherChannel bundle should be enabled.

- None of the bundle ports can be a Switch Port Analyzer (SPAN) port.

- Assign an IP address to the logical Port Channel interface, not the physical ones.

- Put all bundle ports in the same VLAN, or make them all trunks. If they are trunks, they must all carry the same VLANs and use the same trunking mode.

- Configuration you apply to the Port Channel interface affects the entire EtherChannel. Configuration you apply to a physical interface affects only that interface.

Configuring an EtherChannel

Basically, for a Layer 3 EtherChannel, configure the logical interface and then put the physical interfaces into the channel group:

```
interface port-channel number
no switchport
ip address address mask
```

Then, at each port that is part of the EtherChannel:

```
interface { number | range interface - interface}
channel-group number mode {auto | desirable | on}
```

Putting the IP address on the Port Channel interface creates a Layer 3 EtherChannel. Simply putting interfaces into a channel group creates a Layer 2 EtherChannel, and the logical interface is automatically created.

The Cisco proprietary Port Aggregation Protocol (PAgP) dynamically negotiates the formation of a channel. Three PAgP modes exist:

- **On**—The port channels without using PAgP negotiation. The port on the other side must also be set to On.

- **Auto**—Responds to PAgP messages but does not initiate them. Port channels if the port on the other end is set to Desirable. This is the default mode.

- **Desirable**—Port actively negotiates channeling status with the interface on the other end of the link. Port channels if other side is Auto or Desirable.

Also, a non-proprietary protocol called Link Aggregation Control Protocol (LACP), IEEE 802.3ad, does the same thing. LACP has two modes:

- **Active**—Port actively negotiates channeling with the port on the other end of the link. Channel forms if other side is passive or active.

- **Passive**—Responds to LACP messages but does not initiate them. Channel forms if other end is set to active.

If you want to use LACP, specify it under the interface and put the interface in either active or passive mode.

```
channel-protocol lacp
```

Verifying an EtherChannel

Here are some typical commands for verifying an EtherChannel:

- **show running-config interface** *number*
- **show interfaces** *number* **etherchannel**
- **show etherchannel** *number* **port-channel**
- **show etherchannel summary**

Additional Spanning Tree Features

Some additional features available to help you tune spanning tree include

- BPDU Guard
- BPDU Filtering
- Root Guard
- Unidirectional Link Detection (UDLD)
- Loop Guard

BPDU Guard

BPDU Guard prevents loops if another switch is attached to a Port Fast port. When BPDU Guard is enabled on an interface, it is put into an error-disabled state (basically, shut down) if a BPDU is received on the interface. It can be enabled at either global config mode—in which case it affects all Port Fast interfaces—or at interface mode. Port Fast does not have to be enabled for it to be configured at a specific interface.

```
(config)# spanning-tree portfast bpduguard default
(config-if)# spanning-tree bpduguard enable
```

BPDU Filtering

BPDU filtering is another way of preventing loops in the network. It also can be enabled either globally or at the interface and functions differently at each. In global config, if a Port Fast interface receives any BPDUs, it is taken out of Port Fast status. At interface config mode, it prevents the port from sending or receiving BPDUs. The commands are

```
(config)# spanning-tree portfast bpdufilter default
(config-if)# spanning-tree bpdufilter enable
```

Root Guard

Root Guard is meant to prevent the wrong switch from becoming the spanning-tree root. It is enabled on ports other than the root port, on switches other than the root. If a Root Guard port receives a BPDU that would cause it to become a root port, the port is put into "root-inconsistent" state and does not pass traffic through it. If the port stops receiving these BPDUs, it automatically re-enables itself.

```
(config-if)# spanning-tree guard root
```

Unidirectional Link Detection (UDLD)

A switch notices when a physical connection is broken, by the absence of Layer 1 electrical keepalives (Ethernet calls this a link beat). But sometimes, a cable is intact enough to maintain keepalives, but not to pass data in both directions. This is a unidirectional link. UDLD detects a unidirectional link by sending periodic hellos out the interface. It also uses probes, which must be acknowledged by the device on the other end of the link. UDLD operates at Layer 2. The port is shut down if a unidirectional link is found.

- To enable UDLD on all fiber-optic interfaces, use this command:

```
(config)# udld enable
```

Although this command is given at global config mode, it applies only to fiber ports.

• To enable UDLD on non-fiber ports, give the same command at interface config mode.

• To disable UDLD on a specific fiber port, use this command:
(config-if)# `udld disable`

• To disable UDLD on a specific non-fiber port, use this command:
(config-if)#`no udld enable`

• To re-enable all interfaces shut by UDLD:
#`udld reset`

• To verify UDLD status:
#`show udld` *interface*

Loop Guard

Loop Guard prevents loops that might develop if a port that should be blocking inadvertently transitions to the forwarding state. This can happen if the port stops receiving BPDUs (perhaps because of a unidirectional link or a software/configuration problem in its neighbor switch). When one of the ports in a physically redundant topology stops receiving BPDUs, the STP conceives the topology as loop-free. Eventually, the blocking port becomes designated, and moves to forwarding state, thus creating a loop. With Loop Guard enabled, an additional check is made.

If no BPDUs are received on a blocked port for a specific length of time, Loop Guard puts that port into "loop inconsistent" blocking state, rather than transitioning to forwarding state. Loop Guard should be enabled on all switch ports that have a chance of becoming root or designated ports. It is most effective when enabled in the entire switched network, in conjunction with UDLD.

To enable Loop Guard for all point-to-point links on the switch, use the following command:

(config)# `spanning-tree loopguard default`

To enable Loop Guard on a specific interface, type

(config-if)# `spanning-tree guard loop`

Loop Guard automatically re-enables the port if it starts receiving BPDUs once again.

Troubleshooting STP

Some common things to look for when troubleshooting Spanning Tree Protocol include

• **Duplex mismatch**—When one side of the link is half duplex and the other is full duplex. Causes late collisions and FCS errors.

• **Unidirectional link failure**—When the link is up but data only flows in one direction. Can cause loops.

• **Frame corruption**—Physical errors on the line cause BPDUs to be lost, and the port incorrectly begins forwarding. Caused by duplex mismatch, bad cable, or too long of cable.

• **Resource errors**—STP is implemented in software, so a switch with an overloaded CPU or memory can neglect some STP duties.

• **Port Fast configuration errors**—Connecting a switch to two ports that have Port Fast enabled. Can cause a loop.

• **STP tuning errors**—Max Age or Forward Delay set too short can cause a loop. Network diameter set too low causes BPDUs to be discarded and affect STP convergence.

Identifying a Bridging Loop

Suspect a loop if you see the following:

• You capture the traffic on the overloaded link and see the same frames multiple times. This signifies a loop.

• All users in one bridging domain have connectivity problems at the same time.

• An abnormally high activity exists when checking port utilization.

To remedy a loop quickly, shut redundant ports and then enable them one at a time. Some switches allow debugging of STP (not 3550/2950) to help in diagnosing problems.

What to Use Where

Confused by all the acronyms and STP features? The following diagram shows the STP features you might use in your network, and where you might use them.

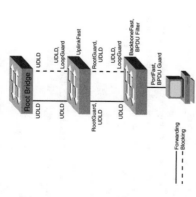

--- Forwarding
- - - - Blocking

Multilayer Switching

Understanding the Switching Process

Here are the steps involved in Layer 2 forwarding:

Input

1. Receive frame
2. Verify frame integrity
3. Apply inbound VLAN access control list (ACL)
4. Lookup destination MAC

Output

1. Apply outbound VLAN ACL
2. Apply outbound QoS ACL
3. Select output port
4. Queue on port
5. Rewrite
6. Forward

Here are the steps involved in Layer 3 forwarding:

Input

1. Receive frame
2. Verify frame integrity
3. Apply inbound VLAN ACL
4. Lookup destination MAC

Routing

1. Input ACL
2. Switch if entry cached
3. Identify exit interface and next-hop address using routing table
4. Output ACL

Output

1. Apply outbound VLAN ACL
2. Apply outbound QoS ACL
3. Select output port
4. Queue on port
5. Rewrite source and destination MAC, IP checksum, and frame check sequence (FCS); decrement Time to Live (TTL)
6. Forward

Understanding the Switching Table

Content Addressable Memory (CAM)

- Used for Catalyst 4000 Layer 2 forwarding tables
- Used for Catalyst 6500 Layer 2 and NetFlow forwarding tables
- Binary values (0 or 1)
- Match must be exact

Ternary Content Addressable Memory (TCAM)

- Used for Catalyst 3550, 4000, and 6500 Layer 3 switching
- Ternary (3) values (0, 1, or wildcard)
- Entries are in VMR form:
  - Value—Pattern to be matched
  - Mask—Masking bits associated with pattern
  - Result—Consequences of a match (permit/deny; or more complex information

BGP Table

Address	Prefix	AS-Path	Next-Hop	Communities	Other Attr.
10.0.0.0	/8	42 13	1.2.3.4	37:12	
...					

BGP Table Map

Next-Hop	Outgoing Interface	Precedence	QoS Group
1.2.3.4	Ethernet 0	3	7
1.5.4.1	Ethernet 0	—	—

IP Routing Table

Protocol	Address	Prefix	Next-Hop
BGP	10.0.0.0	/8	1.2.3.4
OSPF	1.2.3.0	/24	1.5.4.1
Conn.	1.5.4.0	/24	

FIB Table (CEF Cache)

Address	Prefix	Adjacency Pointer
10.0.0.0	/8	1.5.4.1
...		

IP Address	Precedence	QoS Group
1.5.4.1	3	7

Adjacency Table

IP Address	Layer 2 Header
1.5.4.1	MAC Header
...	

ARP Cache

IP Address	MAC Address
1.5.4.1	0c.00.11.22.33.44

Understanding Switch Forwarding Architectures

Centralized Forwarding
- Decision made by single table
- Used by 4000 and 6500

Distributed Forwarding
- Decision made at port or module
- Used by 3550 and 6500 with distributed forwarding card

NetFlow Switching
- Decision made cooperatively by route processor and Multilayer Switching (MLS)
- First packet switched in software; result cached
- Subsequent packets switched in hardware

Cisco Express Forwarding (CEF)
- Topology based switching (via Forwarding Information Base [FIB])
- Can be centralized or distributed

Cisco Express Forwarding (CEF)

CEF does the following:
- Separates control plane hardware from data plane hardware
- Controls control plane runs in software and builds Forwarding Information Base (FIB) and adjacency table
- The data plane uses hardware to forward most IP unicast traffic
- Handles traffic that must be forwarded in software (much slower) including:
  —Packets originating from device
  —Packets with IP header options
  —Tunneled traffic
  —802.3 (IPX) frames
- Supports load sharing
- FIB is an optimized routing table, stored in TCAM
- Builds adjacencies from Address Resolution Protocol (ARP) data

ARP throttling:
- First packet to destination forwarded to route processor
- Subsequent traffic dropped until MAC resolved
- Prevents overwhelming RP with redundant ARP requests
- Helps during denial-of-service attacks; removed when MAC resolved or in 2 seconds

Configuring and Troubleshooting CEF

By default, CEF is on and supports per destination load sharing.

To disable CEF:
- 4000: **no ip cef.**
- 3550: On each interface, use **no ip route-cache cef.**
- 6550 with Policy Feature Card, Distributed FC, and Multilayer Switch FC: Cannot be disabled.

View CEF information:
show interface fastethernet 2/2 | begin L3

View switching statistics:
show interface fastethernet 2/2 | include switched

View FIB: show ip cef

View detailed CEF FIB entry:

show ip cef fastethernet 2/2 10.0.0.1 detail

Troubleshoot CEF drops:

debug ip cef drops

Troubleshoot packets not forwarded by CEF:

debug ip cef receive

Troubleshoot CEF events:

debug ip cef events

Inter-VLAN Routing

Inter-VLAN Routing Using Multilayer Switches

Port roles:

- VLAN port—Acts as Layer 2 switching port with a VLAN
  - Static VLAN—Use **switchport** command to identify VLAN
  - Dynamic VLAN—Use VLAN Membership Policy Server (VMPS)
- Trunk port—Passes multiple VLANs and differentiates by tagging
  - Use **switchport** command to set parameters
  - ISL or 802.1Q
- Switch virtual interface (SVI)—Virtual routed port in a VLAN
  - Use to route or fallback bridge between VLANs
  - Default SVI for VLAN 1 automatically created
  - Associate with VLAN using **interface vlan#**
  - Not associated with VLAN
- Routed port—Acts as Layer 3 routed port
  - Place in Layer 3 mode with **no switchport**
  - Turn on routing using **ip routing**
  - Assign address and enable routing protocols as needed

Inter-VLAN Routing

Multilayer switches do the following:

- Enable IP routing using **ip routing**
- Create SVI using **interface vlan#**
- Assign IP address to each interface

Router-on-a-stick—Attach router to switch using trunk line (ISL or 802.1Q):

- Easy to implement
- Uses existing equipment
- Much more latency than MLS solution
- Configure by creating subinterface—**interface fastethernet 1/0.7**
- Associate VLAN to interface with command **encapsulation isl 7** or **encapsulation dot1q 7**:
  - ISL—No address on main interface
  - 802.1Q—Address on main interface for native (untagged) VLAN

Multilayer Switch Reliability

Equipment Goals

Network hardware should be reliable and fault-tolerant. The network should be optimized and every opportunity to implement redundancy scrutinized.

Opportunities to implement hardware redundancy:

- Supervisor card
  - Second Supervisor provides backup without cost of new switch.
  - Supervisor configuration and switchover maintained by Route Processor Redundancy (RPR) or Route Processor Redundancy Plus (RPR+).
  - RPR—Redundant Supervisor boots, draws configuration, when main Supervisor dies. About 3 minutes failover.
  - RPR+—Redundant Supervisor already booted and maintained in synchronized state. Both Supervisors must use same IOS. Failover in less than minute.
  - FIB table blank at switchover.
  - Enable with command **redundancy.**
  - Identify redundancy protocol using **mode rpr-plus.**
  - View settings with **show redundancy states.**
  - Uplink ports for backup Supervisor are active.
  - Split redundant links between Supervisors so that failure doesn't remove both links.

- Power supply
  —Some switch models allow for redundant power supplies.
  —Place in backup mode with command **power redundancy-mode redundant.**
  —View power supply settings using **show power.**
- Fans
- Hot swap modules

Topological redundancy:

- Provides redundant switching paths so there isn't a single point of failure.
- Implements network monitoring to recognize failures and repair them.
- With redundant paths, device can be offline for upgrades without disrupting network service.
- Does not co-locate devices, so that problems in the space do not affect more than a single piece of equipment.

Use all methods to split traffic between redundant paths, increasing aggregate network bandwidth

Default Gateway Redundancy

Gateway Discovery

Specifying a default gateway leads to a single point of failure.
Many methods exist for hosts to dynamically discover gateways, but all have problems.

- Proxy ARP
  —Host ARPs for all destinations, even remote.
  —Router responds with its MAC.
  —Problem: Slow failover because ARP entries take minutes to timeout.
- ICMP Router Discovery Protocol (IRDP)
  —Routers use IRDP to advertise default routes.
  —IRDP advertisements have a lifetime—If the lifetime expires without hearing a readvertisement, another gateway is chosen.
  —Problem: Slow failover because advertisements have a default lifetime of 30 minutes.
- Routing protocol
  —PC runs routing protocol to discover best routes.
  —Usually RIP.

Router Redundancy

Instead of making the host responsible for choosing a new gateway, router redundancy protocols allow two or more routers to support a shared MAC address. If the primary router is lost, the backup router assumes control of traffic forwarded to that MAC.

Hot Standby Router Protocol (HSRP)

- Cisco proprietary.
- Two or more devices support a virtual router with made up MAC and unique IP address.
- *Active* router forwards traffic.
- *Standby* is backup. Monitors periodic hellos to detect Active failure.
- Active router is chosen because it has higher HSRP priority (default 100).
- A new router with a higher priority does not cause an election unless it is configured to PREEMPT.
- Shared MAC is 0000.0c07.ACxx, where xx is the HSRP group.
- Multiple groups (virtual routers) allowed.
- On failure, standby device starts using IP and MAC of the virtual router.
- Interface tracking allows priority to change if a connection is lost.
- HSRP devices move between these states:
  —Initial—HSRP not running.
  —Learn—The router does not know the virtual IP address and is waiting to hear from the active router.
  —Listen—Router knows IP and MAC of virtual router, but not the identity of other HSRP group members.
  —Speak—Router sends period HSRP hellos and elects active router.
  —Standby—Router monitors hellos from active router and assumes responsibility if active router fails.
  —Active—Router forwards packets on behalf of the virtual router.

Configuring HSRP:

- Configure router as member of HSRP group 39 for virtual router with IP 10.0.0.1:
  Router(config-if)# **standby 39 ip 10.0.0.1**
- Configure priority (default 100, prefers highest):
  Router(config-if)# **standby 39 priority 150**

- Allow router to take over if active router has lower priority:
  Router(config-if)# **standby 39 preempt**

- Change hello timer to 2 seconds and hold timer to 7 seconds. Can be set between 1–255 seconds (default is hello 3 seconds and hold 10 seconds):
  Router(config-if)# **standby 39 timers 2 7**

- Track interface—If serial0 is down, decrement HSRP priority by 100:
  Router(config-if)# **standby 39 track s0 100**

NOTE Other routers must be configured for PREEMPT to take control.

- View HSRP status:
  show standby interface fasteth 0/0 *or* **show standby brief**

- Monitor HSRP activity:
  debug standby

Virtual Router Redundancy Protocol (VRRP)

- Similar to HSRP, but open standard (RFC 2338).
- Two or more devices support either real addresses or virtual router addresses.
- *Master* router forwards traffic. If a real address is being supported, owner of real address *must* be master.
- *Backup* takes over if master fails. Monitors periodic hellos to detect active failure.
- Master chosen because 1) it owns the real address or 2) it has higher priority (default 100).
- Multiple redundancies (real or virtual) allowed.

Gateway Load Balancing Protocol (GLBP)

- Similar to HSRP or VRRP, but simultaneous use of gateways allowed, maximizing bandwidth.
- Automatically detects and routes around gateway failure.
- Three modes:
  —Weighted load balancing—Traffic is balanced proportional to configured weight.
  —Host-dependent load balancing—A given host always uses the same router.
  —Round-robin load balancing—Each router MAC used to respond to ARP requests in turn.

- Active Virtual Gateway (AVG or *master gateway*) is the only router to respond to ARPs. It uses this capacity to balance load.
- GLBP can track interface; if interface goes down ARPs redirect traffic to other routers.

Single Router Mode (SRM):
- Used by switches with redundant MSFC2 cards
- Only one MSFC forwards traffic
- If first MSFC fails, backup starts. Current FIB used until new router starts.
- Both must run same IOS and have same configuration

Configuring Single Router Mode (SRM)

- Enable redundancy:
  L3switch(config)# **redundancy**

- Enable high availability:
  L3switch(config-r)# **high-availability**

- Enable SRM:
  L3switch(config-r-ha)# **single-router-mode**

- Verify:
  L3switch# **show redundancy**

Server Load Balancing (SLB)

SLB distributes client requests between several servers. Clients send traffic to a single virtual address, and SLB intelligently distributes requests to the group.

- Lighter load on each server results in better performance
- Server failures are recognized, and server is removed from group until restored.
- Individual server might be removed for maintenance.

Configuring SLB

- Define a server farm name:
  L3switch(config)# **ip slb serverfarm ponderosa**

- Identify real servers by IP address:
  L3switch(config-slb-sfarm)# **real 10.1.2.3**

- Activate SLB for each real server:
  L3switch(config-slb-real)# **inservice**

- View the list of real servers in server farm:

  L3Switch# **show ip slb real**

- View status of server farm:

  L3Switch# **show ip slb serverfarm**

- Define virtual server farm name:

  L3Switch(config)# **ip slb vserver benjamin**

- Identify virtual server IP address:

  L3Switch(config-slb-vserver)# **virtual 202.101.100.9 255.255.255.0**

- Link virtual server with server farm:

  L3Switch(config-slb-vserver)# **serverfarm**

- Activate virtual server:

  L3Switch(config-slb-vserver)# **inservice**

IP Multicast and IP Telephony in a Switched Network

A multicast is a single data stream sent from one source to a group of recipients. In contrast, a unicast is traffic from one source to one destination. A broadcast is traffic from one source to all destinations. Some features of multicast traffic are as follows:

- Sending host does not know the identity of the receiving hosts; they are all identified by one group IP address.
- Group membership is dynamic. Hosts join a group, notify their upstream router, and the router begins forwarding data to them.
- Hosts can belong to more than one group.
- Hosts in a group can be located in many different places.

Multicast IP Addresses

Multicasts use the IP address range of 224.0.0.0 to 239.255.255.255. The first four bits of the first octet are always binary 1110. The remaining 28 bits identify the multicast group. Some addresses are reserved:

- 224.0.0.1 is the all-hosts group.
- 224.0.0.2 is the all-routers group.
- The rest of the 224.0.0.0/16 range is reserved for network protocols.
- 224.0.1.0 to 238.255.255.255 are for use over the Internet and are called *globally-scoped addresses*.
- Source specific multicast uses 232.0.0.0 to 232.255.255.255 addresses.
- 233.0.0.0 to 233.255.255.255 are used to assign a static multicast address for use by an organization. The second and third octets of the address are the organization's autonomous system number. This is called GLOP—a combination of *global* and *scope*.
- The 239.0.0.0 to 239.255.255.255 range is for local use within an organization. They are called *limited scope* or *administratively scoped* addresses.

Multicast Distribution Trees

Multicasts use two different ways to distribute data between a server and hosts:

- A **source-based tree** is the simplest kind. Its root is the server, and it forms branches out through the network to all the members of the multicast group. A source tree is identified by (S,G) where S is the IP address of the server and G is the group multicast address. It creates optimal paths between the server and the hosts, but takes more router resources. Every router along the path must maintain path information for every server.

- A **shared tree** selects a common root, called a rendezvous point (RP). The server sends traffic to the RP, which forwards it toward hosts belonging to the group. The tree is identified by (*, G) where * means any source and G is the group multicast address. Shared trees use less router resources, but might result in suboptimal paths.

Reverse Path Forwarding

Multicast routers identify upstream ports (pointing toward the server or RP) and downstream ports (pointing toward other receivers) for each multicast group. The upstream port is found using Reverse Path Forwarding (RPF). RPF involves looking at the routing table to see which interface the router would use to send unicast traffic to that server or RP. That interface is the upstream port, or RPF port, for that multicast group. The RPF check is done every 5 seconds. It is used in this way:

- If a multicast packet arrives on the RPF port, the router forwards the packet out the interfaces listed in the outgoing interface list of a multicast routing table.
- If the packet does not arrive on the RPF port, the packet is discarded to prevent loops.

Protocol Independent Multicast (PIM)

PIM is a protocol used between routers to keep track of where to forward traffic for each multicast group. It can use information gathered from any routing protocol. PIM can run in dense mode or sparse mode.

PIM Dense Mode

PIM dense mode uses source-based trees. When running in dense mode, PIM assumes that every router needs to receive multicasts. Any router that doesn't want to receive it must send a prune message upstream toward the server. PIM dense mode is most appropriate when:

- Multicast servers and receivers are near each other.
- There are just a few servers and many receivers.
- You have a high volume of multicast traffic.
- The multicast stream is fairly constant.

PIM Sparse Mode

PIM sparse mode uses shared distribution trees. It does not assume that any routers want to receive the multicast, but instead waits to hear an explicit message from them, joining the group. Then, it adds branches to the tree to reach the hosts behind those routers. PIM sparse mode uses rendezvous points to connect hosts and servers. After the connection is made, PIM switches over to a source tree. Sparse mode is used when:

- Pockets of users are widely dispersed around the network.
- Multicast traffic is intermittent.

PIM Sparse-Dense Mode

An interface can be configured in sparse-dense mode. Then, if the router knows of a RP for its group, it uses sparse mode. Otherwise, it uses dense mode. Additionally, it makes the interface capable of receiving multicasts from both sparse and dense mode groups.

Configuring Multicast Routing and PIM

- Give this command to enable multicast routing:
  ```
  (config)# ip multicast routing
  ```

- PIM mode must be configured at each interface with the following command. Configuring PIM on an interface also enables IGMP on that interface:
  ```
  (config-if)# ip pim {sparse-mode | dense-mode | sparse-dense-mode}
  ```

- When using sparse mode, a RP must be specified. A router knows that it is an RP when it sees its own address in the command:
  ```
  (config)# ip pim rp-address ip-address
  ```

Auto-RP

Auto-RP automates the discovery of RPs in a sparse or sparse-dense PIM network. RPs advertise themselves to a router designated as an RP mapping agent. The mapping agent then decides on one RP per group and sends that information to the other routers.

- To configure a router as an RP, type
  ```
  (config)# ip pim send-rp-announce type number scope ttl group-list access-list-number
  ```

- To configure a router as a mapping agent, type
  ```
  (config)# ip pim send-rp-discovery scope ttl
  ```

PIM Version 2

Cisco routers with recent versions of the IOS use PIM v2 by default. Some differences between PIM v1 and PIM v2 include the following:

- PIM v1 is Cisco proprietary, whereas PIM v2 is standards-based.
- Both versions can dynamically map RPs to multicast groups. PIM v1 uses an Auto-RP mapping agent; PIM v2 uses a bootstrap router (BSR).
- PIM v1 uses a Time-To-Live value to bound its announcements, PIM v2 uses a configured domain border.
- In PIM v2, sparse and dense mode are group properties, not interface properties.

To configure PIM v2, configure at least one router as a BSR and selected routers as RPs. To configure a BSR:
```
(config)# ip pim bsr-candidate interface hash-mask-length [priority]
```

To configure a router as a candidate RP:
```
(config)# ip pim rp-candidate type number ttl group-list access-list-number
```

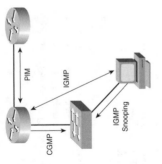

Internet Group Management Protocol

When a host wants to join a multicast group, it sends an Internet Group Management Protocol (IGMP) message to the router. The router periodically checks for group members on each segment. There are three versions of IGMP.

IGMP Version 1

Multicast routers query each segment periodically to see if there are still hosts in multicast groups with a query sent to the all-hosts address of 224.0.0.1. One host on the segment responds. Hosts silently leave a group; the router doesn't know they are gone until it queries and nobody responds.

IGMP Version 2

Version 2 adds explicit leave messages that hosts send when they leave a group. Queries are sent to specific multicast group addresses, not the all-hosts address.

IGMP Version 3

Hosts are able to tell the router not only which multicast groups they belong to, but also which sources they accept multicasts from. It adds two modes for requesting membership in a multicast group:

- **Include mode**—The receiver lists the groups to which it belongs, and the servers it uses.
- **Exclude mode**—The receiver lists the group to which it belongs, and the servers it doesn't use.

Cisco Group Management Protocol

Switches flood multicasts by default. Cisco Group Management Protocol (CGMP) lets a router tell a switch which hosts belong to which multicast group, so the switch can add that information to its port-to-MAC address mapping. Then, when a multicast comes in, the switch forwards it out only to ports that have hosts belonging to that group. CGMP is Cisco proprietary.

IGMP Snooping

IGMP snooping is another way for the switch to find out which ports have multicast hosts. When it is enabled, the switch opens all multicast packets, looking for IGMP join or leave messages. When it finds one, it records that information and uses it for forwarding multicasts. Because every multicast packet has to be opened, this can cause a performance hit on the switch.

Verifying Multicast Routing

Some commands to verify multicast routing include the following:

- **show ip mroute**—This shows the contents of the multicast routing table. For each group, it lists the mode, the RPF neighbor, the group identifier, and outgoing interfaces.
- **show ip mroute summary**—Lists each multicast group without as much detail.
- **show ip mroute active**—Shows the active sources, and the sending rate of each.
- **show ip mroute count**—Shows traffic statistics for each multicast group.
- **show ip pim interface**—Lists each interface doing multicasting, its PIM mode, and number of neighbors
- **show ip pim rp**—Lists RPs the router knows about.
- **show ip pim rp-hash**—Shows the RP selected for each multicast group.
- **show ip pim bsr**—Lists the current BSR.

Cisco IP Telephony

Packet loss is one of the biggest enemies of voice transmissions, and is often caused by jitter and congestion. Jitter (variable delay) causes buffer over- and underruns. Congestion at the interface can be caused by traffic from a fast port being switched to exit out a slower port, which causes the transmit buffer to be overrun.

Cisco switches are well suited to support both voice and video transmission (AVVID) because of the following features:

- They support multiple VLANs on each access port, by using Voice VLANs. This enables the IP Phones to belong to a separate VLAN from the computers.
- They can classify, mark, and police traffic, as well as provide differentiated queuing to different classes of traffic.
- They can be configured to trust the QoS markings provided by the IP phones or other devices.

Preparing the Network

When adding voice or video to an existing network, you should examine several things in advance:

1. **What features are needed?**—Power for IP phones, voice VLANs on the switches, network redundancy for high availability, security for voice calls, QoS settings.
2. **The physical plant**—Cabling at least CAT-5.
3. **Electrical power for the IP phones**—Use either inline power from Catalyst switch or power patch panel. Need uninterruptible power supply (UPS) with auto-restart, monitoring, and 4-hour response contract. Also generator backup. Maintain correct operating temperatures.
4. **Bandwidth**—Commit no more than 75 percent of bandwidth. Consider all types of traffic—voice, video and data. Have more than enough bandwidth if possible. Include both voice and call-control traffic in your planning.

Network and Bandwidth Considerations

The network requirements for Voice over IP (VoIP) include

- Maximum delay of 150–200 ms (one-way)
- No more than 1 percent packet loss
- Maximum average jitter of 30 ms
- Bandwidth of 21—106 kbps per call, plus about 150 bps per phone for control traffic

The network requirements for streaming video include

- Maximum delay of 4–5 sec (one-way)
- No more than 2 percent packet loss
- No jitter requirements
- Bandwidth needed depends on the video stream

The network requirements for video conferencing include

- Maximum delay of 150–200 ms (one-way)
- No more than 1 percent packet loss
- Maximum average jitter of 30 ms
- Bandwidth required is 20 percent more than the size of the videoconferencing stream

A formula to use when calculating bandwidth needed for voice calls is as follows: (Packet payload + all header in bits) * Packet rate per second

Auxiliary (or Voice) VLANs

Cisco switches can be configured to dynamically place IP telephones into a VLAN separate from the data VLANs. They can do this even when the phone and PC are physically connected to the same switch port. A term you might see is VVID—this is the voice VLAN ID, which is the same thing as the number of the auxiliary VLAN. Voice VLANs allow phones to be dynamically placed in a separate IP subnet from hosts, to have QoS (using 802.1Q/p headers) and security policies applied, and makes troubleshooting easier.

Voice in the Building Access Submodule

Include the following in the Building Access Submodule when implementing VoIP:

- Auxiliary VLANs
- 802.1p/Q encapsulation between the phone and the switch, which allows QoS marking
- Use switches that support multiple output queues
- Use switches that support inline power to IP phones
- Configure the following on switch ports connected to IP Phones, and in the network in general:
  —STP Port Fast
  —Root Guard
  —Unidirectional Link Detection (UDLD)
  —Uplink Fast

Support for Voice in the Building Distribution Submodule

To support VoIP, use the following in the Building Distribution Submodule:

- Make sure VoIP ports do not participate in routing—either use passive interface or configure the network statements under the routing protocols properly.
- Use HSRP for Layer 3 redundancy.
- Tune the routing protocol to allow for fast detection of a lost path and quick convergence when the network changes.

Implementing QoS in a Switched Network

Quality of service (QoS) configurations give special treatment to certain traffic at the expense of others. Using QoS in the network addresses these problems:

- Packet loss due to data being dropped at a congested interface
- Delay of sensitive data such as voice and video
- Jitter (variable delay)

People sometimes think that there is no need for QoS strategies in a LAN. However, switch ports can experience congestion because of port speed mismatches, many people trying to access the switch backbone, and many people trying to send traffic to the same switch port (such as a server port). QoS is disabled by default on switches. It is enabled at the interface configuration mode with the following command:

`(config-if)# mls qos`

QoS Techniques

Three QoS strategies are commonly implemented on interfaces where traffic enters the switch:

- **Classification**—Distinguishing one type of traffic from another. After traffic is classified, other actions can be performed on it. Examples: access lists, class maps, NBAR.
- **Marking**—Placing class of service (CoS), IP Precedence, or DiffServ Code Point (DSCP) values on the classified traffic.
- **Policing**—Determining whether or not a specific type of traffic is within preset bandwidth levels. If so, it is usually allowed and might be marked. If not, the traffic is typically marked or dropped. Example: CAR and class-based policing.

Some other QoS techniques are typically used on outbound interfaces:

- **Traffic shaping and conditioning**—Attempts to send traffic out in a steady stream, at a specified rate. Buffers traffic that goes above that rate and sends it when there is less traffic on the line.
- **Queuing**—Once traffic is classified and marked, one way it can be given special treatment is to be put into different queues on the interface, to be sent out at different rates and times. Examples: priority queuing, weighted fair queuing, custom queuing. The default queuing method for a switch port is FIFO.

- **Dropping**—Normally, interface queues accept packets until they're full and then drop everything after that. You can implement prioritized dropping, so that less important packets are dropped before more important ones. Example: Weighted Random Early Detection (WRED).

Integrated Services (IntServ)

Integrated services is a QoS model that guarantees a specific amount of bandwidth to the identified traffic, throughout the entire network. A check is made of the path from sender to receiver, and each router along the way has to reserve bandwidth for that flow. This is done using RSVP—Resource Reservation Protocol. If the network cannot provide the required bandwidth, the session is not allowed. RSVP is typically used for voice applications.

Differentiated Services (DiffServ)

Differentiated services provide levels of service based on the value of certain bits in the IP or ISL header, or the 802.1Q tag. Each hop along the way must be configured to treat the marked traffic the way you want—this is called per-hop behavior (PHB).

- In the Layer 3 IP header, you use the 8-bit ToS field. You can set either IP Precedence, using the top 3 bits, or Differentiated Services Code Points (DSCP) using the top 6 bits of the field. The bottom 2 bits are not used. The default DSCP value is 0, which corresponds to best-effort delivery.
- At Layer 2, with ISL, you can set 3 of the 4 bits in the ISL priority field to set the class of service (CoS). With 802.1Q, you set the 3 802.1p bits to the COS. The values of these 3 bits correspond to the IP Precedence values.

IP Precedence/Class of Service

Using three bits for IP Precedence gives you 8 possible values. The following table shows the values and their meaning. Precedence 5 is usually used for voice traffic; 6 and 7 are reserved for such things as routing protocols. Normal data is typically given Precedence 0. These same values apply for CoS bits also.

Precedence/CoS	Name
7	Network
6	Internet
5	Critical

Precedence/CoS	Name
4	Flash-override
3	Flash
2	Immediate
1	Priority
0	Routine

Translating Between DSCP and CoS

When traffic comes into the switch already marked with a COS or IP Precedence value and the switch trusts that, it assigns a DSCP value for its own internal use. If the frame has an existing DSCP value and the switch trusts that, it assigns the same value for the internal DSCP. Similarly, the switch can also translate a DSCP value into a CoS setting when sending data out a trunk port. The default CoS to DSCP mappings are shown in this table:

CoS	DSCP	CoS	DSCP
0	0	4	32
1	8	5	40
2	16	6	48
3	24	7	56

The default mappings of DCSP to COS are shown in this table:

DSCP	CoS
0–7	0
8–15	1
16–23	2
24–31	3

DSCP	CoS
32–39	4
40–47	5
48–55	6
56–63	7

DiffServ Assured Forwarding

The 6 DSCP bits can be broken down into two sections: the first 3 bits define the DiffServ Assured Forwarding (AF) class, and the next 2 bits define the drop probability within that class. The sixth bit is 0 and unused. AF classes 1–4 are defined, and within each class, 1 is low drop probability, 2 is medium, and 3 is high (meaning that traffic is more likely to get dropped if there is congestion). Each hop still needs to be configured for how to treat each AF class.

	Low Drop	Medium Drop	High Drop
Class 1	AF11	AF12	AF13
Class 2	AF21	AF22	AF23
Class 3	AF31	AF32	AF33
Class 4	AF41	AF42	AF43

DiffServ Expedited Forwarding

Another predefined DiffServ classification is Expedited Forwarding (EF). This is equivalent to DSCP 46 and is for use by your highest priority traffic, such as voice. You configure each hop in the network for the type of service you want EF traffic to receive.

Classifying Traffic and Marking for QoS

Mark traffic for QoS as close to the source as possible. If the source is an IP telephone, it can mark its own traffic. If not, the building access module switch can do the marking. If those are not under your control, you might need to mark at the distribution layer. Classifying and marking slows traffic flow, so don't do it at the core. All devices along the path should then be configured to trust the marking and provide a level of service based on it. The place where trusted marking is done is called the *trust boundary*. To configure a switch to trust the markings at an interface:

```
(config-if)#mls qos trust {dscp | cos}
```

When IP traffic comes in already marked, the switch has some options about how to handle it. It can

- Trust the DSCP value in the incoming packet, if present
- Trust the IP Precedence value in the incoming packet, if present
- Trust the CoS value in the incoming frame, if present
- Classify the traffic based on an IP access control list, or a MAC address ACL

Handling Non-IP Traffic

Non-IP traffic does not have fields in the header for Type of Service. The switch can handle this in the following ways:

- Use the default port CoS value if the frame does not have a value assigned
- Trust the already-assigned CoS value in the incoming frame, if present
- Classify the traffic based on a MAC address access control list

Classifying and Marking Using MQC

Modular QoS command-line interface (MQC) is a method of classifying traffic, marking the traffic, and setting policies for that traffic that can be used on most devices with most kinds of policies. Here are the general steps:

1. Create the necessary access control lists, if classifying traffic by ACL, or configure NBAR if your switch supports that (e.g., 6500).
2. Create the class maps that specify matching such things as ACLs, protocol, DSCPs, or IP Precedence values.
3. Create a policy map that calls each class map and defines the policy for each.
4. Apply the policy map to the appropriate switch ports.

When access control lists (ACLs) are used to classify traffic, the way a switch reacts to specific access control entries (ACEs) is different in a QoS context than with security-based ACLs. In a QoS access list,

- If the traffic matches a *permit* statement, the designated QoS action is taken
- If the traffic matches a *deny* statement, the rest of the ACEs in that ACL are skipped, and the switch goes to the next ACL.
- If there are multiple ACLs in a policy applied to an interface, the switch stops reading them as soon as a permit statement match is found for the traffic.

- If the traffic does not match any ACL entry, the switch just gives best-effort delivery to the traffic.

Configuring MQC

First, configure the access lists if using them.

Second, configure a class map for each classification of traffic:

```
(config)# class-map [match-any | match-all] name
(config-cmap)# match match options, such as ACL
```

Third, configure a policy map that calls the class maps and sets policies or types of treatment for each class:

```
(config)#policy-map name
(config-pmap)#class class-map name
(config-pmap-c)#policy options, such as    set DSCP
```

Finally, apply the MQC policy to the desired interface(s), either inbound or outbound. Note: Policy maps that classify traffic using ACLs, that set DSCP or IP Precedence, or that tell the interface to trust existing markings can be applied only inbound.

```
(config-if)#service-policy {output | input} name
```

Queuing Methods

FIFO (First-In, First-Out)

The default on switch ports. If QoS is not enabled, there is one software queue. If QoS is enabled, there are four software queues per port, but they are all weighted and serviced equally, with best-effort delivery. Traffic is placed in them based on CoS value:

Queue 1—CoS values 0 and 1
Queue 2—CoS values 2 and 3
Queue 3—CoS values 4 and 5
Queue 4—CoS values 6 and 7

Priority Queuing (PQ)

Queues are assigned different priority values, and the high priority queue gets serviced before anything else. Priority queuing is done on the 3550 using the expedite queue, which is a strict priority queue. It is serviced ahead of the other queues until it is empty. This queue is configured on the 3550 at interface configuration mode with the command: priority-queue out.

Custom Queuing (CQ)

Reserves a part of the interface bandwidth for the different queues. Can classify and place specific traffic into the queues.

Weighted Fair Queuing (WFQ)

Gives weights to different types of traffic, and allows lower weighted traffic more bandwidth. Traffic can be weighted by flow (conversation) or using class maps.

Low Latency Queuing (LLQ)

Has one priority queue and usually voice traffic is put into this. Uses class-based WFQ for the rest of the interface traffic. Configure this under the class statement in the policy map:

(config-pmap-c)# priority bandwidth

IP RTP Priority

Is similar to LLQ in that is has a priority queue and uses WFQ for other traffic. However, here the priority queue is completely for voice traffic. RTP is Real Time Protocol, the protocol used by Voice over IP. It is configured at the interface:

(config-if)# ip rtp priority start-port port-range BW

Weighted Round Robin (WRR)

This is the process that takes packets from the queues, decides which queue goes when, and how many packets can be sent from each queue at a time. During times of interface congestion, WRR weights queues, and more packets are sent from higher weighted queues, thus giving them more bandwidth.

What Happens When the Software Queues Get Full?

By default, when a software queue is full (congested) the switch just drops all other traffic bound for that queue. This is called *tail drop*. It can cause some problems:

- TCP global synchronization.
- TCP buffer starvation.
- Delay and jitter.
- High priority traffic is dropped while low priority traffic is sent.

Congestion avoidance is accomplished by using Weighted Random Early Detection (WRED). WRED starts dropping lower priority traffic (based on DSCP or IP Precedence values) as the queue starts to fill, and drops high priority traffic only when the queue is almost full. The drop thresholds and the drop ratios are configurable. WRED works best with TCP traffic, because TCP dynamically adjusts its sending rate when packets are dropped. Do not use WRED for voice traffic. If the queue fills completely, tail drop is used.

On the 3550, the gigabit Ethernet ports can use either tail drop or WRED (Weighted Random Early Detection). The 10/100 ports can use only tail drop. WRED is enabled either in a policy map or at the interface—the command is the same:

random-detect dscp-based

Traffic Policing

By using the QoS policing function, bandwidth use can be controlled on physical interfaces in the switch. Traffic cannot be policed per VLAN or on an SVI. Policing specifies an amount of bandwidth allowed for a particular type of traffic, and generally drops traffic over that amount. It can also be configured to allow the excess traffic, but mark it with a different DSCP value.

The 3550 switch can police bandwidth use either for each individual class of traffic (individual policing), or it can limit bandwidth use for all traffic (aggregate policing).

Traffic Shaping

Traffic shaping also controls the amount of traffic used by a specified type of traffic, but shaping buffers the excess traffic instead of dropping it. Because data is usually bursty, the buffered traffic can be sent out between bursts. It thus smooths out the flow of traffic.

Creating Bandwidth by Compression

Compressing the traffic on a line creates more useable bandwidth; because each frame is smaller, there are fewer bits to transmit. You can compress the whole payload, or just compress the protocol headers with TCP or RTP header compression. Cisco supports three Layer 2 payload compression algorithms:

- Stacker
- Predictor
- Microsoft Point-to-Point Compression (MPPC)

Link Fragmentation and Interleave (LFI)

A typical network has a range of packet sizes. Small packets can be delayed waiting for a large packet to be sent out the interface. LFI breaks large packets into smaller segments and intersperses the smaller packets between the pieces of the big ones. This reduces delay and jitter.

In summary, options that are available to you when configuring a switch's outbound (egress) queues include

- Changing the CoS-to-queue map
- Assigning drop thresholds to each queue
- Mapping DSCPs to the drop thresholds
- Enabling either WRED or tail drop
- Changing the size of buffer space allotted to each queue
- Changing the relative weight of each queue

QoS at the Building Access Layer

Enable QoS at the building access layer, then classify and mark the traffic, and perhaps do policing. If the traffic is already classified by a trusted end station, configure the switch to trust the markings. Configure voice VLANs if using IP phones.

QoS at the Building Distribution Layer

Enable QoS at the building distribution layer and then configure the switch to trust the priority marking it receives from the access layer switches. If the markings are from an untrusted source, configure the switch to override them. You might then want to modify the switch's default per-hop behavior based on these values. If using WRED, you might change the DSCP-to-threshold mappings. You might also change the DSCP-to-CoS mappings, to put traffic in different egress queues. Lastly, you typically change the relative weights of the queues on the egress interface.

QoS at the Campus Backbone

No classification or marking should be done at the core layer, as this slows down traffic. A congestion avoidance mechanism such as WRED might be used, along with interface queuing techniques such as class-based weighted fair queuing or low latency queuing to guarantee bandwidth to critical applications.

QoS for Voice over IP

In a network with voice traffic, configure either the end stations or the switch to mark the voice traffic with IP Precedence 5 or DSCP 46. Configure the egress interface for priority queuing, then configure the DSCP-to-CoS mappings to put the voice traffic in the Expedite queue (on the 3550) or the highest priority queue (on the 2950).

Verifying QoS

Use the following commands to verify your QoS configurations and actions:

- show class-map [*name*]—Displays the configured class maps, or just the one named.
- show policy-map [*name*]—Displays the configured policy maps, or just the one named.
- show policy-map [interface [*interface-spec* [*input* | *output*] [class *class-name*]]]—Displays the policy maps and statistics by interface and/or class.
- show queuing [interface *interface-no.*]—Shows the queuing strategy and statistics for any queues configured on the interface.
- show policy interface *interface-no.*—Displays the policies for all classes applied to the interface, along with statistics.
- debug ip rsvp—If using RSVP for voice, shows information about packets received and sent.
- debug priority—Shows information on the priority queue.

Optimizing Performance of Campus Networks

Techniques to Optimize Performance

- Monitor network continuously
- Understand nominal behavior (baseline)
  —Utilization
  —Response times
  —Errors
- Anticipate capacity issues—New hardware or circuits can take weeks to be installed

Protocol Analysis tools in Cisco switches

Switched Port Analyzer (SPAN)

- Copies network traffic from a switch port or VLAN to a listening port. Can monitor incoming, outgoing, or both.
- Captures the traffic with a protocol analyzer (such as Sniffer or Ethereal) attached to listening port.

- Multiple SPAN sessions are supported.
- The following example configures SPAN to copy traffic from port fastethernet 2/2 (incoming and outgoing) to fastethernet 2/48 as session number 7.

```
L3Switch(config)# monitor session 7 source interface fastethernet 2/2 both
L3Switch(config)# monitor session 7 destination interface fastethernet 2/48
```

VLAN-Based SPAN (VSPAN)

- Same idea as SPAN but copies all traffic incoming or outgoing on ports in a VLAN to monitor port.
- Traffic internally routed to VLAN not monitored (does not come in or go out a VLAN port).
- Monitor port might be in same or different VLAN.

Remote SPAN (RSPAN)

- Same idea as SPAN but copies traffic to a remote monitor port.
- Supports source ports and source VLANs.
- VTP pruning can block monitored traffic.
- Monitored traffic carried over a single-purpose VLAN.

```
L3Switch(config)# vlan 999
L3Switch(config-vlan)# remote-span
```

- The following example configures RSPAN to copy traffic from port fastethernet 2/2 (incoming and outgoing) to VLAN 999 as session number 8:

```
L3Switch(config)# monitor session 8 source interface fastethernet 2/2 both
L3Switch(config)# monitor session 7 destination remote vlan 999
```

- View SPAN settings:

```
L3Switch# show monitor session 7
```

Network Analysis Module (NAM)

- Module for Catalyst 6000/6500
- Accumulates flow information using Remote Monitoring (RMON) and by monitoring VLANs
- Uses TrafficDirector or any RMON application to analyze data

To configure NAM, assign IP settings and start web server:

```
L3Switch# session slot processor 1
root@localhost#ip address 10.0.0.2 255.255.255.0
root@localhost#ip broadcast 10.0.0.255
root@localhost#ip host MyNAM
root@localhost#ip gateway 10.0.0.1
root@localhost#ip domain stewart.hickory.nc.us
root@localhost#ip nameserver 10.0.0.254
root@localhost#snmp location At home
root@localhost#snmp contact Brent Stewart
root@localhost#snmp community public ro
root@localhost#snmp community private rw
```

- Identify the set of information you want collected. Choose from these collections:
  - addressmap
  - art (application response time)
  - etherstat
  - priostats
  - vlanstats

  ```
  root@localhost#autostart addressmap enable
  ```

- Configure the NAM collection port 1. NAM must monitor session 1.

```
L3Switch(config)# monitor session 1 destination interface gigabit 8/0
```

Viewing NAM:

```
show module
show interface gigabit 8/1
```

Security in the Campus Network

Securing Cisco Devices

Here are some basic security suggestions for network devices:

- Use passwords that are not susceptible to dictionary attack. Add numbers or substitute numbers and symbols for letters, for example, substituting 0 for o and using cisc0.
  - Console
  - AUX
  - Enable
  - SNMP
  - VTP

- Limit Telnet access using access lists.

- Physically secure access to the device.
- Use banners that warn against unauthorized access.
- Remove unused services:

```
no service finger
no service config
no service tcp-small-services
no service udp-small services
no cdp enable
no ip http
```

- Set up and monitor syslog.
- Disable automatic trunking on all non-trunk ports

Authentication, authorization, and accounting (AAA):

- Verifies ID.
- Limits privileges.
- Logs usage for billing or monitoring.
- Configures authentication:

```
L3switch(config)# aaa new-model
```

  —Identify authentication methods (RADIUS first and then the local username/password database in this example):

```
L3switch(config)# aaa authentication login default radius local
```

  —Apply to a line:

```
L3switch(config)# line vty 0 4
L3switch(config-line)# login authentication default
```

- Configure authorization:

  —Identify authorization methods (RADIUS in this example):

```
L3switch(config)#aaa authorization network default radius
```

  —Apply to interface:

```
L3switch(config)# interface s0/1
L3switch(config-line)# ppp authorization default
```

- Configure accounting:

  —Identify accounting method:

```
L3switch(config)# aaa accounting network default start-stop radius
```

  —Apply to interface:

```
L3switch(config)# interface s0/1
L3switch(config-line)# ppp accounting default
```

Limiting MAC Access

- Port security limits the number of MAC addresses learned on a port:

```
L3switch(config-if)# switchport port-security max 1 violation shutdown
```

- 802.1X limits network access by authenticating at data link before allowing access:

```
L3switch(config)# aaa new-model
L3switch(config)# aaa authentication dot1x default group radius
L3switch(config)# dot1x system-auth-control
L3switch(config)# int fasteth2/1
L3switch(config-if)# dot1x port-control auto
```

- View security settings:

```
L3switch# show port-security
```

Access Lists

Cisco switches support

- Traditional Router ACL (RACL)
- QoS ACL
- VLAN ACL (VACL)

VLAN ACL (VACL)

- Applied against all VLAN traffic.
- Similar to route-maps:

  —Statements contain match and set conditions

  —Statements numbered for ordering

- Actions: Permit, Deny, Redirect
- The following is a sample VACL to drop traffic that matches ACL 101:

```
L3switch(config)# vlan access-map Kaitlyn 5
L3switch(config-access-map)# match ip address 101
L3switch(config-access-map))# action drop
L3switch# vlan filter Kaitlyn vlan_list 10
```

- View VACL settings:

```
show vlan access-map Kaitlyn
show vlan filter access-map Kaitlyn
```

Private VLAN (PVLAN)

PVLANs allow service providers to isolate customers into separate multiaccess domains. Using a VLAN for each customer isn't scalable. PVLANs isolate a set of ports from other ports in a VLAN.

Port and VLAN types

- **Community**—Communicate with a community, plus promiscuous
- **Isolated**—Communicate just with promiscuous
- **Promiscuous**—Communicate with all

To configure VLAN, enter the following at the prompt:

```
L3switch(config)# vlan 777
L3switch(config-vlan)# private-vlan isolated
```

Metro Ethernet

Ethernet as a metropolitan area solution provides attractive features.

For consumers:

- Low cost
- High bandwidth (>1 G)

For service providers:

- Provisioned over dark fiber or existing services
- Profitable
- Supports new services

Transparent LAN Service (TLS)

- Customer switches see MAN as single VLAN
- Supports point-to-point and multipoint
- All locations must peer. Some routing protocols have trouble peering more than 40 devices.
- Easy to implement.
- Broadcast and multicasts aren't controlled, QoS is difficult, and it's not scalable.

Directed VLAN Service (DVS)

- Customer switches see MAN as multiple VLANs, each going to a specific neighbor.
- Supports point-to-point and multipoint.
- VLAN identifies destination, scalable, SPs prefer.
- Requires many VLANs.

Metro Ethernet Over SONET

Metro Ethernet over Synchronous Optical Network (SONET) uses existing bandwidth and redundancy of SONET to facilitate simulated Ethernet service.

- SONET has ring structure.
- Metro Ethernet over SONET emulates hub.
- SONET generally available, quick failover.
- Customer buys bandwidth in chunks of 51.84 M. (OC-x)

Metro Ethernet Over DWDM

Metro Ethernet over dense wavelength division multiplexing (DWDM) uses dark fiber or wavelength.

- Metro Ethernet over SONET emulates hub.
- Gigabit plus bandwidth, and easy to configure.
- Built on dark fiber or wavelength (not generally available).

Metro Ethernet Over CWDM

Metro Ethernet over Course Wave-Division Multiplexing (CWDM) uses dark fiber or wavelength.

- Last mile technology
- Doesn't use bandwidth as efficiently
- Last mile technology
- Cheap (comparatively)

Metro Ethernet Tunneling Options

Traffic crossing the service provider can be encapsulated to preserve private VLAN tags across the backbone.

No Tunneling

- Customer traffic isolated in one or more VLANs in shared definition set.
- Easy to implement.
- Doesn't scale—Service provider runs out of VLANs!
- Used to build low-cost MAN services.

802.1Q-in-Q

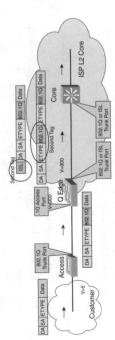

- Two dot1q tags associated with frame—One for enterprise and one for service provider.
- Also called *tag stacking*.
- SP reads their tag, removes before passing back.
- Isolates enterprises from each other.
- Enterprise sees Q-in-Q as trunk service between sites.
- Spanning tree used to prevent loops.
- STP can cause issues with backbone.
- Redundant links supported with EtherChannel.
- Easy to set up and support.

MPLS Secret Decoder Ring

Before we discuss Metro Ethernet over MPLS, here's a reminder of important MPLS acronyms is appropriate:

- **Label Switch Router (LSR)**—Device that forwards traffic inside an MPLS domain.
- **Label Distribution Protocol (LDP)**—Protocol that synchronizes label definitions between LSR.
- **Label Switch Controller (LSC)**—MPLS router that works with ATM switch to forward MPLS traffic.
- **Label Edge Router (LER)**—Device that sits between Ethernet and MPLS. Maps Ethernet traffic to MPLS labels.

EoMPLS

- VLAN mapped to MPLS tunnel.
- Point-to-point only.
- Requires either full mesh, or traffic to exit MPLS to a switch and be passed back to MPLS (a *hairpin turn*).
- Very scalable.
- Supports Transport Layer Security (TLS) functionality—makes disparate networks appear as one LAN.
- Uses a tunnel label and a virtual circuit label applied by LER.
- Ingress LER uses Forwarding Equivalence Class (FEC) to map traffic to Label Switch Path.
- LSRs along LSP just use tunnel label to direct traffic.
- Virtual circuit label used by LER to demux.
- CoS mapped to 3 bit EXP field in label.

EoMPLS Point-to-Multipoint

- Provides features of EoMPLS plus multipoint configurations.
- Service acts like an Ethernet switch.
- Efficiently handles traffic (solves hairpin turn).

Part III

CIT

Section 1
Network Baselining and Troubleshooting Methodologies

Section 2
Troubleshooting TCP/IP

Section 3
Troubleshooting Switched Ethernet Networks

Section 4
Troubleshooting PPP

Section 5
Troubleshooting Frame Relay

CIT Quick Reference Sheets

Section 1

CIT

Network Baselining and Troubleshooting Methodologies

It's almost comical, but most network engineers hate to document networks. At the same time, however, they are frustrated when things don't work as they should. The interesting fact is that time spent documenting your network is effectively spent learning and understanding it. The goal of network baselining is to establish a point of reference to which the operation of the network can be compared. Without a baseline, how do you know if your network is operating properly? Or more importantly, how do you convey (or if necessary prove) to others that it is not operating correctly?

Although troubleshooting approaches and methodologies vary as widely as our personalities, several characteristics are common across all successful troubleshooting mindsets. As a CCNP candidate, you are expected to understand these characteristics and more importantly leverage them to your advantage.

This section challenges your understanding of network baselining, documentation, and troubleshooting topics that are covered in the CCNP Support exam.

Question 1

What is the point of a baseline?

Question 2

Which of the following should be recorded for a router in a network configuration table?

A. Network addresses

B. Data link addresses

C. Memory and CPU

D. Routing protocol configuration

E. All of the above

Question 1 Answer

An established baseline helps you determine the normal operating characteristics of the network. This baseline can be used as a reference when implementing changes. The difference between the baseline and the new operating characteristics helps you assess the positive or negative impact a change has had.

Question 2 Answer

Letter E, All of the above, is the correct answer. Every piece of information that is relevant to the operation of the router should be recorded. Having this information in a central, available repository greatly aids in network troubleshooting.

Question 3

What is one of the most critical items to document for a router running Open Shortest Path First (OSPF)?

Question 4

What type of information should be recorded for a switch in a network configuration table?

Question 3 Answer

The OSPF Router ID should be recorded for every router running OSPF.

Question 4 Answer

The network configuration table of a switch should include all the following:

- Switch name
- IP address and mask
- STP bridge priority
- VTP domain and role
- Per-port information
  - STP state
  - Port Fast configuration
  - VLAN
  - Trunk configuration
  - Speed and duplex

Question 5

What is the purpose of a topology diagram?

Question 6

What types of information should be contained in a topology diagram?

Question 5 Answer

A good topology diagram helps you visualize the configuration of network elements (routers, switches, etc.) while giving you an understanding of the network design and configuration as a whole.

Question 6 Answer

A topology diagram should contain the following information as a minimum:

- Device names
- Device location
- Network addressing
- Physical interface names
- Device-to-device connections
- Routing protocol configuration
- Diagram date or versioning information

Question 7

Put the following network discovery steps in order:

Discover the directly connected devices.

Document the current device name and addresses.

View details about connected devices.

Document all active interfaces.

Question 8

What commands help you gather information about any connected devices?

Question 7 Answer

The correct order for these discovery steps is

1 Document the current device name and addresses.

2 Document all active interfaces.

3 Discover the directly connected devices.

4 View details about connected devices.

Question 8 Answer

The following commands can help in determining device interconnections:

- **show cdp neighbors [detail]**
- **show ip ospf neighbor**
- **show ip eigrp neighbors**
- **show ip route**
- **show ip arp** [*interface-type interface-number*]

Question 9

Put the following device documentation steps in order:

Interface discovery

Diagram

Document

Login

Device discovery

Question 10

As documented in the CIT course, what are the five guidelines for creating network documentation?

Question 9 Answer

The correct order is

1 Login

2 Interface discovery

3 Document

4 Diagram

5 Device discovery

Question 10 Answer

The five guidelines are

- Determine the scope.
- Know your objective.
- Be consistent.
- Keep the documents accessible.
- Maintain the documentation.

Question 11

What command displays all possible information about the IP configuration of a Windows 2000 workstation?

Question 12

Which command displays the interfaces and IP addresses in use on a UNIX-based computer?

Question 11 Answer

The command **ipconfig /all** displays the IP configuration of the workstation. The output of this command includes the IP address, subnet mask, Domain Name System (DNS) servers, Windows Internet Naming Service (WINS) servers, default gateway, and MAC address.

Question 12 Answer

The command **ifconfig –a** displays information about each of the configured interfaces on a UNIX-based computer.

Question 13

At what layers of the OSI reference model does a router typically operate?

Question 14

The data link layer of the OSI reference model maps to which TCP/IP layer?

Question 13 Answer

Routers typically operate in Layers 1 through 3 of the OSI reference model. However, applications like Network Address Translation (NAT), Dynamic Host Configuration Protocol (DHCP), and policy routing might require the router to operate in the upper OSI layers as well.

Question 14 Answer

The OSI data link layer maps to the network interface layer in the TCP/IP model. The OSI physical layer also maps to the network interface TCP/IP layer.

Question 15

How many layers are in the TCP/IP model?

Question 16

What are the three stages to the general troubleshooting process?

Question 15 Answer

The TCP/IP model is made up of four layers. Those layers are the network interface layer, the Internet layer, the transport layer, and the application layer.

Question 16 Answer

The three stages of the general troubleshooting process are gather symptoms, isolate the problem, and correct the problem.

Question 17

Put the five parts of the gather symptoms troubleshooting stage in order:

Determine ownership.

Narrow scope.

Determine symptoms.

Analyze existing symptoms.

Document symptoms.

Question 18

What are the three troubleshooting methodologies?

Question 17 Answer

The correct order for steps of the gather symptoms stage is as follows:

1 Analyze existing symptoms.

2 Determine ownership.

3 Narrow scope.

4 Determine symptoms.

5 Document symptoms.

Question 18 Answer

The three troubleshooting methodologies are

- Bottom-up
- Top-down
- Divide and conquer

Question 19

How do you view the routing table of a Windows workstation?

Question 20

What command displays the routing table of a UNIX-based computer?

Question 19 Answer

The command **route print** displays the routing table of the local Windows workstation.

Question 20 Answer

The command **netstat –r** displays the routing table on a UNIX-based computer.

Question 21

Internet Control Message Protocol (ICMP) exists in which layer of the TCP/IP model?

Question 22

What are the three stages to the general troubleshooting process?

Question 21 Answer

ICMP exists within the same layer as IP, the Internet layer.

Question 22 Answer

The three stages of the general troubleshooting process are gather symptoms, isolate the problem, and correct the problem.

Question 23

At which layer of the OSI reference model does the Bottom-Up troubleshooting approach begin?

Question 23 Answer

The Bottom-Up approach starts at the physical layer of the OSI reference model. This approach is best if you suspect that the problem is in the bottom layers of the OSI reference model.

Section 2

Troubleshooting TCP/IP

Thanks largely to its success on the Internet, TCP/IP has become the most widespread networking protocol ever, and it is certain to remain as such for the foreseeable future. With this in mind, it is critical that CCNP candidates understand all aspects of the protocol suite. Cisco IOS provides many troubleshooting tools that can aid in the resolution of IP connectivity problems. Used wisely, tools like **ping** and **traceroute** can help you quickly determine the failure domain. After the failure is located, a myriad of **show** and **debug** commands can help you further isolate the problem.

After you complete this section, your understanding of TCP/IP troubleshooting should not only be refreshed, but enhanced. This section includes flash cards on IP troubleshooting tools and commands, including **ping** and **traceroute**.

Question 1

How does ping work?

Question 2

Can you source a ping from a particular router IP address? Why is this useful?

Question 1 Answer

Ping uses the Internet Control Message Protocol (ICMP) to test connectivity between two IP devices. The ping request is an ICMP echo packet; the response is an ICMP echo-reply packet.

Question 2 Answer

Yes. By using the extended options of the **ping** command, you can select the source IP address used by the ping process. This is useful in testing connectivity from different IP subnets using one router.

Question 3

What is traceroute and how does it work?

Question 4

What command displays which routing protocols are being redistributed into other routing protocols?

Question 3 Answer

The **traceroute** command determines the path IP packets take to the destination IP address. This determination is accomplished by sending UDP packets towards the source but with a limited Time-To-Live (TTL) value. By default, the TTL starts at one and is incremented one at a time. When the TTL expires, the intermediate router sends an ICMP time exceeded message to the source device. This message includes the IP address of the intermediate device encountering the TTL expiration error, thus reporting the next hop to the origin device.

After the packets reach their intended destination, the destination device processes the UDP packet for port 33434 and returns an ICMP port-unreachable message to the source device. Because this is a different ICMP message than that returned by the intermediate routers, the **traceroute** program knows that the packet has reached its destination.

Question 4 Answer

The EXEC command **show ip protocols** displays information about the configuration of each IP routing protocol, including redistribution.

Question 5

What is route redistribution?

Question 6

When does IP route redistribution take place automatically?

Question 5 Answer

Route redistribution is the process of making routes from one routing protocol available to routers running another routing protocol.

Question 6 Answer

Routing redistribution takes place automatically between Enhanced Interior Gateway Router Protocol (EIGRP) and Interior Gateway Router Protocol (IGRP) processes with the same autonomous system number.

Question 7

What is a null interface?

Question 8

What are the ICMP messages used by ping and traceroute?

Question 7 Answer

A null interface is a logical interface that automatically discards packets. It is often used with static or summary routes to discard packets for a particular destination, or in the case of summary routes to discard packets to destinations without a more specific route.

Question 8 Answer

Ping uses the following two ICMP messages:

- echo
- echo-reply

Traceroute uses the following ICMP messages:

- time-exceeded
- port-unreachable
- echo (Windows tracert)
- echo-reply (Windows tracert)

Question 9

What are the available options when running an IP extended ping?

Question 10

How can you limit which routes are redistributed from one protocol to another?

Question 9 Answer

An IP extended ping provides the following options:

- Repeat count
- Datagram size
- Timeout
- Source address or interface
- IP type of service
- Don't fragment
- Validate reply data
- Data pattern
- Source routing
- Sweep packet sizes
- Record route
- Timestamp

Question 10 Answer

A route map can be used to filter routes during the redistribution process. The syntax of the redistribute router configuration command with the route-map option is

```
redistribute protocol route-map map-tag
```

Question 11

What is *count to infinity*?

Question 12

When might a connected route not exist in the routing table?

Question 11 Answer

Count to infinity is a situation where the routing protocol on two neighboring routers continuously increases the metric of a route until the route reaches the maximum metric and is removed from the routing table on both routers. This can occur with distance vector routing protocols when a route becomes unavailable.

Question 12 Answer

A connected route does not exist in the routing table if the route's outbound interface is down.

Question 13

How can you limit the output from the debug ip packet command?

Question 14

How can you determine if packets have been matched by an access list?

Question 13 Answer

It is possible to apply an access list to the **debug ip packet** command to limit the information produced. The following is a sample command using this syntax:

```
debug ip packet access-list-number
```

Question 14 Answer

The output of the **show access-lists** EXEC command includes the number of matches by each single access list entry. If the annotation (X matches) is not shown to the right of an access list entry, no packets have matched that entry.

Question 15

Is the following configuration valid?

```
interface Ethernet 0
 ip address 10.1.1.1 255.255.0.0
 !
interface Serial 0
 ip address 10.1.2.200 255.255.255.0
 !
```

Troubleshooting
TCP/IP

Question 16

How can you determine if packets are being dropped by an interface?

Troubleshooting
TCP/IP

Question 15 Answer

No. The IP addresses configured on Ethernet 0 and Serial 0 are for overlapping subnets. When attempting to apply this configuration, you would receive the error message "10.1.2.200 overlaps with Ethernet 0".

Question 16 Answer

The EXEC command **show interfaces** shows many interface statistics, including the number of output queue drops.

Question 17

How and when can default metrics be used?

Question 18

How does the log access control list (ACL) option aid troubleshooting?

Question 17 Answer

By using the router configuration command **default-metric**, you can apply a metric to routes that did not have a metric set during redistribution.

Question 18 Answer

Applied to individual entries of an access control list, the **log** option causes packets matching that entry to be logged. When logging to the console has been enabled via the **logging console** global configuration command, the **log** ACL option can provide real-time insight into traffic flows.

Question 19

What are the primary concerns when redistributing one routing protocol into another?

Question 20

What state is a route in if a show ip route shows the route as "possibly down"?

Question 19 Answer

The concerns when performing route redistribution include

- Creation of routing loops
- Suboptimal routing
- Metric incompatibilities
- Routing protocol overhead

Question 20 Answer

When a route is shown as "possibly down," the router has placed the route in a hold down state. While a route is in hold down, the router is waiting for better information regarding the route before the route is made available or removed from the routing table.

Question 21

What does every access list include?

Troubleshooting
TCP/IP

Question 22

How do you clear a router's ARP cache?

Troubleshooting
TCP/IP

Question 21 Answer

Every access list includes an implicit deny any as the last access list entry.

Question 22 Answer

The privileged EXEC command **clear arp** clears the contents of a router's ARP cache.

Question 23

How does the router choose between routes learned via different sources? How can you influence this choice?

Question 23 Answer

An administrative distance (AD) value establishes a preference among the configured routing protocols. Although each protocol has a default AD, it is possible to use the **distance** router configuration command to change the AD of a routing protocol or specific routes within the protocol.

Section 3

Troubleshooting Switched Ethernet Networks

As today's networks grow, you are almost certainly faced with the task of troubleshooting a switched network. Given that, it is critical that you understand switched network troubleshooting not only to pass the CCNP exams, but also to be a successful network engineer.

Switched networks include many technologies and protocols. Capabilities from VLAN trunking to Gigabit EtherChannel and protocols from VLAN Trunking Protocol (VTP) to the Spanning Tree Protocol (STP) provide the ability to craft a network that is resilient, extensible, and efficient. Unfortunately, all these protocols and technologies increase the skill level required for successful implementation and support of switched Ethernet networks.

The flash cards in this section challenge your understanding of switched network troubleshooting, and your knowledge of the design characteristics and protocol operation needed within today's networks.

Question 1

How do you view a switch's forwarding (CAM) table?

Question 2

How does a switch configured as VTP transparent interact with VTP servers and clients?

Question 1 Answer

On an IOS-based switch, the command **show mac-address-table** is used to view the switch's forwarding table.

Question 2 Answer

A VTP transparent switch disregards VTP packets received. However, it forwards those packets onto neighboring switches. A VTP transparent switch can be configured with locally defined VLANs, but makes no attempt to distribute those VLANs to other switches.

Question 3

What is a CAM table?

Question 4

What are the types of CAM entries?

Question 3 Answer

On a CatOS switch, the CAM table contains the bridge forwarding table of the switch. It can be viewed by using the **show cam** command. On an IOS switch, this table is called the MAC address table.

Question 4 Answer

There are three types of CAM entries:

- **Dynamic**—These entries are learned and aged out during normal switch operation.
- **Static**—These entries are not aged out of the CAM table.
- **Permanent (CatOS only)**—These entries are not aged out of the CAM table and are saved in the switch NVRAM.

Question 5

How do you determine the root switch for a VLAN?

Question 6

What are the types of possible STP configurations?

Question 5 Answer

On an IOS switch, the command **show spanning-tree vlan** *number* displays the STP configuration state for a particular VLAN. On a CatOS switch, the command **show spantree** *number* displays the STP status for VLAN *number.* In either case, the Bridge ID (BID) of the root bridge is shown.

Question 6 Answer

The Spanning Tree Protocol (STP) can be configured in one of three manners:

- **Per-VLAN spanning tree plus (PVST+)**—In this mode, the STP algorithm is run in each VLAN individually allowing more efficient use of redundant connections.

- **Multiple Spanning Tree Protocol (MSTP)**—When configured for MSTP, a switch can share a single STP instance on multiple VLANs.

- **Common Spanning Tree (CST)**—Using this configuration option, all VLANs in the network share one instance of the Spanning Tree Protocol. This single instance is typically run on VLAN number 1.

Question 7

After a switch port has been error disabled, how does it become enabled again?

Question 8

What are some of the reasons that a switch port could become error disabled?

Question 7 Answer

An error-disabled port can be reenabled in two ways. The first requires administrator intervention by entering the command **set port enable** *mod/port* on CatOS switches and the IOS interface configuration commands **shutdown** and **no shutdown**. Error disabled ports can be automatically reenabled by entering the CatOS configuration command **set errdisable-timeout interval** *interval* or the IOS global configuration command **errdisable recovery interval** *interval*.

Question 8 Answer

The following types of errors might cause a port to become error disabled:

- BPDU detected on Port Fast enabled port
- EtherChannel misconfiguration
- Too many interface state changes
- Port security violation
- Detection of an unidirectional link

Question 9

What is VTP pruning?

Question 10

How is pruning enabled?

Question 9 Answer

VTP pruning removes unused VLANs from trunk ports. This reduces trunk port traffic as broadcasts from all VLANs are not unnecessarily forwarded over every trunk port in the network.

Question 10 Answer

Pruning is enabled VTP domain-wide by entering either the **set vtp pruning enable** (CatOS) or **vtp pruning** (IOS VLAN configuration mode) command on a VTP server.

Question 11

What are the available VLAN trunking methods?

Troubleshooting Switched Ethernet Networks

Question 12

Which VLAN Trunking Protocol includes the idea of a native VLAN?

Troubleshooting Switched Ethernet Networks

Question 11 Answer

VLAN trunking can be accomplished by using Inter-Switch Link (ISL) or IEEE 802.1Q. 802.1Q is the preferred protocol because it is a defined standard.

Question 12 Answer

In 802.1Q, traffic on the native VLAN does not contain a VLAN tag. Traffic on all other VLANs contains the 802.1Q header.

Question 13

Which VLAN carries Cisco Discovery Protocol (CDP) and VTP messages on trunk ports?

Question 14

What is the default VLAN?

Question 13 Answer

VLAN 1, which is not eligible for pruning, transports VTP and CDP packets on trunk ports.

Question 14 Answer

The default VLAN is always VLAN number 1. This VLAN is named default and cannot be renamed.

Question 15

What can you do on a VTP server that you cannot do on a VTP client?

Question 16

How many links can be aggregated using Fast EtherChannel?

Question 15 Answer

VLANs must be added or removed on a VTP server. VTP clients are not able to add or remove VLANs from the VTP domain.

Question 16 Answer

Up to eight ports can be placed into a single EtherChannel.

Question 17

What command shows you the current VTP configuration revision number?

Question 18

What does SPAN stand for and what does it accomplish?

Question 17 Answer

The CatOS command **show vtp domain** and the IOS EXEC command **show vtp status** show the current VTP configuration revision number. These commands also show other important information, including the VTP domain name and the number of active VLANs.

Question 18 Answer

SPAN, or the Switch Port Analyzer, provides visibility into switched traffic flows. With SPAN, traffic from a port or VLAN can be replicated to another port for use with a network sniffer, intrusion detection system, or monitoring station.

Question 19

Workstations attached to a new switch in your network are unable to receive an IP address upon startup. What should you check first?

Question 20

You are unable to Telnet to a switch from certain parts of your network. What switch configuration parameter should you check first?

Question 19 Answer

This is the most common symptom of spanning-tree port enablement delays. To solve this problem, ensure that spanning-tree Port Fast has been enabled via the following IOS interface configuration command:

```
spanning-tree portfast
```

Question 20 Answer

Verify the configuration of CatOS permit lists or IOS access classes.

Question 21

How does a switch determine which operating system image to use during the boot process?

Question 22

If you require greater than 1000 VLANs, which VLAN trunking protocol must you use?

Question 21 Answer

First, any explicitly configured operating system images are attempted. On CatOS, these can be specified with the command **set boot system flash** *device:filename*. On IOS-based switches, this command is **boot system** *device:filename*. If these commands have not been entered or are incorrect, the switch automatically attempts to boot any valid image present in Flash memory.

Question 22 Answer

802.1Q includes support for VLANs numbered up to 4095. In contrast, ISL includes support only for VLANs numbered through 1005.

Question 23

What CatOS show command provides a summary of the configuration and status of all switch ports?

Question 23 Answer

The CatOS command **show port** [*mod/port*] is used to display information about switch ports.

Section 4

Troubleshooting PPP

A derivative of High-Level Data Link Control (HDLC), the Point-to-Point Protocol (PPP) has enjoyed widespread implementation. Through support for nearly all network layer protocols, strong authentication options, and bandwidth efficiency mechanics, PPP can be adapted to almost any use. PPP has been used for years as the remote access protocol of choice for Internet connectivity. Recently, this functionality has been extended to include broadband users with PPP over Ethernet (PPPoE) and PPP over ATM (PPPoA). Although running PPP over a broadcast multiaccess technology, such as Ethernet, might initially seem unnatural, it provides authentication, address management, and accounting capabilities that many broadband deployments require. The configuration of PPP on Cisco routers is flexible and nearly all features can be enabled or disabled independently.

The flash cards in this section apply your knowledge of PPP to troubleshooting. Available **show** and **debug** commands help you gain insight into almost all aspects of PPP's operation. In addition to flash cards on these commands, this section contains flash cards on general protocol operation and configuration.

Question 1

What debug command shows the authentication process as it occurs?

Question 2

What command shows the status of each NCP?

Question 1 Answer

The command **debug ppp authentication** shows the details of any active authentication process.

Question 2 Answer

The **show interfaces** EXEC command shows which Network Control Protocols (NCPs) are in an Open, Closed, or Listen state. An Open state indicates that the protocol has been negotiated and is operating across the PPP connection. A Closed state is the result of a protocol being explicitly disabled on the connection. If a protocol has not successfully been negotiated, it shows a Listen state.

Question 3

What tasks are accomplished using IPCP?

Troubleshooting PPP

Question 4

Besides the ability to add additional bandwidth, what benefit does multilink PPP provide?

Troubleshooting PPP

Question 3 Answer

The Internet Protocol Control Protocol (IPCP) establishes IP connectivity across a PPP connection. It is also used to pass the IP configuration from the server to an asynchronous PPP client. Information that can be exchanged includes IP address, DNS server, and domain name.

Question 4 Answer

Multilink PPP also includes link fragmentation and interleaving capabilities. Although fragmentation is enabled by default for interfaces using multilink PPP, interleaving must be manually enabled. When interleaving is enabled via the interface configuration command **ppp multilink interleave**, small packets can be sent without waiting for an entire large packet to be transmitted. This reduces the serialization delay, and as such, decreases the latency seen by small packets traversing the network.

Question 5

Is authentication required on PPP links?

Question 6

What is LCP and what does it accomplish?

Question 5 Answer

No, authentication is not required for PPP to operate correctly. However, authentication is highly recommended on asynchronous interfaces.

Question 6 Answer

LCP is the Link Control Protocol. LCP is responsible for the testing and configuration of Layer 2 connectivity across a PPP link. The Network Control Protocols (NCPs) are not run until LCP has completed successfully.

Question 7

What type of functionality does LQM provide?

Question 8

While examining the output of a show interfaces command, you notice that CDPCP is shown in a Listen state. What could this mean?

Question 7 Answer

The PPP Link Quality Monitoring (LQM) enables a router to monitor and potentially disable links that are encountering errors. When LQM is enabled via the **ppp quality** *percentage* interface configuration command, an interface is disabled when the percentage of packets successfully sent and received drops below the configured threshold.

Question 8 Answer

This indicates the CDPCP failed to successfully negotiate with the remote PPP peer. This could mean that either the remote peer is not capable of CDP, or that the remote router has had CDP disabled.

Question 9

What command shows details of each link quality report sent and received by the router?

Question 10

What is an advantage of using PPP as opposed to HDLC for point-to-point links?

Question 9 Answer

The privileged EXEC command **debug ppp packet** shows information about link quality reports (LQRs) as they are sent and received. The LQRs include statistics about the number of packets successfully transmitted and received over the PPP interface.

Question 10 Answer

The advantages of PPP over HDLC include the following:

- Vendor interoperability
- Authentication
- Link fragmentation and interleaving

Question 11

What must you do to configure multilink PPP on a group of point-to-point interfaces?

Question 12

What control protocol appears if compression is enabled on an interface?

Question 11 Answer

Two configuration options exist for multilink PPP on synchronous interfaces. The first uses the global configuration command **multilink virtual-template** *number* to assign all multilink PPP interfaces to a particular virtual access interface. The second option uses the **multilink-group** *number* interface configuration command to link serial interfaces to a multilink logical interface. The multilink logical interface holds the Layer 3 information for the multilink group and is configured using the **interface multilink** *number* global configuration command.

Question 12 Answer

The EXEC command **show interfaces** shows CCP (the Compression Control Protocol) with an Open state after compression is negotiated. A Listen state indicates that the local router is attempting to negotiate compression unsuccessfully.

Question 13

When compression is configured, does the same compression algorithm need to be configured in both directions?

Question 14

What EXEC command displays statistics on the performance of compression?

Question 13 Answer

No, it is possible to use different compression algorithms for the data sent in each direction. The EXEC command **show compress detail-ccp** displays the compression algorithm used in each direction.

Question 14 Answer

The EXEC command **show compress** details per interface statistics for compression.

Question 15

**What are the ways that an IP address can be
allocated for a dialup user?**

Question 16

**In what case is a host route entered into the
routing table when a PPP peer connects?**

Question 15 Answer

Several ways exist in which an IP address can be assigned to a PPP dialup user. The following is a prioritized list of the address allocation options:

- AAA server IP pool
- Local IP pool or DHCP configuration
- Dialer map address
- Address specified via the **ppp** or **slip** EXEC commands
- The **peer default ip address** *address* interface configuration command
- Peer provided IP address

Question 16 Answer

By default, the IP address of the PPP peer is entered into the local routing table. To disable this functionality, use the **no peer neighbor-route** interface configuration command.

Question 17

When multilink PPP has been configured, how do you disable packet fragmentation?

Question 18

At what point does PPP authentication take place?

Question 17 Answer

When multilink PPP is configured, multilink fragmentation is enabled by default. To disable fragmentation, use the **no ppp multilink fragmentation** interface configuration commands.

Question 18 Answer

PPP authentication takes place after the LCP completes and before any NCPs are run.

Question 19

What protocols can PPP transport?

Troubleshooting PPP

Question 20

After the command ppp quality 75 is configured, what happens if the router detects errors in half of the packets it receives?

Troubleshooting PPP

Question 19 Answer

PPP can be used to carry protocols for which a NCP exists. NCPs exist for IP, IPX, AppleTalk, XNS, DECnet, CLNS, and VINES. It might also be possible to support other protocols through bridging over PPP, which uses the BridgeCP NCP.

Question 20 Answer

After the quality of the link drops below the configured threshold, 75 percent in the example, the serial interface is disabled. Link quality is determined to be the percentage of traffic successfully transmitted and received. Traffic is measured in both packets and bytes.

Question 21

Can a loopback test be used with PPP?

Question 22

Does LQM need to be enabled on both sides of a PPP connection?

Question 21 Answer

No, once a loopback is placed on a circuit with PPP encapsulation, line protocol on the router interface goes down. This down state makes it impossible for the router to send any traffic.

Question 22 Answer

No. When LQM is enabled, LQRs are sent in place of interface keepalives. When an interface not configured for LQM receives a LQR, it responds with a LQR.

Question 23

When LQM is enabled, packets are monitored in which direction?

Question 23 Answer

The quality determined by LQM is computed using both inbound and outbound traffic statistics from LQRs.

Section 5

Troubleshooting Frame Relay

Frame Relay is possibly the most ubiquitous of wide-area networking topologies. As such, its configuration options are as flexible as the technology itself. However, like most technologies, once implemented, the support and troubleshooting of Frame Relay can be challenging. Lucky for you, many show and debugging commands are available. These commands are specific to Frame Relay and provide traffic statistics, PVC information, and detailed information on the operation of the Frame Relay protocol.

The following flash cards challenge your Frame Relay network support knowledge. They cover **debug** and **show** commands relevant to Frame Relay, information to help you verify your router configurations, and material to give you a greater understanding of the protocol.

CIT

Question 1

After Local Management Interface (LMI) is properly configured, what command details the status of each provisioned permanent virtual circuit (PVC)?

Question 2

What command shows any address to data-link connection identifier (DLCI) mappings?

Question 1 Answer

The EXEC command **show frame-relay pvc** shows the PVCs configured on the router and its Frame Relay switch. It also shows the status and statistics for each PVC.

Question 2 Answer

The command **show frame-relay map** shows the DLCI to Layer 3 address mappings active on the router.

Question 3

How is a router notified of congestion in a Frame Relay network?

Question 4

How can you determine how many times a router has received FECNs or BECNs?

Question 3 Answer

The router is notified of congestion in the network through FECNs and BECNs. FECNs (Forward Explicit Congestion Notifications) notify the router that congestion has occurred in the direction that the frame traveled. BECNs (Backward Explicit Congestion Notifications) alert the router to congestion in the network in the reverse direction.

Question 4 Answer

The EXEC command **show frame-relay pvc** displays statistics on the number of FECNs and BECNs received on each PVC.

Question 5

Which command shows detailed statistics regarding the operation of Frame Relay Local Management Interface (LMI)?

Question 6

What options does the encapsulation frame-relay interface configuration command have?

Question 5 Answer

The command **show frame-relay lmi** shows detailed statistics about the operation of LMI over each Frame Relay interface.

Question 6 Answer

The **encapsulation frame-relay** command has a single option, **ietf**. When **ietf** is specified, the router uses Frame Relay encapsulation compliant with RFCs 1490 and 2427.

Question 7

Must DLCIs match at both ends of a Frame Relay PVC?

Question 8

If the output from show frame-relay pvc shows a PVC's status as DELETED, what does that mean?

Question 7 Answer

No. The Frame Relay DLCI is of local significance only. This value must be shared between the router and the local Frame Relay switch, but the router at the far end of the PVC can use a different DLCI.

Question 8 Answer

When a PVC has been configured on the local router but not the Frame Relay switch, **show frame-relay pvc** shows that PVC with a status of DELETED. Other possible statuses include ACTIVE and INACTIVE.

Question 9

What are the two possible types of address mappings?

Question 10

What is the lowest number DLCI that you should ever configure?

Question 9 Answer

The two types of address mappings are static and dynamic. Static address mappings are created with the **frame-relay map** interface configuration command; dynamic mappings are created automatically using Frame Relay Inverse Address Resolution Protocol (ARP).

Question 10 Answer

All three LMI types reserve the DLCIs numbered from 0 to 15. Therefore, DLCI numbering should begin at 16.

Question 11

Should congestion occur in a Frame Relay network, can you specify frames that should be dropped first?

Question 12

Can a loopback test be used with Frame Relay?

Question 11 Answer

Yes, it is possible to set the DE bit on outgoing Frame Relay frames by using the **frame-relay de-list** and **frame-relay de-group** configuration commands. Here is a sample configuration showing these two commands:

```
!
frame-relay de-list 1 protocol ipx
!
interface s0/0
 encapsulation frame-relay
 frame-relay interface-dlci 16
 frame-relay de-group 1 16
!
```

Question 12 Answer

Yes, while it prevents proper communication from occurring, placing a loopback on the circuit and validating traffic sent through the loopback can serve as a helpful troubleshooting step.

Question 13

What is LMI autosense?

Question 14

Which debug command shows you information relative to a serial interface?

Question 13 Answer

LMI autosense allows the router to detect the LMI type utilized by the Frame Relay switch. When LMI autosense is enabled but the LMI type has not yet been determined, the router sends LMI status requests in all three types (ANSI, Q933a, and Cisco) and listens to see which format the Frame Relay switch responds to.

Question 14 Answer

The command **debug serial interface** shows you information about sent and received keepalives, LMI information, and interface resets.

Question 15

Which debug command shows Frame Relay ARP activity?

Troubleshooting Frame Relay

Question 16

How can you determine if a Frame Relay circuit has been looped within the wide-area network?

Troubleshooting Frame Relay

Question 15 Answer

The command **debug frame-relay events** shows ARP activity. To clear the Inverse ARP cache, use the EXEC command **clear – frame-relay-inarp**.

NOTE

In some versions of IOS, the command **clear frame-relay-inarp** is actually **clear frame-relay inarp**.

Question 16 Answer

The EXEC command, **show interfaces** shows "looped" if a loopback has been placed on a locally attached interface. Here is a sample output showing a looped interface:

```
Serial0/0 is up, line protocol is down (looped)
  Hardware is PowerQUICC Serial
  Internet address is 192.168.1.1/30
-- output truncated --
```

Question 17

What types of events would cause the serial interface to reset?

Troubleshooting
Frame Relay

Question 18

What command clears the Frame Relay Inverse ARP table?

Troubleshooting
Frame Relay

Question 17 Answer

The following situations cause a router to reset an interface:

- The **clear interface** command was used to reset the interface.
- The router was unable to send packets in the interface's output queue.
- There is a hardware problem.
- A loopback has been placed on the circuit.

Question 18 Answer

The EXEC command **clear frame-relay-inarp** clears the Inverse ARP table.

NOTE

In some versions of IOS, the command **clear frame-relay-inarp** is actually **clear frame-relay inarp**.

Question 19

What command shows whether or not IP split horizon has been disabled on an interface?

Question 20

Two spoke sites using Enhanced Interior Gateway Routing Protocol (EIGRP) on a Frame Relay network are not receiving each others routes. What is the first thing to check?

Question 19 Answer

Use the EXEC command **show ip interface** to display the IP configuration of each router interface.

Question 20 Answer

If a multipoint Frame Relay subinterface is used at the hub site, IP split horizon might prevent routes from one spoke site from being seen from the other spoke sites. To disable IP split horizon, use the interface configuration command **no ip split-horizon.**

Question 21

Must the Frame Relay LMI type be manually configured?

Question 22

What command shows the number of received frames with the DE bit set?

Question 21 Answer

No, when the Frame Relay LMI type is not explicitly configured, the router attempts to use LMI autosense. When LMI autosense is used, the router sends LMI status requests in all three formats while determining the LMI type to use. Once the correct LMI type has been discovered, status requests are sent only in the proper format.

Question 22 Answer

The command **show frame-relay pvc** shows statistics about the Frame Relay PVC, including the number of frames sent and received with the Discard Eligible (DE) bit set.

Question 23

What is the default interface type when Frame Relay encapsulation is configured on a physical interface?

Question 23 Answer

Physical interfaces configured for Frame Relay default to multipoint. To use a point-to-point configuration, subinterfaces must be used.

CIT Quick
Reference Sheets

Network Troubleshooting and Baselining

The General Troubleshooting Process

You can characterize troubleshooting by using a three-stage process. Unfortunately, you might need to repeat this process until a resolution is found. The three steps of the process are

1. **Gather symptoms**—During this step, you must gather and document symptoms of the problem. It is also during this step that problem ownership is determined.
2. **Isolate the problem**—At this point in the process, you must choose and apply the correct troubleshooting strategy.
3. **Correct the problem**—Use the information that you have gained in the previous steps to correct the problem. It is important that the operational status of the network be assessed once this step is complete to ensure that the changes have not had a negative impact.

Gathering Symptoms

The first step in the troubleshooting process, which is to gather the symptoms, has five steps itself:

1. **Analyze existing symptoms**—During this step, you must examine the currently documented symptoms and document any others that are known, but undocumented.
2. **Determine ownership**—At this point, you need to leverage your understanding of the technical and organizational environment to determine ownership of the problem. If the problem is within a system you are responsible for, continue the process. If not, contact and work with the responsible party.
3. **Narrow the scope**—Combining the information from the first two steps, narrow the scope of the problem by eliminating symptoms of symptoms and focusing on the root cause. In general, use this step to focus on what you know and eliminating superfluous information.
4. **Determine symptoms**—If necessary, gather additional symptoms attempting to gain new insight into the problem.
5. **Document symptoms**—Simply document the symptoms you know.

Types of Troubleshooting Methodologies

Three general troubleshooting methodologies help you in the fault-finding process:

- **Top-down**—This approach begins the troubleshooting process at Layer 7 of the OSI model and works down.
- **Bottom-up**—This methodology starts at the physical layer, Layer 1 of the OSI model, and works up.
- **Divide and conquer**—Leverages past experiences to begin troubleshooting in the middle of the OSI model. This model initially troubleshoots in both directions and is considered to be a more advanced technique when compared to the top-down or bottom-up methodologies.

Guidelines for Network Documentation

- **Determine your scope**—Determine which portion of the network or what aspects of the network this documentation covers. Without this determination, it is likely that the resultant documentation will not cover the appropriate material at an appropriate depth.
- **Know your objective**—Understand what your document is trying to accomplish. Then, make sure that each component works towards accomplishing that goal.
- **Be consistent**—Being consistent aids others in understanding your documentation. Consistent conventions also help troubleshooters cross reference information they need.
- **Keep the document accessible**—What good is the network documentation if you can't access it during a network outage? It is critical to keep documentation accessible to the people who need it. Otherwise, its creation was just an exercise.
- **Maintain the documentation**—The only thing that is possibly worse than no documentation is old incorrect documentation. It is important that troubleshooters trust the documentation and do not have to waste time validating or correcting it.

Reasons to Baseline a Network

- Give yourself or others an understanding of the network.
- Document the normal operation for comparison during troubleshooting and fault isolation.

Steps in the Network Discovery Process

The network discovery process is made up of four steps. By using these steps consistently, your network documentation is more accurate and complete:

1. **Document the current device name and addresses**—In this step, you must detail the network layer properties of the current device.

2. **Document all active interfaces**—Not only is this information important to the present device, it is used in the discovery process, which happens next.

3. **Discover the directly connected devices**—Use the network layer addressing and interface information documented in the previous steps to discover adjacent network devices. Several **show** commands can help you in discovering the network; they are detailed in the section, "Helpful Commands in Network Discovery and Documentation."

4. **View details about connected devices**—Leverage available tools to view and document information about connected devices.

Network Topology Diagrams

Network topology diagrams greatly aid the troubleshooting process. Once created, they give the troubleshooter the following information:

- A quick overview of the network
- A visual representation of how devices are connected
- A list the device names and locations
- An overview of the routing protocol configurations, such as area definitions and points of summarization

Components of a Network Configuration Table

A vital component of any set of network documentation, the network configuration tables need to capture all-important aspects of a router or switch configuration. The following critical points need to be included in network configuration tables for routers and switches alike:

- System name
- Software version and filename
- Interface types
- Network layer addresses
- Data-link addresses
- Router memory and central processing unit (CPU)

- Routing protocol configuration
- Any other critical configuration or hardware component

Important Points to Document for Ethernet Switches

Specific to an Ethernet switch, the following items allow the reader to quickly understand the switch configuration, and if needed, quickly recreate it:

- Switch name
- IP address
- STP bridge priority
- VLAN Trunking Protocol (VTP) domain name
- VTP role
- Per-port information
  - STP state
  - Speed and duplex configuration
  - VLAN assignment
  - Trunking configuration
  - EtherChannel configuration

Important Points to Document for Routers

The following items are critical to the operation of a router. As such, it is important that these details be found in any relevant network configuration tables:

- Router name
- Network layer addresses
- Interface types
  - Per interface settings
  - Speed and duplex
- Routing protocol configuration
  - Router ID
  - Open Shortest Path First (OSPF) and Intermediate System-to-Intermediate System (IS-IS) area definition
  - Summarization
  - Autonomous system number

Helpful Commands in Network Discovery and Documentation

This table lists some EXEC commands that are useful when discovering or documenting a network.

Command	Description
show cdp neighbors [detail]	Used to display the adjacent Cisco devices. The **detail** option displays additional information, including any configured network layer addresses.
show ip ospf neighbor	Displays all active OSPF neighbors.
show ip eigrp neighbors	Displays the Enhanced Interior Gateway Routing Protocol (EIGRP) adjacencies.
show ip route	Displays the IP routing table.
show ip arp [interface *type number*]	Shows the Address Resolution Protocol (ARP) cache. The output of this command can be displayed per-interface using the interface argument.
show ip bgp summary	Displays the Border Gateway Protocol (BGP) peers configured on this router.
show clns neighbor	Used to display information about neighboring IS-IS routers.

Troubleshooting TCP/IP

Static Routes

Static routes can be good and bad. They are often the source of network problems, but at the same time, understanding their operation and benefits can aid in troubleshooting. To create a static route, use the following global configuration command:

`ip route prefix mask {ip-address | interface-type interface-number [ip-address]} [distance] [permanent]`

This command has few, but nonetheless important, options. The following table explains these options.

Option	Description
prefix	The destination network.
mask	The mask to apply to the entered prefix.
ip-address	The next hop for the static route.
interface-type interface-number	Configures a specific output interface for the static route; should only be used on point-to-point interfaces. When used on multi access interfaces, this causes the router to ARP for any destination included in that route.
distance	The administrative distance for the route.
permanent	Specifies that the route should not be removed from the routing table when the associated interface is down.

Administrative Distance

The router assigns a value called administrative distance (AD) to sources of routing information. This value is used to select a route when multiple routes to the same destination are available from different sources. A lower AD indicates a higher level of preference. The following table shows the default AD for each available source of IP routing information.

0	Connected routes
1	Static routes
5	EIGRP summary route
20	External BGP (EBGP)
90	Internal EIGRP

100	IGRP
110	OSPF
115	IS-IS
120	Routing Information Protocol (RIP)
140	Exterior Gateway Protocol (EGP)
160	On-Demand Routing (ODR)
170	External EIGRP
200	Internal BGP (IBGP)
255	Unknown

The AD can be changed for any routing protocol using the router configuration command:

distance *distance* {*ip-address* {*wildcard-mask*} [*ip-standard-list*] [*ip-extended-list*]

For EIGRP and BGP, the commands are slightly different. To change the AD for EIGRP, use the router configuration command:

distance eigrp *internal-distance external-distance*

For BGP, use the router configuration command:

distance bgp *external-distance internal-distance local-distance*

Route Redistribution

Redistribution is the process of importing routes from an outside source. Examples of redistribution include the advertising of static routes to OSPF neighbors, and the broadcasting of OSPF routes to other routers running RIP.

Within the context of IP, redistribution takes place automatically in one instance, when a router is running both EIGRP and IGRP with the same autonomous system numbers.

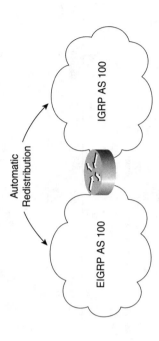

Automatic Redistribution

EIGRP AS 100   IGRP AS 100

For all other cases of redistribution, manual administrator intervention is required. When performing redistribution, the following items must be taken into account:

- **Incompatible metrics**—The metrics used by different routing protocols are not compatible and must be manually configured.
- **Routing loops**—It is possible to introduce routing loops when multiple routers are performing redistribution; to prevent this, configure filtering to limit the routes that are redistributed.

Route redistribution is configured with the following router configuration command:

redistribute *protocol* [*process-id*] {**level-1** | **level-1-2** | **level-2**} [**metric** *metric-value*] [**metric-type** *type-value*] [**match** {**internal** | **external 1** | **external 2**}] [**route-map** *map-tag*] [**subnets**]

The following table explains the many options to the **redistribute** command.

Option	Description
protocol	The routing protocol to redistribute routes from.
process-id	The process ID of the routing process to import from.
level-1	For IS-IS, redistribute only L1 routes.

IOS TCP/IP Troubleshooting Commands

Many IOS commands can aid in the troubleshooting of TCP/IP problems. The following table explains these commands and their usefulness.

Command	Description
clear arp	Removes all entries in the router's ARP cache.
clear ip route [* | ip-address [mask]]	Removes a specific route from the router's routing table.
ping ip-address	Tests ICMP connectivity between the router and a remote IP address.
ping (Extended)	An extended ping allows you to specify the following items: • Repeat count • Datagram size • Timeout • Source address or interface • IP type of service • Don't Fragment bit • Validate reply data • Data pattern • Source routing • Sweep packet sizes
show ip access-list [access-list]	Shows the configured access lists and how many times each access list entry (ACE) has been matched; the output can be limited by specifying a particular access list.
show interfaces [type number]	Shows the operational status of a router interface and the IP address and mask in use.

Option	Description
level-1-2	For IS-IS, redistribute both L1 and L2 routes.
level-2	For IS-IS, redistribute only L2 routes.
metric metric-value	Set the default metric in this routing protocol for the redistributed routes.
metric-type type-value	For OSPF, redistributed routes can be either external type 1 or external type 2. Enter either 1 or 2 to select the external route type for redistributed routes. For IS-IS, redistributed routes can be either internal or external. Enter either internal or external to configure the IS-IS type for redistributed routes.
match [internal | external 1 | external 2]	Redistribute OSPF routes only of the specified type.
route-map map-tag	Use the specified route map to filter or alter redistributed routes.
subnets	For OSPF, redistribute networks using masks longer than the appropriate natural mask.

If you decide not to set the default metric for redistributed routes on the redistribute command, you can use one of the following.

BGP	default-metric metric
EIGRP	default-metric bandwidth delay reliability loading mtu
IGRP	default-metric bandwidth delay reliability loading mtu
OSPF	default-metric metric
RIP	default-metric metric

The following command, common to Windows and UNIX, can help determine if an IP address is reachable from the designated workstation:

ping *ip-address*

The following commands display the IP configuration of all configured network interfaces:

(Windows) **ipconfig /all**
(UNIX) **ipconfig -a**

The following commands output the routing table of the workstation they are issued on. Just like a router's routing table, these commands display the network, mask, and next hop information for all routes in the table:

(Windows) **route print**
(UNIX) **netstat -rn**

The following commands display an approximation of the path packets between the workstation and specified IP address take:

(Windows) **tracert** *ip-address*
(UNIX) **traceroute** *ip-address*

NOTE: It is important to use the output of any **traceroute** command (from a router, Windows, or UNIX workstation) with a grain of salt. Because of asymmetric routing, policy routing, and other factors, the path reported by traceroute might or might not reflect the actual path of user traffic.

TCP/IP Debugging Commands

The following commands can be used to debug IP-related problems.

This command displays ARP requests sent and answered by the router:

debug arp

This command displays information about EIGRP packets sent and received by the router:

debug ip eigrp

Command	Description
show ip arp [*ip-address*] [interface *type number*]	Shows the contents of the router ARP cache; can be limited to a specific IP address or interface.
show ip interfaces [*type number*]	Displays detailed information about the IP operation of all interfaces or a specific interface. The information includes the IP address, mask, routing protocol metrics, route cache flag, MTU, and applied access lists.
show ip protocols	Displays the configuration and status of any configured routing protocols.
show ip route [*source*]	Displays the contents of the routing table; output can be limited to a specific routing protocol.
trace *ip-address*	Displays the path that UDP packets take to the remote IP address.
trace (Extended)	Traces the path through the network that UDP packets take from the router to a remote destination. Using the extended form of this command, you can set: • Target IP address • Source addresses • Numeric display • Timeout • Probe count • Minimum Time-To-Live (TTL) • Maximum TTL • UDP port number • Source routing options

Workstation Troubleshooting Commands

Several commands can be issued on Windows and UNIX workstations to aid in the IP troubleshooting process.

The debug command:

```
debug ip ospf events
```

displays information about the following OSPF events:

- Adjacency management
- Link State Advertisement (LSA) flooding
- Designated router elections
- SPF calculations

This command displays real-time information about OSPF packets sent and received by the router. The output can be limited by specifying an access list:

```
debug ip ospf packet [access-list]
```

The following command displays information about packets routed by the router. The output can be limited by specifying an access list:

```
debug ip packet [access-list]
```

The following command displays information about the operation of the Routing Information Protocol (RIP):

```
debug ip rip
```

Troubleshooting Switched Ethernet Networks

Protocols Used on a Switched Network

- VLAN Trunking Protocol (VTP)—Used to disseminate information about VLANs throughout the network. Switches are grouped into a VTP domain. Allows for simple security using VTP domain passwords. VTP pruning, which is disabled by default, automatically removes unneeded VLANs from trunk ports.

  Switches can be configured for one of these three VTP roles:

  —Server—Can make changes to the VTP database. Servers multicast changes to other VTP servers and VTP clients in the domain.

  —Client—Cannot make changes to the VTP database. Clients listen for VTP database announcements from servers.

  —Transparent—Can configure VLANs locally. Although transparent switches do not advertise VTP messages, they forward those VTP messages heard unaltered.

- Dynamic Trunking Protocol (DTP)—Used to automatically configure VLAN trunking on switch links. Available modes include on, off, desirable, and auto. Should be disabled on workstation ports.

- Spanning Tree Protocol (STP)—Used to remove loops from the network. Defined as the 802.1d standard. Port Fast reduces edge port enablement time from 50 to about 5 seconds. STP has several available modes of operation, such as

  —Per VLAN Spanning Tree Plus (PVST+)

  —Multiple Spanning Tree Protocol (MST)

  —Common Spanning Tree Protocol (CST)

- Inter-Switch Link (ISL)—This Cisco proprietary protocol allows multiple VLANs to traverse one link. Adds VLAN tag to each packet. Supports VLANs numbered 1 through 1005.

- 802.1Q Trunk Protocol—Standards-based protocol. Allows multiple VLANs to travel across one link. Adds VLAN tag to each packet. Traffic on Native VLAN does not have 802.1Q header added. 802.1Q header includes 802.1P class of service bits. Supports VLANs number from 1 to 4094.

- EtherChannel—Provides additional bandwidth through the aggregation of multiple ports. Appears as one port to the Spanning Tree Protocol. Can support up to eight interfaces. (Interfaces can be added or removed seamlessly.) EtherChannel can use the following load distribution methods: per source MAC, per destination MAC, per source IP address, per destination IP address, per source IP port, and per destination IP port. EtherChannel has three current flavors: EtherChannel, Fast EtherChannel (FEC), and Gigabit EtherChannel (GEC).

- Cisco Discovery Protocol (CDP)—Allows devices and administrators to learn information from neighboring network devices. The information carried in CDP includes

  —Model

  —Capabilities

  —Software revision

  —Layer 3 addresses

  —Interface

Using SPAN and RSPAN

Switched networks inherently limit the visibility of network analyzers because traffic is directed to specific switch ports and not simply replicated to all ports.

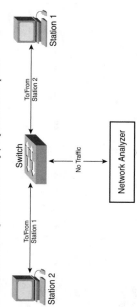

To gain visibility into network traffic when troubleshooting must take place, a Switch Port ANalyzer (SPAN) port replicates traffic to or from a switch port or VLAN to the port connected to a network analyzer.

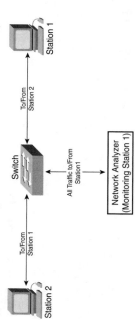

The syntax to enable a SPAN differs between CatOS and IOS switches; both syntaxes are shown as follows:

CatOS

set span {*src_mod/src_ports* | *src_vlans* | **sc0**} {*dest_mod/dest_port*}
[**rx** | **tx** | **both**]

IOS

monitor session *session* **source** {**interface** *type* | **vlan** *vlan-id* [**rx** | **tx** | **both**]}

and

monitor session *session* **destination** {**interface** *type* | **vlan** *vlan-id*}

Troubleshooting Error Disabled Ports

A port might become error disabled when one of the following occurs:

- Excessive collisions.
- Late collisions.
- EtherChannel misconfiguration.
- BPDU port-guard is violated.
- A unidirectional link is detected via Unidirectional Link Detection (UDLD).

To reenable an error disabled port, one of the following commands must be used:

(CatOS) **set port enable** *mod/port*
(IOS) **shutdown**

then

no shutdown

Alternatively, error disabled ports can be automatically enabled after a period of time using the commands:

(CatOS) **set errdisable-timeout interval** *timeout*
(IOS) **errdisable recovery interval** *interval*

Important Troubleshooting Commands

Although not categorized as debug commands, these commands can be of great assistance when troubleshooting switched networks.

The following CatOS command configures a proven set of parameters for workstation ports. Specifically, it turns on STP Port Fast and disables trunking and channeling:

set port host *mod/port*

Although the following command is not a **debug** command, it does allow direct access to intelligent Catalyst 6500 modules. Such modules contain their own configuration and must be accessed directly to be configured:

(CatOS) **session slot** *module* **processor** *proc*
(IOS) **session** *slot*

The following commands are used to view the switch's Layer 2 forwarding table:

(CatOS) **show cam**
(IOS) **show mac-address-table**

This CatOS command displays counter information for all or the specified ports. These counters include the number of bytes transmitted and received, as well as the number and types of errors received:

show port {*mod/port*}

The following commands display information about the state of STP on the specified VLAN. This information includes the root bridge ID and the switch's designated and root ports:

(CatOS) **show spantree** *number*
(IOS) **show spanning-tree vlan** *number*

These commands display information about ports that have been blocked by the STP:

(CatOS) **show spantree blockedports**
(IOS) **show spanning-tree blockedports**

Debugging Commands

The Cisco IOS Software allows for extensive debugging facilities. The commands detailed as follows give you insight into the operation of your network, and aid in the troubleshooting process. These commands are not available on CatOS devices.

The following debug command displays information about the establishment and maintenance of EtherChannel groups:

debug etherchnl

The following debug command displays information about interface state changes on the designated interface:

debug interface *mod/port*

The following debug command displays real-time information about the operation of multilayer switching (MLS) for switches that are acting as an MLS Route Processor (RP):

debug mls rp {**all** | **error** | **events** | **ip** | **ipx** | **locator** | **packets** | **verbose packets**}

The following debug command displays information about the operation of any configured SPAN sessions:

debug monitor

The following command provides real-time information into the Spanning Tree Protocol. With many options, the output can be granular:

debug spanning-tree {**all** | **bpdu** | **bpdu-opt** | **etherchannel** | **config** | **events** | **exceptions** | **general** | **pvst+** | **root** | **snmp**}

Troubleshooting PPP

Components of PPP

The Point-to-Point Protocol (PPP) is modular and is made up of many components. The following sections attempt to detail many of the most used protocol components.

- The Link Control Protocol (LCP) establishes and tests Layer 2 connectivity.
- Authentication can take place in one or both directions and takes place before any Network Control Protocols (NCPs) are run.
  —Challenge Handshake Authentication Protocol (CHAP) uses a three-way handshake in which passwords are never sent over the network.
  —Password Authentication Protocol (PAP) sends username and password information unencrypted.
- Network Control Protocols (NCPs)
  —A NCP exists for each protocol.
  —Negotiates protocol specific parameters.
  —Example NCPs include IPCP, IPXCP, ATALKCP, CDPCP, and BridgeCP.
- Link Quality Monitoring (LQM)
  —Measures link quality
  —Disables unreliable links
  —Replaces regular keepalives
  —Can be enabled on one or both PPP endpoints
- Multilink PPP
  —Allows bonding of multiple physical interfaces into a single logical interface
  —Packet fragmentation
  —Fragment interleaving
  —Works on synchronous and asynchronous connections

Debugging PPP Connections

A suite of commands can help you troubleshoot PPP connection establishment problems. The following table details these commands.

debug ppp authentication	Displays information relevant to the operation of PAP and CHAP.
debug ppp compression	Displays information about the negotiation of compression.
debug ppp errors	Outputs errors and error statistics during connection establishment.
debug ppp multilink events	Displays information about system events affecting the multilink PPP connection.
debug ppp multilink fragments	Displays information about multilink PPP fragments sent and received over the connection.
debug ppp multilink negotiation	Outputs information about the negotiation of multilink PPP during connection establishment.
debug ppp negotiation	Displays information about the negotiation of parameters via LCP and the NCPs.
debug ppp packet	Outputs the details of keepalives and Link Quality Reports (LQRs) as they traverse the connection.

Client IP Address Assignment

A PPP client can be assigned an IP address in several ways. The following is a prioritized list of the available methods:

- AAA server IP pool
- Local IP pool or Dynamic Host Configuration Protocol (DHCP) configuration
- Dialer map address
- Address specified via the ppp or slip EXEC commands
- The **peer default ip address** *address* interface configuration command
- Peer provided IP address

The default address allocation method can be controlled with the following global configuration command:

ip address-pool {dhcp-proxy-client | local }

An IP address pool is configured using the following command:

ip local pool *pool-name start-address end-address*

After the pool is created, it can be applied with the interface configuration command that follows:

peer default ip address pool *pool-name*

To configure the access server to use DHCP to determine addresses available for client assignment, use the global configuration command that follows:

ip dhcp-server {*ip-address* | *name*}

After the DHCP servers are configured and the default address allocation method set to DHCP, the following interface configuration command enables IP address assignment from the DHCP retrieved addresses:

peer default ip address pool dhcp

A specific address can be assigned to user dialing into a particular access server interface with the following interface configuration command:

peer default ip address *ip-address*

Configuring and Tuning Multilink PPP

The following commands configure and customize the implementation of multilink PPP. The following command allows you to determine at what point additional connections are established using other rotary group members:

dialer load-threshold *load* **[inbound | outbound | either]**

The following command creates a virtual multilink interface. Member interfaces are linked to this interface using the **multilink-group** interface configuration command:

interface multilink *number*

The following global configuration command links all synchronous interfaces configured for multilink PPP to a single virtual-template interface:

multilink virtual-template *number*

The following interface configuration command links physical interfaces to a single multilink virtual interface. The virtual interface is configured with the global configuration command interface multilink *number*:

multilink-group *number*

The following interface configuration command enables multilink PPP on an interface:

ppp multilink

The following command enables multilink PPP fragmentation on an interface. This is enabled by default and can be disabled using the command **ppp multilink fragment disable**:

no ppp multilink fragment disable

The following interface configuration command enables interleaving of multilink PPP fragments. This is disabled by default for interfaces using multilink PPP encapsulation:

ppp multilink interleave

Verification of a PPP Configuration

The following commands can be used to view the status of a configured PPP configuration:

- ping *ip-address*
- show compress
- show interfaces [*type number*]
- show ppp multilink
- show users [all]

Supporting Frame Relay

Key Frame Relay Troubleshooting Terminology

Frame Relay is an extremely widespread protocol. Understanding its mechanisms greatly increases your effectiveness in troubleshooting its problems.

- **Backwards Explicit Congestion Notification (BECN)**—Sent by the Frame Relay network to indicate congestion on a virtual circuit (VC) in the opposite direction. If a router receives a BECN, it is an indication of congestion from that router toward the other end of the VC.

- **Forward Explicit Congestion Notification (FECN)**—Sent by the Frame Relay network to indicate congestion on a VC in the same direction as the FECN traveled.

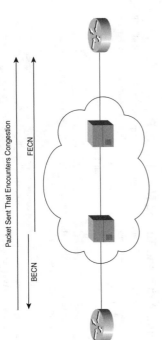

Packet Sent That Encounters Congestion

FECN

BECN

- **The Discard Eligible (DE) bit**—Set in the Frame Relay header of packets that are in excess of the Committed Information Rate (CIR) on a VC. The DE bit can be set by the network or transmitting Frame Relay endpoint.
- **The Local Management Interface (LMI)**—A means of communication between Frame Relay switch and Frame Relay endpoint. The status of VCs is communicated using LMI.

Configuring a Router to Interact with a Congested Frame Relay Network

The map class configuration command

frame-relay adaptive-shaping becn

instructs the router to slow transmission into the network when a BECN is received. The slower transmission rate is applied on a per-VC basis and is by default half of the configured CIR. This value, called MinCIR, can be explicitly configured with the map class configuration command:

frame-relay mincir *mincir*

Using the **frame-relay de-group** and **frame-relay de-list** commands, it is possible to selectively set the DE bit in outgoing packets. The following example sets the DE bit in all outgoing IPX packets and IP packets larger than 512 bytes; all other packets are unchanged:

```
Router(config)# frame-relay de-list 1 protocol ipx
Router(config)# frame-relay de-list 1 protocol ip gt 512
Router(config)# interface Serial 0.16
Router(config-subif)# frame-relay interface-dlci 16
Router(config-fr-dlci)# frame-relay de-group 1 16
```

Viewing the Status of Frame Relay Connections

The following commands help you view the status of any configured Frame Relay connections.

The following command displays configuration and statistic information about the Frame Relay Local Management Interface (LMI). The important troubleshooting information includes the LMI type, interface type, and the number of LMI status messages sent and received:

show frame-relay lmi [interface *type number*]

The output of the following command includes the mappings of data-link connection identifiers (DLCIs) to Layer 3 addresses, as well as other characteristics of the connection, such as compression and LMI type:

show frame-relay map

When the following command displays information about an interface configured with Frame Relay encapsulation, it displays the Frame Relay specific information such as LMI and encapsulation types, LMI statistics, and DLCI used for LMI:

show interfaces [*type number*]

The following command displays the status and statistics for each VC. Statistics displayed include the number of BECN, FECN, and DE packets received for each VC. After LMI is configured, any VCs configured on the Frame Relay switch are display, including those not configured on the router:

show frame-relay pvc [interface *name number*] [*dlci*]

The following command shows the number of Frame Relay ARP request and replies sent and received:

show frame-relay traffic

The following command shows the configuration of traffic shaping on each VC. The output includes the target and peak rates, time interval (Tc), and the status of adaptive shaping:

show traffic-shape [*type number*]

The output of the following command includes statistics relative to the operation of traffic shaping on each VC. These statistics include the number of bytes and packets shaped, the queue depth, and if adaptive shaping is enabled:

show traffic-shape statistics [*type number*]

Debugging Frame Relay Connections

These debug commands provide real-time insight into the operation of Frame Relay. The following command displays Frame Relay LMI messages as they are sent and received by the router. Once every 60 seconds, your router receives an LMI message including the configured permanent virtual circuits (PVCs) and their CIRs from the Frame Relay switch:

debug frame-relay lmi [interface *type number*]

Not restricted to just Frame Relay debugging, the following command displays keepalive messages sent and received:

debug serial interface

The following command displays real-time information about Frame Relay ARP messages sent and received:

debug frame-relay events

The following command displays information about each outgoing packet for all interfaces or the selected interface. The information displayed includes the DLCI, packet type, and packet size:

debug frame-relay packet [interface *type number*]

Part IV

BCRAN

Section 1
Wide-Area Network Technologies

Section 2
Configuring Asynchronous Serial Connections

Section 3
Configuring PPP with CHAP and PAP

Section 4
Dial-on-Demand Routing

Section 5
Configuration of Frame Relay Connections

Section 6
Network Redundancy and Backup Connections

Section 7
Queuing and Compression

Section 8
Network Address Translation

Section 9
Cable and DSL Technologies

Section 10
Understanding Virtual Private Networks

BCRAN Quick Reference Sheets

Section 1

Wide-Area Network Technologies

BCRAN

Wide-area network (WAN) technologies make it possible to connect disparate locations with an appropriate amount of bandwidth. Extremely different, dedicated connections, ISDN, and Frame Relay each approach wide-area networking in a different fashion. Dedicated connections are exactly that—bandwidth for use between exactly two sites. ISDN, a circuit-switched technology, can be used to connect many sites as needed and is often billed on a per minute basis. A Frame Relay network can take almost any shape, from point-to-point to partial mesh to full mesh. Whichever technology is used, the design of the network should match the connectivity requirements of the organization, while managing cost and providing the required level of redundancy.

These flash cards review the technologies and protocols used to establish WAN connectivity. Although the configuration of these protocols is covered in subsequent chapters, this chapter provides foundational topics for ISDN, Frame Relay, and dedicated connections.

Question 1

What are the two types of ISDN interfaces?

Wide-Area Network
Technologies

Question 2

What is a B channel?

Wide-Area Network
Technologies

Question 1 Answer

ISDN is available over two interface types: Basic Rate Interface (BRI) and Primary Rate Interface (PRI). An ISDN BRI connection provides two 64 Kbps B channels and one 16 Kbps D channel. In North America and parts of Asia, an ISDN PRI interface provides 23 64 Kbps B channels and one 64 Kbps D channel. In other parts of the world, an ISDN PRI includes 30 B channels, one D channel, and one channel used for framing and CRC information.

Question 2 Answer

An ISDN B, or Bearer channel, transports voice or data between two ISDN end points. This is in contrast to the D channel, which sends and receives call setup and disconnect messages.

Question 3

What is a D channel?

Question 4

How many B channels exist on each type of ISDN interface?

Question 3 Answer

The ISDN D channel is used for signaling call control information. On an ISDN BRI interface, the D channel is 16 Kbps, while on ISDN PRI interfaces, the D channel is 64 Kbps.

When used in North America and parts of Asia, the D channel is the twenty-fourth channel on the PRI. When used elsewhere, the D channel is sixteenth channel.

Question 4 Answer

An ISDN BRI interface has two 64 Kbps B channels. In North America and parts of Asia, a PRI has 23 B channels. In other parts of the world, the PRI interface has 30 B channels.

Question 5

What are the ISDN reference points?

Question 6

What are the two signaling protocols used by ISDN on the D channel?

Question 5 Answer

The ISDN reference points identify different interfaces within the ISDN specification. The defined reference points are

- **R**—The point at which non-ISDN terminal equipment (TE2) connects to the ISDN Terminal Adapter (TA).

- **S**—The point where an ISDN TA or terminal equipment (TE1) connects customer-owned switching equipment (NT2).

- **T**—Where the customer-owned equipment (NT2) connects to the NT1.

- **U**—The NT1-to-telephone company connection. This is important only in North America. Elsewhere, the NT1 function is provided by the telephone carrier.

Question 6 Answer

ISDN uses two protocols for D channel signaling: Q.921 and Q.931. Q.921 is also known as Link Access Procedure, D channel (LAPD). Q.921 is used for Layer 2 signaling over the ISDN D channel.

Q.931 is a Layer 3 protocol used to establish, manage, and disconnect ISDN connections between two ISDN interfaces.

Question 7

What is a SPID?

Question 8

What is the default encapsulation on a synchronous serial interface?

Question 7 Answer

A SPID, or Service Profile Identifier, is used on BRI interfaces in North America to identify the ISDN end point. Not all ISDN switch types require the use of SPIDs. When SPIDs are used, one SPID is assigned to each B channel.

Question 8 Answer

The default encapsulation on a synchronous serial connection is HDLC. Encapsulation can be changed using the interface configuration command **encapsulation** *encapsulation-type*.

Question 9

What is another name for an ISDN PRI router interface?

Question 10

What is Q.921 used for?

Question 9 Answer

An ISDN PRI router interface is often called a channelized T1, or channelized E1 interface because the PRI specification uses either a T1 or E1 for the underlying connectivity.

Question 10 Answer

Q.921 establishes Layer 2 ISDN connectivity between the ISDN network and the ISDN end point.

Question 11

What does Q.931 accomplish?

Question 12

ISDN uses what type of switching technology?

Question 11 Answer

Q.931 is used in ISDN to establish Layer 3 communication between two end points in an ISDN network. Its messages are used to set up, manage, and disconnect circuit-switched connections.

Question 12 Answer

ISDN is a circuit-switched networking technology. Circuits are established using the Q.931 protocol. Once established, all data between the end points is switched over the same network path.

Question 13

Frame Relay uses what type of switching technology?

Question 14

What is the difference between a T1 and an E1?

Question 13 Answer

Frame Relay is a packet-switched network technology. A field within the Frame Relay frame, the DLCI determines the frame's destination. Every frame received by the network has its DLCI individually examined.

Question 14 Answer

Used in North America, the T1 is made up of 24 timeslots and provides 1.544 Mbps of bandwidth. The E1 is made up of 32 timeslots and supports data rates of 2.048 Mbps.

Question 15

What happens when congestion occurs in a Frame Relay network?

Question 16

If a router has an ISDN S/T interface, what piece of equipment is required to connect the router to the North American ISDN network?

Question 15 Answer

When congestion occurs in a Frame Relay network, switches simply drop frames that they are not able to transmit or receive. When this occurs, the switch might send a Forward or Backward Explicit Congestion Notification to the receiving or sending stations.

Question 16 Answer

A NT1 is required to connect an S/T interface to the ISDN network in North America.

Question 17

**Can analog modem calls be terminated on a
router over an ISDN connection?**

Question 18

**Is additional equipment required to connect an
ISDN U interface to the ISDN network?**

Question 17 Answer

Yes. Inbound analog calls can be supported over ISDN when the router is equipped with a digital modem. Without digital modems, the ISDN router can support connections only from other ISDN connected devices.

Question 18 Answer

No. An ISDN U interface includes the NT1 and can be connected directly to the ISDN network in North America.

Question 19

What type of error recovery does the Frame Relay network provide?

Question 19 Answer

A Frame Relay network provides absolutely no error recovery. If an error is found in a frame, the network simply drops the packet without notifying the source or destination. Frame Relay leaves error recovery to the upper layer protocols and applications.

Section 2

Configuring Asynchronous Serial Connections

To provide dialup connectivity to an organization's remote users, some sort of asynchronous access must be configured. This type of scenario requires the configuration of lines, modems, and optionally Group-Async interfaces. The modemcap database holds default configurations for several modem types and can be extended to include any configuration desired. Group-Async interfaces provide a means to configure a pool of physical lines with a shared configuration. Leveraging a flexible expect-send syntax, chat scripts can interact with modems and remote devices as desired.

These flash cards review the configuration of asynchronous connectivity on a Cisco router. The configuration of chat scripts, interfaces, and lines is covered.

Question 1

What is reverse Telnet used for?

Configuring
Asynchronous Serial
Connections

Question 2

What is the formula for determining the port number that should be used with a reverse Telnet session?

Configuring
Asynchronous Serial
Connections

Question 1 Answer

Reverse Telnet, or a Telnet session to a line, is used to test the modem connected to that line. Individual AT commands, including dialing a remote modem, can be entered using this session.

Question 2 Answer

Character mode reverse Telnet sessions can be opened by connecting to TCP port 2000 + line number. To determine the line number, enter the **show line** EXEC command.

Question 3

What type of logical interface configures many asynchronous interfaces simultaneously?

Question 4

What command binds a Group-Async interface to a line?

Question 3 Answer

A Group-Async logical interface can be created to configure many asynchronous interfaces at one time. The interface configuration command **group-range** *start end* is applied to Group-Async interface and is used to specify the asynchronous interfaces that make up the group.

Question 4 Answer

The Group-Async interface configuration command **group-range** *start end* associates asynchronous interfaces to the Group-Async interface.

Question 5

What interface configuration command conserves an IP subnet by using the IP address of another interface?

Question 6

What type of flow control is used between a router and a modem?

Question 5 Answer

By using **ip unnumbered** *type number,* your asynchronous interfaces can use the IP address of another interface. This command is typically used to configure the router to use the IP address of a loopback or Ethernet interface for the local side of PPP connections.

Question 6 Answer

Routers are capable of two types of flow control: hardware or CTS/RTS, and software or XON/XOFF. Use the line configuration command **flowcontrol** {**none** | **hardware** | **software**} to configure the desired type of flow control on a particular line.

Question 7

When connected to a modem using reverse Telnet, how do you end the session?

Question 8

What is the command modemcap used for?

Question 7 Answer

Reverse Telnet sessions can be suspended using the key sequence Ctrl-Shft-6 then x. Once suspended, you can disconnect the session using the EXEC command **disconnect**.

Question 8 Answer

The global configuration command **modemcap** allows you to edit or add entries to the router's modem capabilities database. This database stores modem configuration information and is used by the **modem autoconfigure** line configuration command.

Question 9

What line configuration command enables the modem for use in the inbound, outbound, or both directions?

Question 10

What is a chat script?

Question 9 Answer

The line configuration command **modem** {**inout** | **callin** | **callout**} configures the direction in which calls can be placed or received.

Question 10 Answer

A chat script interacts with the modem during initialization or while attempting to connect to a remote device. Chat scripts can prepare the modem, dial the remote phone number, and optionally, log on to the remote computer.

Question 11

What is the autoselect line configuration command used for?

Question 12

What is the result of applying the line configuration command async mode dedicated?

Question 11 Answer

The **autoselect** command informs the router which protocols to attempt when an inbound connection is established. Different protocols can be selected with the following syntax:

```
autoselect {ppp | arap | slip}
```

The following syntax provides additional options:

```
autoselect {during-login | timeout seconds}
```

If the **during-login** option is specified, the router presents the caller with the login prompt without the user pressing the Return key. After the user logs in, the autoselect function begins. The timeout option configures the length of time for which the router attempts protocol autoselection.

Question 12 Answer

The **async mode dedicated** line configuration command forces a caller to use PPP or SLIP for inbound calls. The caller is not presented with an EXEC shell after logging on.

Question 13

When supporting terminal sessions, what command forces the caller to authenticate?

Question 14

What is modem autoconfiguration?

Question 13 Answer

Enter the line configuration command **login local** to force users to authenticate. When this variant of the **login** command is used, users are authenticated against usernames and passwords configured on the router using the **username** global configuration command.

Question 14 Answer

Modem autoconfiguration uses the local modemcap database to retrieve the correct modem configuration settings. Autoconfiguration is enabled with the **modem autoconfigure** {**discovery** | **type** *modem-name*} line configuration command.

Question 15

Which AT command string tells the modem to answer an inbound call on the specified ring?

Question 16

How do you determine the modems supported by the modemcap database?

Question 15 Answer

The AT command **ATS0=n** configures the modem to answer inbound calls on the *n*-th ring. Entering **ATS0=0** disables auto answer.

Question 16 Answer

Entering the EXEC command **show modemcap** displays the modems currently in the modemcap database.

Question 17

What is modem autodiscovery? What does it accomplish for you?

Question 18

Can the modemcap database by edited by the router administrator?

Question 17 Answer

Modem autodiscovery enables the router to detect the appropriate modemcap entry for the attached modem. After the line configuration command **modem autoconfigure discovery** is entered, the router detects the appropriate modem type.

Question 18 Answer

Yes, individual modemcap entries can be modified with the global configuration command **modemcap edit** *modem-name attribute value*. Additionally, modems can be entered into the modemcap database with the global configuration command **modemcap entry** *modem-name*. After a modem is entered, the **modemcap edit** command must be used to edit the particular attributes of the modem.

Question 19

How is modem autoconfiguration enabled for a range of physical lines?

Question 20

What command enables flow control on a physical line?

Question 19 Answer

Modem autoconfiguration is configured by applying the **modem autoconfigure** {**discovery** | **type** *modem-name*} line configuration command. A range of lines can be configured (via any line configuration command) by specifying a range of lines when entering line configuration mode. Enter line configuration mode by entering the command **line** *start end*.

Question 20 Answer

The **flowcontrol** {**none** | **software** | **hardware**} line configuration command is used to configure flow control. It is critical that the router and modem have identical flowcontrol settings.

Section 3

Configuring PPP with CHAP and PAP

Whether it is a dial-on-demand connection or remote access dialup, the Point-to-Point Protocol (PPP) exists in almost every organization. Defined in RFC 1661, PPP has proven to be an extensible protocol and suitable for most situations. With support for almost every protocol, a PPP connection can simultaneously support IP, IPX, and bridging of non-routed protocols. Through integration with the Password Authentication Protocol (PAP) and the Challenge Handshake Authentication Protocol (CHAP), PPP authentication provides a simple yet secure method for the authentication of remote peers. Although PAP is a simpler protocol than CHAP, CHAP increases security as passwords are not sent over the network. Multilink PPP further extends scalability with the ability to create multilink PPP bundles of multiple PPP connections; these bundles act as one higher bandwidth logical interface.

The following flash cards review the configuration of a router for connectivity over a PPP connection. They include questions on encapsulation, using PAP or CHAP for authentication, multilink PPP, and general interface configuration.

Question 1

What command enables PPP encapsulation on an interface?

Question 2

What is the main difference between PAP and CHAP?

Question 1 Answer

To configure PPP encapsulation, use the interface configuration command **encapsulation ppp**.

Question 2 Answer

With PAP, usernames and passwords are sent over the network as cleartext. With CHAP, hashed values are computed and transmitted so passwords are never sent over the network.

Question 3

What command configures CHAP on an interface?

Question 4

Does PPP provide for authentication of the remote device?

Question 3 Answer

The interface configuration command **ppp authentication chap** configures an interface to use CHAP authentication exclusively.

Question 4 Answer

Yes. PPP can use PAP, CHAP, or Microsoft Challenge Handshake Authentication Protocol (MS-CHAP) to authenticate remote devices.

Question 5

Which command configures a PAP username other than the router host name to be sent to the server during authentication?

Question 6

What is IPCP and what does it do?

Question 5 Answer

The interface configuration command **ppp pap sent-username**
username **password** {0 *password* | 7 *encrypted-password*}
explicitly configures the username and password to be sent to the
remote device during PAP authentication.

Question 6 Answer

The Internet Protocol Control Protocol (IPCP) negotiates the
IP configuration of the remote end of a PPP connection.
Information such as IP address and the location of DNS
servers is configured via IPCP.

Question 7

What is LCP and what does it do?

Configuring PPP
with CHAP and PAP

Question 8

What technology allows for an additional connection to be established when additional bandwidth is needed?

Configuring PPP
with CHAP and PAP

Question 7 Answer

LCP, which stands for the Link Configuration Protocol, establishes, tests, and configures the data link layer connection. Information specific to any network layer protocols is negotiated after LCP has completed by the Network Control Protocol (NCP) specific to that protocol (for example, IP Control Protocol [IPCP] or IPXCP).

Question 8 Answer

Multilink PPP allows for multiple PPP connections to be bundled into a single logical connection. By using the **dialer load-threshold** *load* in conjunction with the **ppp multilink** interface configuration command, it is possible to establish at what point additional links are established and disconnected.

Question 9

What command enables multilink PPP framing on an interface?

Question 10

What command configures compression on a PPP connection?

Question 9 Answer

The interface configuration command **ppp multilink** configures multilink PPP framing.

Multilink framing is often configured on a single PPP connection as it allows large packets to be broken up and smaller packets to be interleaved within the large packet. This allows the smaller, more delay-sensitive data to be sent without having to wait for the entire large frame to traverse the link.

Question 10 Answer

The interface configuration command **compress** {**stac** | **predictor** | **mppc**} configures compression on an interface. For compression to be used, it must be configured on both ends of the connection. However, it is not necessary to use the same compression algorithm in both directions.

Question 11

At what point during PPP connection establishment does authentication occur?

Question 12

What command configures the interface load at which additional links are removed from a multilink PPP bundle?

Question 11 Answer

PPP authentication takes place after LCP negotiations have completed and before any Network Control Protocols (NCPs) have run.

Question 12 Answer

The interface configuration command **dialer load-threshold** *load-value* [**inbound** | **outbound** | **either**] configures the interface load at which additional connections are established or disconnected. When the interface load rises above the *load-value*, additional connections are established. When the total load of all connections minus one is less than *load-value,* one interface is disconnected.

Question 13

What interface configuration commands configure a PPP client to negotiate callback?

Configuring PPP with CHAP and PAP

Question 14

What interface configuration command configures a server to require PPP callback?

Configuring PPP with CHAP and PAP

Question 13 Answer

The command **ppp callback request** configures the interface to use PPP callback.

Question 14 Answer

The interface configuration command **ppp callback accept** in conjunction with the dial-on-demand routing (DDR) command **dialer callback-secure** forces an initiating station to use PPP callback.

Question 15

What is the autoselect line configuration command used for?

Question 16

Which PPP authentication protocols are supported by Cisco routers?

Question 15 Answer

The **autoselect** {ppp | arap | slip | during-login | timeout *seconds*} line configuration command tells the router which remote access protocol to start when initiating a new connection. If autoselect cannot complete before the timeout expires, an EXEC process is started.

Question 16 Answer

PPP supports the PAP, CHAP, and MS-CHAP.

Question 17

When two PPP peers finish IPCP negotiation, a host route is entered into the local routing table for the remote PPP peer. What command disables this functionality?

Question 18

When using multilink PPP with synchronous interfaces, how is the multilink bundle configured?

Question 17 Answer

The interface configuration command **no peer neighbor-route** disables the automatic creation of host routes for connected PPP peers.

Question 18 Answer

Individual interfaces are placed in the multilink bundle using the **multilink-group** *number* interface configuration command. A virtual interface is then configured using the command **interface multilink** *number* where the interface number matches the multilink-group number. Network layer information is configured on the virtual interface and is shared across all bundle members. Link layer configurations such as authentication and compression are configured on the individual interfaces.

Question 19

What does CHAP stand for?

Question 20

Can both CHAP and PAP be configured at the same time on an interface?

Question 19 Answer

CHAP is the Challenge Handshake Authentication Protocol.

Question 20 Answer

Yes, it is possible to use the interface configuration command **ppp authentication** with any combination of chap, pap, or ms-chap to indicate which protocols are to be supported.

Section 4

Dial-on-Demand Routing

BCRAN

As the foundation of many types of remote access and dial backup configurations, dial-on-demand routing (DDR) is flexible. Dialer profiles allow for the separation of physical and logical interface configuration, while Legacy DDR requires that dialer configurations be placed directly on physical interfaces. Dialer pools and rotary groups are used with dialer profiles to create a grouping of physical interfaces that can be used by a dialer interface. Legacy DDR does not support this type of pooling; however, it does include additional protocol support.

These flash cards challenge your understanding of DDR. They present questions on the basic configuration of dialer profiles, legacy DDR, dialer pools, dialer rotary groups, and dialer maps, as well as dialer class maps and callback.

Question 1

What is a dialer profile?

Dial-on-Demand
Routing

Question 2

What is interesting traffic and how is it defined?

Dial-on-Demand
Routing

Question 1 Answer

Simply, a dialer profile is a dialer interface. Dialer interfaces are created with the global configuration command **interface dialer** *number*. Dialer profiles allow for the separation of physical interface and logical interface. As a benefit of this, multiple dialer profiles can share one or more physical interfaces.

Question 2 Answer

Interesting traffic is network traffic that triggers the dialing of a DDR interface. After an interface is brought up, all traffic, interesting or not, flows over the interface. Only interesting traffic resets the idle timeouts that have been configured.

Question 3

What is a dialer pool?

Question 4

**What does the interface configuration
command dialer-group *number* do?**

Question 3 Answer

A dialer pool is a grouping of physical interfaces that can be used by one or more dialer profiles. Physical interfaces are put into the dialer pool with the **dialer pool-member** *pool-number* interface configuration command. Dialer interfaces are configured to use a specific pool with the **dialer pool** *pool-number* interface configuration command.

Question 4 Answer

The interface configuration command **dialer-group** *number* associates a set of **dialer-list** commands to the interface for the specification of interesting traffic.

Question 5

Without using a dialer map, how can the remote phone number be specified?

Question 6

What show command shows the status of any dialer interfaces?

Question 5 Answer

The remote phone number can be entered with the interface configuration command **dialer string** *dial-string*.

Question 6 Answer

The command **show dialer** shows the status of all configured dialer interfaces.

Question 7

What makes a DDR configuration a legacy DDR configuration?

Question 8

How do you configure the idle timeout for a DDR interface?

Question 7 Answer

The direct configuration of physical interfaces makes a DDR configuration a legacy DDR configuration. Put a different way, the absence of dialer interfaces makes a DDR configuration legacy DDR.

Question 8 Answer

The interface or map class configuration command **dialer idle-timeout** *timeout* sets the idle time out for an interface or dialer class. Only traffic that has been defined as interesting resets the idle timer to 0.

Question 9

What is a dialer rotary group?

Dial-on-Demand
Routing

Question 10

How is a dialer rotary group different than a dialer pool?

Dial-on-Demand
Routing

Question 9 Answer

A dialer rotary group is a group of physical interfaces that is used by a single dialer interface.

Question 10 Answer

A dialer pool can be used by any number of dialer interfaces, whereas a dialer rotary group can be used by exactly one dialer interface.

Dialer interfaces are linked to a dialer pool using the **dialer pool** *number* interface configuration command. Dialer interfaces are associated with a rotary group when the interface number (set via **interface dialer** *number*) matches the rotary group number set with the **dialer rotary-group** *number* interface configuration command.

Question 11

What do dialer map classes accomplish?

Dial-on-Demand Routing

Question 12

Can physical interfaces in a dialer rotary group be prioritized? If so, how?

Dial-on-Demand Routing

Question 11 Answer

A dialer map class can be configured and applied to any **dialer map** commands by specifying the **class** option. Dialer map class configuration mode is entered by using the **map-class dialer** *map-class-name* global configuration command, in which a limited subset of configuration commands are available. The available commands include the following:

- **dialer callback-server** {**dialstring** | **username**}
- **dialer enable-timeout** *seconds*
- **dialer fast-idle** *seconds*
- **dialer idle-timeout** *seconds*
- **dialer isdn** {**speed** *speed* | **spc**}
- **dialer outgoing** {**accunet** | **megacomm** | **sdn**}
- **dialer voice-call**
- **dialer wait-for-carrier-time** *seconds*

Question 12 Answer

Yes. A priority value is assigned to each physical interface that is part of a rotary group. The command **dialer priority** *priority* sets the priority. Valid priority values range from 0 to 255 with a higher number indicating a higher priority. The default is 0.

Question 13

What does the interface configuration command dialer fast-idle do?

Dial-on-Demand Routing

Question 14

Which show command details the static and dynamic dialer map entries?

Dial-on-Demand Routing

Question 13 Answer

The command **dialer fast-idle** *seconds* configures the idle timeout to be used when another dialer interface is waiting for the physical interface to become available. The default is 20 seconds.

Question 14 Answer

The command **show dialer map** details all the dialer map entries currently being used by the router.

Question 15

What does the broadcast argument of the dialer map ip interface configuration command do?

Question 16

Is a dialer-group *number* command required for all legacy DDR or dialer interfaces?

Question 15 Answer

When the **broadcast** argument is specified, IP broadcasts are sent to this DDR peer. Whether or not the IP broadcast causes connection establishment to take place depends on the configuration of the applied dialer list.

Question 16 Answer

Although a **dialer-group** *number* command is not required, an interface without it accepts only incoming calls. Because no interesting traffic has been defined, the interface never dials a remote router.

Question 17

What global configuration commands would you use to define all Telnet and Simple Mail Transport Protocol (SMTP) traffic as interesting?

Question 18

Which interface configuration command configures the priority of an individual rotary group member?

Question 17 Answer

The following global configuration commands define Telnet and SMTP traffic as interesting for dialer group 1:

```
access-list 100 permit tcp any any eq 23
access-list 100 permit tcp any any eq 25
dialer-list 1 protocol ip list 100
```

Question 18 Answer

The interface configuration command **dialer priority** *number* explicitly configures the interface priority. Priority values can range from 0 to 255 with a higher number indicating a higher priority. Higher priority interfaces are used for connection establishment before lower priority interfaces.

Question 19

Which command configures the amount of time that a dialer interface waits before making or accepting another call?

Question 20

During DDR session establishment, are interesting packets dropped?

Question 19 Answer

The interface configuration command **dialer enable-timeout** *seconds* configures the delay between when a dialer interface becomes available and when it is used again. This timeout applies to both incoming and outgoing calls.

Question 20 Answer

Yes, while interesting traffic causes the link to be established, these packets are dropped by default. To configure the queuing of these packets until connection establishment completes, use the interface configuration command **dialer hold-queue** *packets* **timeout** *seconds*.

Section 5

Configuration of Frame Relay Connections

Frame Relay is possibly the most prevalent of wide-area network technologies. As such, few networks do not have some sort of Frame Relay connectivity. The configuration of Frame Relay on a Cisco router is extremely flexible. From the design process through configuration, you are presented with numerous options to customize your router's interaction with the network. This section challenges your understanding of a Cisco router's operation with a Frame Relay network.

The following flash cards review the configuration of a router for connectivity to a Frame Relay network. They include questions on interface configuration, supported encapsulation and Local Management Interface (LMI) types, and Frame Relay Traffic Shaping, as well as items on general Frame Relay operation and design principles.

Question 1

What is split horizon?

Question 2

Disabling split horizon solves what problem?

Question 1 Answer

Split horizon dictates that a router does not advertise a route on the same interface from which it was learned. Its primary design goal is to eliminate the count to infinity situation that can occur with distance vector routing protocols.

Question 2 Answer

Disabling split horizon allows the router to advertise routes on the same interface from which they were received. In situations where you have a dynamic routing protocol configured on a Frame Relay physical or multipoint subinterface, this enables a spoke router to learn routes from other spoke routers as the routes are readvertised by a hub router.

Question 3

When a physical interface is configured for Frame Relay encapsulation, does it default to becoming a multipoint or point-to-point interface?

Question 4

What is a DLCI?

Question 3 Answer

Physical interfaces configured for Frame Relay are always multipoint interfaces.

Question 4 Answer

A DLCI, or data-link connection identifier, is a value used by the Frame Relay network to identify a particular virtual circuit. This value is assigned by the Frame Relay provider and is only of significance to the local router-to-Frame Relay switch connection. Each Frame Relay switch in the network reads this value from an incoming frame, changes the value if necessary, and then routes the frame to the next Frame Relay switch or the appropriate end device.

Question 5

True of False: Two routers configured to communicate over a Frame Relay network must be using the same DLCI.

Question 6

What type of error checking and recovery does the Frame Relay network provide?

Question 5 Answer

False. The DLCI is of significance only to the local connection. The router and the Frame Relay switch that it is connected to must share the same DLCI for each configured virtual circuit. However, no guarantee exists that both routers use the same DLCI.

Question 6 Answer

None. The Frame Relay network discards any frames that contain errors without sending a notification to either the sending or receiving stations. Error recovery is left to the higher layer protocols and applications.

Question 7

What command would you use to enable Frame Relay on an interface?

Question 8

What is a CIR?

Question 7 Answer

The correct interface configuration command is **encapsulation frame-relay** *encapsulation-type*. By using the *encapsulation-type* argument, you can specify the type of Frame Relay encapsulation to be used. Although this command defaults to Cisco encapsulation, it is possible that IETF must be specified when connecting to devices from other manufacturers.

Question 8 Answer

The Committed Information Rate, or CIR, is a value negotiated between a Frame Relay customer and provider that indicates the amount of traffic the provider is willing to guarantee through its network. The CIR is measured in kilobits per second (kbps).

Question 9

What does Frame Relay Traffic Shaping do?

Question 10

When configuring Frame Relay Traffic Shaping, what is Tc?

Question 9 Answer

Frame Relay Traffic Shaping ensures that the traffic sent by the router on a particular permanent virtual circuit (PVC) matches the contracted CIR. If traffic is sent by the router in excess of the CIR, there's no guarantee that the Frame Relay network would be able to deliver it to its destination exists.

Question 10 Answer

In Frame Relay Traffic Shaping, Tc is the time interval in which other Traffic Shaping specific measurements are taken. The default for Tc is 125 ms; this value is rarely changed.

Question 11

When configuring Frame Relay Traffic Shaping, what is Bc?

Question 12

When configuring Frame Relay Traffic Shaping, what is Be?

Question 11 Answer

Bc, or the Burst Committed value, is the amount of guaranteed data to send in each time interval (known as Tc). With Tc at its default value of 125 ms, Bc should be equal to the Committed Information Rate (CIR) divided by 8.

To derive Bc when Tc has been changed to a non-default value, multiply the CIR by Tc, as shown in the following formula:

$$Bc = CIR \times Tc$$

Question 12 Answer

Be, or the Excessive Burst, is the amount of additional data to send in the first Tc when a bandwidth credit has been earned. Bandwidth credits are earned when the router has no data to transmit.

This is implemented using a token bucket. With token buckets, a token represents the permission to transmit one bit. Tokens are placed into the bucket at a fixed rate equal to the configured CIR or average rate values. When bandwidth is not used, tokens accumulate in the bucket up to the maximum bucket size of Bc + Be.

Question 13

Why would you use a Frame Relay map class?

Configuration of
Frame Relay
Connections

Question 14

What Frame Relay LMI types does a Cisco router support?

Configuration of
Frame Relay
Connections

Question 13 Answer

Frame Relay map classes allow you to apply a consistent configuration to many Frame Relay PVCs. Items such as Traffic Shaping and priority or custom queuing can first be configured on the map class and then applied to all PVCs that share that configuration.

Question 14 Answer

Cisco routers support the following Frame Relay LMI types:

- ANSI
- Cisco
- Q933a

Question 15

What is the default Frame Relay LMI type on a Cisco router?

Question 16

What types of Frame Relay encapsulation does a Cisco router support?

Question 15 Answer

The default Frame Relay LMI type for a Cisco router is Cisco.

Question 16 Answer

Cisco routers support the following types of Frame Relay encapsulation:

- Cisco
- IETF

Question 17

Can Frame Relay IETF encapsulation be set on a per-PVC basis?

Question 18

What is the DE bit in the Frame Relay header?

Question 17 Answer

Yes, by using the **IETF** option to the **frame-relay map** or **frame-relay interface-dlci** interface configuration commands.

Question 18 Answer

The Discard Eligible (DE) bit within the Frame Relay header indicates to the Frame Relay network that this frame should be dropped before others when congestion occurs.

Question 19

What are the advantages of a topology that uses point-to-point subinterfaces exclusively?

Question 20

What does Frame Relay Traffic Shaping do?

Question 19 Answer

The advantages of point-to-point subinterfaces are as follows:

- Broadcasts are not replicated over each PVC.

- Split horizon becomes a non-issue.

- Compatibility with IS-IS is guaranteed.

Question 20 Answer

Frame Relay Traffic Shaping is used to ensure that the traffic sent by the router on a particular permanent virtual circuit (PVC) matches the contracted CIR. If traffic is sent by the router in excess of the CIR, no guarantee that the Frame Relay network would be able to deliver it to its destination exists.

Section 6

BCRAN

Network Redundancy and Backup Connections

Several options exist for the configuration of backup connections: floating static routes, backup interfaces, and dialer watch. With a varying level of complexity, each of these provides its own set of advantages and disadvantages.

The following flash cards challenge your understanding of the available options for the configuration of backup interfaces. These flash cards present questions on configuration commands and the trade-offs associated with each technology.

Question 1

What is a floating static route?

Question 2

What command configures the backup interface to establish a connection when the traffic levels on the primary interface reach a certain level?

Question 1 Answer

A floating static route is a static route that has had its administrative distance set to a value higher than any active dynamic routing protocols. This high administrative distance tells the router to prefer the dynamically learned routes. Should the router not have the dynamically learned routes because of network or neighbor failure, the floating static route takes effect and instructs the router to use a backup connection.

Question 2 Answer

The interface configuration command **backup load** {*enable-threshold* | **never**} {*disable-threshold* | **never**} allows you to configure the percentage of bandwidth utilization to establish and disconnect the backup link. This command must be used in conjunction with the **backup interface** command.

Question 3

When using the backup interface command, can multiple primary interfaces share a backup interface?

Question 4

When using the backup interface command, when does the backup interface establish a connection?

Question 3 Answer

No, there must be a one-to-one mapping of primary interfaces to backup interfaces.

To overcome this, it is possible to configure a dialer interface as a backup interface. Multiple dialer interfaces can share a physical interface by using the **dialer pool** *pool-number* command on the dialer interfaces and the **dialer pool-member** *pool-number* physical interface configuration command.

Question 4 Answer

A backup interface is used only when line protocol goes down on the primary interface.

Question 5

What is one advantage to using a floating static route over the backup interface command?

Question 6

How long does the router wait by default to establish a connection with the backup interface? Can this timeout be explicitly configured?

Question 5 Answer

The **backup interface** command establishes a connection over the backup interface only when line protocol goes down on the primary interface. There are instances where line protocol does not go down, but there is no connectivity over the link. If a floating static route were used in this scenario, the backup connection is activated in any situation in which the dynamic route is removed from the routing table, whether it is because of line protocol failure or route aging.

Question 6 Answer

By default, the backup delay time is set to 0 seconds. By using the **backup delay** {*enable-delay* | **never**} {*disable-delay* | **never**} command, you can configure the delay for both connection establishment and disconnection. Using the **never** keyword causes the connection not to be established or disconnected.

Question 7

What command creates a floating static route?

Question 8

How can multiple interfaces use the same interface as a backup interface?

Question 7 Answer

To create a floating static route, use the *distance* option of the **ip route** command. The relevant syntax of this command is as follows:

```
ip route network mask {next-hop I outbound-interface} distance
```

The *distance* argument must be set higher than any of the routing protocols present on the router. As a general rule, setting the distance to 220 is sufficient.

Question 8 Answer

Through the use of dialer interfaces and dialer pools, it is possible to have one physical interface back up more than one primary interfaces. Each of the primary interfaces must be configured to use a different dialer as the backup interface. The dialer interfaces must then be configured to use a dialer pool with the **dialer pool** *pool-number* interface configuration command. The physical interface is then configured as a dialer pool member with the interface configuration command **dialer pool-member** *pool-number*.

Question 9

What show command shows you the status of any backup interfaces?

Network Redundancy and Backup Connections

Question 10

What is dialer watch?

Network Redundancy and Backup Connections

Question 9 Answer

The command **show backup** shows the status of all primary and backup interfaces.

Question 10 Answer

Dialer watch provides the ability to watch the system routing table for the existence of one or more routes. If at any point all the watched routes do not exist in the routing table, the backup interface is brought up.

Question 11

When using dialer watch, what happens when the primary interface goes down?

Question 12

When using dialer watch, what happens when the primary interface changes to up?

Question 11 Answer

When the primary interface changes to a down state, all routing information associated with that interface is invalidated and immediately removed from the routing table. At that point, the watched routes do not exist, causing the backup connection to be established.

Question 12 Answer

When the primary link is reestablished, the backup link is taken down. Using the interface configuration command **dialer watch-disable** *seconds* on the backup interface, you can configure a time period that the backup interface remains connected once the primary interface becomes available.

Question 13

What are the advantages to using dialer watch over floating static routes?

Question 14

What are the advantages to using dialer watch over the backup interface command?

Question 13 Answer

The advantages of dialer watch over floating static routes include the following:

- Dialer watch does not require a static route.
- Backup interfaces are brought up instantly, without waiting for interesting traffic.

Question 14 Answer

Dialer watch provides the following advantages when compared to the **backup interface** command:

- Interfaces used for failover are not tied to a single primary interface.
- Dialer watch provides greater fault detection capabilities in Frame Relay networks where connectivity can be lost over interfaces that remain up.

Question 15

What command configures the routes that should be monitored by a dialer watch configuration?

Question 16

What interface configuration command associates a dialer watch list to an interface?

Question 15 Answer

The global configuration command **dialer watch-list** *list-number* **ip** *ip-address mask* adds a route to the watch list numbered *list-number*. Multiple routes can be added to the same watch list.

Question 16 Answer

The interface configuration command **dialer watch-group** *list-number* configures an interface to use a specific watch list.

Question 17

Can a single dialer profile be configured for dialer watch backup of multiple primary interfaces?

Question 18

What are the three options for configuring backup dial-on-demand routing (DDR) interfaces?

Question 17 Answer

Because dialer watch looks for the existence of entries in the IP routing table, it is not directly tied to an interface. As long as the watched routes are learned over an interface other than the interface configured for dialer watch, the backup interface remains down.

Question 18 Answer

The three options for configuring backup DDR interfaces are

- Backup interfaces
- Floating static routes
- Dialer watch

Question 19

Which interface configuration command places an interface in the standby mode state?

Question 20

What does the command ip ospf demand-circuit do?

Question 19 Answer

Once the interface configuration command **backup interface** *type number* has been entered on the primary interface, the backup interface enters the standby mode state.

Question 20 Answer

The **ip ospf demand-circuit** interface configuration command causes the router to suppress the sending of Open Shortest Path First (OSPF) hellos and Link State Advertisement (LSA) Refreshes when the network is stable. This allows the dialer connection to remain down until needed. This command needs to be configured on only one end of the point-to-point or point-to-multipoint connection.

Section 7

Queuing and Compression

Queuing is a vast topic and possibly the most complex non-protocol related configuration activity. Largely responsible for enforcing the quality of service (QoS) policy of an organization, the available queuing methods are weighted fair queuing (WFQ), first in, first out (FIFO), custom queuing (CQ), priority queuing (PQ), low latency queuing (LLQ), and class-based weighted fair queuing (CBWFQ). Starting in IOS version 12.0, a new QoS configuration framework was created; the modular QoS command-line interface (MQC). Within this framework, it is possible to configure all types of queuing methods. More importantly, it is possible to configure combinations of queuing methods for a single interface. This section also includes another topic that can further help an organization implement effective QoS: compression. From link compression to Reliable Transport Protocol (RTP) compression, many options are presented.

The following flash cards present questions that test your knowledge of the different queuing methods, their application, and their differences, as well as questions on link-layer and payload compression.

Question 1

What does queuing accomplish for you?

Question 2

What is the default queuing algorithm for serial interfaces slower than 2.048 Mbps?

Question 1 Answer

Queuing allows the network architect to give priority to certain classes of traffic. Configured correctly, queuing can guarantee that critical traffic reaches its destination as quickly as possible during periods of network congestion.

For example, a queuing implementation might guarantee excellent network transit times for traffic to or from an application server, while limiting the amount of bandwidth that FTP sessions are given to 256 kbps.

Question 2 Answer

The default queuing method for serial interfaces that are not using SDLC or X.25 encapsulations at E1 (2.048 Mbps) speeds or slower is weighted fair queuing. The default queuing method for all other interface types is First In, First Out (FIFO) queuing.

Question 3

What is the main difference between priority and custom queuing?

Question 4

When does class-based weighted fair queuing (CBWFQ) become low latency queuing (LLQ)?

Question 3 Answer

In priority queuing, the queues with lower priority can possibly be starved of network bandwidth. This can happen because higher priority queues are serviced without regard for the data in lower queues. This type of queuing is appropriate for delay-sensitive traffic.

In custom queuing, a limit exists to the amount of data that is emptied from a queue before the next queue is serviced (1500 bytes by default).

Question 4 Answer

CBWFQ becomes LLQ when the **priority** class map configuration command is used.

Question 5

What factors change the behavior of weighted fair queuing (WFQ)?

Question 6

What command configures an interface for WFQ?

Question 5 Answer

The following factors can change the behavior of WFQ:

- **IP precedence**—IP traffic with a higher IP precedence value receives a higher portion of the bandwidth.

- **Resource Reservation Protocol (RSVP)**—WFQ is aware of RVSP reserved bandwidth and treats traffic flows accordingly.

Question 6 Answer

The interface configuration command to configure WFQ on an interface is the following:

```
fair-queue [congestive-discard-threshold [dynamic-queues
[reservable-queues]]]
```

The *congestive-discard-threshold* argument configures the length of each queue. The default is 64 messages and can be any power of 2 between 16 and 4096.

The *dynamic-queues* argument configures the number of queues and can be any of the following values: 16, 32, 64, 128, 256, 512, 1024, 2048, or 4096. The default number of queues depends on the bandwidth of the interface and ranges from 16 (for a 64 kbps link) to 256 (for links greater than 512 kbps).

The *reservable-queues* argument defines the number of RSVP reservable queues. When set at the default of 0, the number of queues is automatically determined by dividing the interface bandwidth by 32 kbps. When manually configured, this value can range from 0 to 1000.

Question 7

What command applies a custom queuing configuration to an interface?

Question 8

What techniques can be used to classify traffic for a custom, priority, or class-based weighted fair queuing configuration?

Question 7 Answer

The interface configuration command **custom-queue-list** *queue-list-number* applies a custom queuing configuration to an interface. The *queue-list-number* argument must match a previously defined custom queue list and can range from 1 to 16. The following shows the relevant parts of a custom queuing configuration:

```
interface Serial 0
 custom-queue-list 1
!
queue-list 1 queue 1 byte-count 2000
queue-list 1 protocol ip 1 list 100
queue-list 1 default 10
!
access-list 100 permit tcp any any eq 23
access-list 100 permit udp any any eq 53
```

Question 8 Answer

The following techniques can be used to classify traffic for a queuing configuration:

- Incoming interface
- Packet length
- Protocol
- TCP or UDP port number

In addition, an access list can be used. When using an IP access list, the following criteria can also be used to classify traffic:

- IP precedence
- Source address
- Destination address
- IP type (ICMP, GRE, TCP, UDP, and so on)

Question 9

Which global configuration command would you use to configure priority queuing?

Question 10

Which global configuration command would you use to configure custom queuing?

Question 9 Answer

The priority queuing configuration commands all begin with the command **priority-list**. The following are the global configuration commands specific to priority queuing:

- **priority-list** *priority-list-number* **default** *priority*

- **priority-list** *priority-list-number* **interface** *type number priority*

- **priority-list** *priority-list-number* **protocol** *protocol priority*

- **priority-list** *priority-list-number* **queue-limit** *high-limit medium-limit normal-limit low-limit*

Question 10 Answer

The custom queuing configuration commands all begin with the command **queue-list**. The following are the global configuration command specific to custom queuing:

- **queue-list** *list-number* **default** *queue-number*

- **queue-list** *list-number* **interface** *type number queue-number*

- **queue-list** *list-number* **protocol** *protocol queue-number*

- **queue-list** *list-number* **queue** *queue-number* **byte-count** *count*

- **queue-list** *list-number* **queue** *queue-number* **limit** *count*

Question 11

Which queuing methods should be used to give guaranteed priority to a particular type of traffic?

Question 12

How many queues are available per interface in custom queuing?

Question 11 Answer

Either low latency queuing or priority queuing gives strict priority to traffic classes.

Question 12 Answer

Seventeen queues are numbered from 0 to 16 in custom queuing. Queue 0 is used for high-priority packets generated by the router and is emptied before any of the other queues are serviced. User traffic cannot be assigned to this queue.

Question 13

How many queues are available per interface in priority queuing?

Question 14

During the configuration of a policy map, how do you configure the behavior of traffic that has not been otherwise configured?

Question 13 Answer

Priority queuing has four queues: high, medium, normal, and low. The higher priority queues are emptied before the lower queues are serviced at all.

Question 14 Answer

The policy definition for traffic that has not been otherwise categorized into a class is accomplished using a special class called *class-default*.

Question 15

Which interface configuration command enables PPP compression?

Question 16

Can payload compression be enabled over an interface or subinterface configured for Frame Relay encapsulation?

Question 15 Answer

The interface configuration command **compress {predictor | stac | mppc [ignore-pfc]}** configures PPP compression.

Question 16 Answer

Yes, by using the interface configuration command **frame-relay payload-compress**. The complete syntax for this command is as follows:

```
frame-relay payload-compress {packet-by-packet | frf9 stac
  [hardware-options] | data-stream stac [hardware-options]}
```

Question 17

In class-based weighted fair queuing and weighted fair queuing, what makes up a flow?

Question 18

How do you set the size of a queue in custom queuing?

Question 17 Answer

A flow is made up of communication between a source IP address and port number to a destination IP address and port number using a specific protocol and IP ToS value. For example, the following TCP connections would be categorized as two distinct flows:

Source IP, Source Port	Destination IP, Destination Port
192.168.1.1, 1024	10.1.1.1, 25
192.168.1.1, 1025	10.1.1.1, 25

Question 18 Answer

The command **queue-list** *queue-list* **queue** *queue* **limit** *limit* sets the size of the queue in packets.

Question 19

What command applies a priority queuing configuration to an interface?

Question 20

Which interface configuration command enables PPP compression?

Question 19 Answer

The interface configuration command **priority-group** *list-number* applies a priority queuing configuration to an interface. The *list-number* argument must match a previously defined priority queue list and can range from 1 to 16.

Question 20 Answer

The interface configuration command **compress** {**predictor** | **stac** | **mppc** [**ignore-pfc**]} configures PPP compression.

Section 8

Network Address Translation

BCRAN

Initially driven by the need to conserve public IP addresses, many organizations have implemented private IP addressing as specified in RFC 1918. Today, however, many organizations implement RFC 1918 addressing to gain access to the abundant addresses made possible by that RFC. Regardless of the reason, not using publicly registered IP addresses on your network posses a challenge—how to connect to the public Internet. Network Address Translation (NAT) solves this problem. NAT allows an organization to translate one IP address to another at the edge of the network. Typically, addresses are translated from a private RFC 1918 address to a public IP address range, but this is not a requirement. NAT makes it possible for even the largest organizations to translate from many private addresses to just a few public addresses. You can also use NAT to implement simple TCP load distribution and to compensate for overlapping address spaces.

The following flash cards review the configuration of a router for NAT. They cover the configuration commands, terminology, and implementation possibilities.

Question 1

What is the inside global address?

Question 2

What is the outside local address?

Question 1 Answer

The inside global address is the IP address of a local device as seen on the outside network.

Question 2 Answer

The outside local address is the IP address of a device on the outside network as seen on the inside network.

Question 3

What are the different kinds of Network Address Translation (NAT)?

Question 4

Before NAT will operate correctly on a router, what interface configuration commands must be used?

Question 3 Answer

Primarily, three kinds of Network Address Translation exist:

- One-to-one or static
- Many-to-many
- One-to-many or Port Address Translation (PAT)

In addition to these kinds of NAT configurations, Cisco IOS can leverage NAT to provide the following functionality:

- TCP load distribution
- Translation of overlapping addresses

Question 4 Answer

The inside and outside interfaces must be defined using the commands **ip nat inside** and **ip nat outside**. NAT is applied only between the inside and outside interfaces.

Question 5

Which show command shows the current NAT translations?

Question 6

What global configuration command configures a static NAT mapping?

Question 5 Answer

The command **show ip nat translations** shows all the current NAT translations.

Question 6 Answer

To translate an inside local to a global address, use the command **ip nat inside source static** *inside-local inside-global*.

Question 7

When one-to-many NAT is configured, how is the internal address range defined?

Network Address Translation

Question 8

Which option to the ip nat inside source list command configures the router to use PAT for outbound traffic?

Network Address Translation

Question 7 Answer

The internal address range is checked against a standard access control list (ACL). After this ACL is defined, the *list-number* argument of the **ip nat inside source list** *list-number* **pool** *pool-name* [**overload**] command ties the standard ACL to a previously defined NAT pool.

Question 8 Answer

The optional argument **overload** configures the specified NAT pool for PAT operation.

Question 9

Which command clears the current dynamic NAT translations?

Question 10

When using many-to-many NAT, can the translation timeouts be changed?

Question 9 Answer

The command **clear ip nat translations** * clears all current NAT translations.

Question 10 Answer

The global configuration command **ip nat translation timeout** *timeout-seconds* command changes the timeout for simple NAT translations. Simple translations are a one-to-one dynamic NAT mapping.

Question 11

For one-to-many NAT, how many NAT pools are defined?

Question 12

What command configures a NAT pool?

Question 11 Answer

One pool is required for one-to-many NAT (which is also known as PAT).

A pool configures an address or address range that addresses are translated to. In the case of PAT, the address pool contains only one IP address. In the case of many-to-many NAT, the address pool contains more than one IP address.

Question 12 Answer

The command **ip nat pool** creates a NAT pool; its syntax is as follows:

```
ip nat pool pool-name start-ip end-ip {netmask mask |
   prefix-length prefix-length} [type rotary]
```

The *pool-name* argument is used to tie the configured pool to an **ip nat inside source list** or **ip nat outside source list** command. The *start-ip* and *end-ip* arguments define the IP address range; for PAT, the *start-ip* and *end-ip* are the same.

Question 13

When using NAT to provide connectivity to a network with an overlapping address space, how many NAT pools are defined?

Question 14

When configuring TCP load distribution, how is the virtual IP address defined?

Question 13 Answer

In the overlapping address scenario, two NAT pools need to be defined: one to represent the inside global addresses, and one to represent the outside local addresses. The following sample configuration provides connectivity between two networks that are both using the 10.1.1.0/24 subnet by mapping the inside network to 192.168.2.0/24, and the outside network to 192.168.1.0/24.

```
ip nat pool OUTSIDE-POOL 192.168.1.1 192.168.1.254 prefix-
  length 24
ip nat pool INSIDE-POOL 192.168.2.1 192.168.2.254 prefix-
  length 24
ip nat outside source list 1 pool OUTSIDE-POOL
ip nat inside source list 1 pool INSIDE-POOL
!
access-list 1 permit 10.1.1.0 0.0.0.255
!
interface Ethernet 0
 ip address 10.1.1.1 255.255.255.0
 ip nat inside
interface Serial 0
 ip address 172.16.1.1 255.255.255.252
 ip nat outside
```

Question 14 Answer

A standard IP access control list (ACL) is defined permitting the IP address of the virtual host. As packets arrive at the router, they are checked against the ACL to see if the TCP load distribution should be used. The following configuration sample load balances TCP traffic to 192.168.1.1 across eight servers whose IP addresses are 10.1.1.1 through 10.1.1.8.

```
ip nat pool SERVERS-POOL 10.1.1.1 10.1.1.8 prefix-length 29
  type rotary
ip nat inside destination list 1 pool SERVERS-POOL
!
access-list 1 192.168.1.1
!
interface Ethernet 0
 ip address 192.168.1.254 255.255.255.0
 ip nat outside
!
interface Ethernet 1
 ip add 10.1.1.254 255.255.255.0
 ip nat inside
```

Question 15

When configuring TCP load distribution, how are the real hosts defined?

Question 16

When using NAT to compensate for overlapping address spaces, how is the duplicate range defined?

Question 15 Answer

A NAT pool is created that contains the inside local IP addresses of the real hosts. Because the pool is created with the command **ip nat pool** *pool-name start-ip end-ip* {**netmask** *mask* | **prefix-length** *prefix-length*} **type rotary**, the inside local IP addresses of the servers must be contiguous.

Question 16 Answer

To use NAT to compensate for an overlapping address range, an ACL is defined to represent the common address space. This access list is then referenced in the **ip nat inside source list** and **ip nat outside source list** commands.

Question 17

Does NAT alter any packet contents other than the Layer 3 header?

Question 18

How does NAT interact with DNS?

Question 17 Answer

NAT alters the contents of any Domain Name System (DNS) response records traversing the router if a one-to-one NAT translation is present for the address contained in the response. This is used not only when a DNS server services both internal and external clients, but also to overcome the name resolution challenge in overlapping networks.

Question 18 Answer

A router configured for NAT alters the data within any DNS responses to match any statically or dynamically configured one-to-one NAT translations. This is used to solve name resolution problems with overlapping address spaces, and can be used so that one DNS server can serve both internal and external DNS clients.

Question 19

What is the ip nat inside interface configuration command used for?

Question 20

Can NAT be used for load distribution of UDP traffic?

Question 19 Answer

This interface configuration command tells the router which interface is connected to the inside network. All routers configured for NAT must have at least one inside interface.

Question 20 Answer

No, only TCP traffic can be used with TCP load distribution.

Section 9

Cable and DSL Technologies

Cable and DSL technologies have changed the remote access world dramatically. Without them, remote and Internet access would be limited to the 56 kbps typical of dialup. In order to bring high-speed Internet access to as many users as possible as quickly as possible, technologies had to be developed to leverage existing infrastructure. Broadband cable and DSL are those technologies. Broadband cable uses the RF modulation techniques of cable television. DSL provides high-speed Internet and remote access over existing telephone service. DSL uses either Carrierless Amplitude Phase (CAP) or Discrete Multi-Tone (DMT) to transmit data without interfering with voice communications.

The flashcards in this chapter test and expand your knowledge of these technologies. Recently added to the BCRAN exam, this knowledge is critical to your successful completion of the CCNP certification.

Question 1

What does the abbreviation DOCSIS stand for?

Question 2

What is the current version of the DOCSIS standard?

Question 1 Answer

The abbreviation DOCSIS stands for Data Over Cable Service Interface Specification. DOCSIS is the standardized method of transmitting and receiving data over a cable television network.

Question 2 Answer

DOCSIS is presently at version 2.0. Previous versions of DOCSIS include 1.1, which is very widely deployed, and 1.0.

Question 3

What are the two primary hardware components of a broadband cable deployment?

Question 4

What type of information is included in a DOCSIS-compliant cable modem configuration file?

Question 3 Answer

A Cable Modem Termination System (CMTS) is installed at the cable head end and is used to service many cable modems installed at customer locations.

Question 4 Answer

The following types of information are included in a DOCSIS cable modem configuration file:

- Radio frequency configuration
- Class of service information
- Management information
- Vendor-specific information

Question 5

What protocol does a cable modem use to download its configuration and system image?

Cable and DSL
Technologies

Question 6

What are the two modes in which a cable modem can operate?

Cable and DSL
Technologies

Question 5 Answer

Cable modems use TFTP to download their configurations. Software downloads also utilize TFTP.

Question 6 Answer

Cable modems can be configured in either a bridging or routing mode. In bridging mode, Layer 2 frames are simply bridged from a cable modem's Ethernet interface to its cable interface. In routing mode, IP packets are routed by the cable modem.

Question 7

In which cable modem operational mode might NAT be used?

Question 8

In a broadband cable network bandwidth is dedicated to individual users. True or false?

Question 7 Answer

Because Layer 3 handling of packets only takes place when the CPE is routing, NAT only makes sense in that type of configuration.

Question 8 Answer

False. Because cable networks where built around a shared infrastructure, data bandwidth is shared among several users.

Question 9

Why are PPP over Ethernet and PPP over ATM typically deployed?

Question 10

What type of WAN connection is used at the central site to support DSL connectivity?

Question 9 Answer

PPP over Ethernet and PPP over ATM provide three major benefits: user authentication, service selection, and address management.

Question 10 Answer

Although implementations may vary, remote DSL users are typically provided central site connectivity over an ATM PVC terminated on a customer owned router.

Question 11

Which of the following is not a type of DSL?

- Asymmetric
- Symmetric
- Variable

Question 12

DSL is not limited by distance. True or false?

Question 11 Answer

Variable is not a type of DSL. Asymmetric refers to DSL variants in which the upstream speed is different than the downstream speed. Symmetric refers to DSL variants where the upstream and downstream speeds are identical.

Question 12 Answer

False. In order for DSL to operate correctly, the total length of the local loop must typically be less than 15,000 feet.

Question 13

DSL technologies fall into two broad categories. What are they?

Cable and DSL Technologies

Question 14

In a DSL implementation, what piece of equipment terminates the copper connection from the CPE?

Cable and DSL Technologies

Question 13 Answer

The two categories of DSL variants are symmetric and asymmetric. In symmetric DSL, the upstream and downstream data rates are identical. With asymmetric DSL, the downstream data rate is higher than the upstream rate.

Question 14 Answer

Within the phone company central office, a DSL Access Multiplexer (DSLAM) is used to terminate many customer connections. The DSLAM performs aggregation to one or two ATM backbone connections.

Question 15

What two pieces of equipment terminate each end of a DSL connection?

Question 16

What are two modulation methods used with ADSL?

Question 15 Answer

CPE is used to terminate DSL connection in the customer's residence or business. The DSL provider uses a DSL Access Multiplexer to terminate many customer connections.

Question 16 Answer

The two modulation methods typical in ADSL deployments are Carrierless Amplitude Phase (CAP) and Discrete Multi-Tone (DMT). CAP is not an industry standard, while DMT is. Although widely deployed, CAP is not typically used in new DSL deployments.

Question 17

How large is an ATM cell?

37 bytes

53 bytes

69 bytes

101 bytes

Question 18

What does RFC 1483 detail?

Question 17 Answer

An ATM cell is 53 bytes in length. 48 of the 53 bytes are used for cell payload with the remaining 5 bytes serving as a cell header.

Question 18 Answer

RFC 1483 discusses how to transport connectionless LAN data across an ATM network. This RFC offers two types of connections: bridged and routed.

Question 19

When configuring an ATM interface, the VCI must be in what range?

Cable and DSL Technologies

Question 20

What interface configuration command links a PVC to an ATM interface?

Cable and DSL Technologies

Question 19 Answer

Valid VCI values include 0 through 65535. However, values 0 through 31 have been reserved. Therefore, any configured VCI must be between 32 and 65535.

Question 20 Answer

The interface configuration command **pvc** links a PVC to an ATM interface or subinterface. The complete syntax for the **pvc** command is **pvc** [*number*] *vpi vci*.

Question 21

What encapsulation type should be used on an ADSL ATM connection?

Question 22

What command configures the largest frame that can be sent or received on an interface?

Question 21 Answer

AAL5SNAP encapsulation is used on asymmetric DSL ATM PVCs.

Question 22 Answer

The interface configuration command **ip mtu** *mtu* is used to configure the largest packet that can be sent or received on an interface.

Question 23

What type of authentication server is used with PPP over Ethernet or PPP over ATM?

Question 24

What authentication protocols are used to authenticate PPP over Ethernet or PPP over ATM users?

Question 23 Answer

A RADIUS server is used by the DSL service provider to authenticate PPP over Ethernet and PPP over ATM users.

Question 24 Answer

PPP over Ethernet and PPP over ATM can use either PAP or CHAP to authenticate users. CHAP provides an additional level of security as passwords are never sent over the network.

Question 25

Why must an Ethernet interface using PPP over Ethernet have an MTU less than or equal to 1492 bytes?

Question 26

Which ETHER_TYPE values represent PPP over Ethernet?

Question 25 Answer

PPP over Ethernet (PPPoE) adds a total of 8 bytes to an Ethernet frame; the PPPoE header is 6 bytes and the PPP protocol ID field is 2 bytes. These 8 bytes must be included in every frame and reduce the effective MTU from 1500 bytes to 1492 bytes.

Question 26 Answer

PPP over Ethernet (PPPoE) uses two ETHER_TYPE fields. A value of 0x8863 represents the PPPoE Discovery phase while 0x8864 represents the PPPoE Session phase.

Question 27

What mechanism is used to transmit data over a broadband cable network?

Question 28

When configuring an ATM connection, the VPI must fall in what range?

Question 27 Answer

Broadband cable networks use an RF transmission scheme identical to that used to transmit television programming. Downstream transmissions use the 55 MHz to 750 MHz band while upstream transmissions use the 5 MHz to 42 MHz band.

Question 28 Answer

Valid VPI values range from 0 to 255.

Question 29

Which RFC documents PPP over ATM encapsulation?

Question 30

Which RFC documents PPP over Ethernet encapsulation?

Question 29 Answer

RFC 2364, "PPP over AAL5," describes PPP over ATM.

Question 30 Answer

RFC 2516, "A Method for Transmitting PPP over Ethernet (PPPoE)," describes the operation of PPP over Ethernet.

Question 31

What are the frequency bands used by a cable modem and CMTS to communicate?

Question 32

Which of the following is not a valid PPP over Ethernet packet?

PADI

PADV

PADR

PADS

Question 31 Answer

Downstream (to CPE) uses the 55 MHz to 750 MHz band, while upstream (to CMTS) uses the 5 MHz to 42 MHz band.

Question 32 Answer

PADV is not a valid PPP over Ethernet (PPPoE) packet. There are five valid PPPoE packets: the PPPoE Active Discovery Initiation (PADI), the PPPoE Active Discovery Offer (PADO), the PPPoE Active Discovery Request (PADR), the PPPoE Active Discovery Session confirmation (PADS), and the PPPoE Active Discovery Terminate (PADT) packet.

Question 33

What are the valid PPP over Ethernet session discovery and initiation packets and in what order are they sent and received during session establishment?

Question 34

Why use PPP over ATM instead of PPP over Ethernet?

Question 33 Answer

The four PPP over Ethernet (PPPoE) session discovery and initiation packets are

PPPoE Active Discovery Initiation (PADI)

PPPoE Active Discovery Offer (PADO)

PPPoE Active Discovery Request (PADR)

PPPoE Active Discovery Session (PADS) confirmation

Question 34 Answer

PPP over ATM is used when the CPE is configured for a routed DSL connection. PPP over Ethernet requires that the customer client computer have Layer 2 connectivity with the service provider's PPP access concentrator.

Question 35

What CPE functionality is required to support PPP over Ethernet?

Question 36

What asymmetric DSL modulation technique, Carrierless Amplitude Phase (CAP) or Discrete Multi-Tone (DMT), is an industry standard?

Question 35 Answer

Since the customer computer must have Layer 2 connectivity to the service provider access concentrator, the CPE must be configured for RFC 1483 bridging.

Question 36 Answer

Although CAP was once dominant, DMT is an industry standard and is, therefore, the preferred modulation technique for new asymetric DSL installations.

Question 37

How can cable modem software images be standardized by a broadband cable service provider?

Question 38

Does PPP over Ethernet or PPP over ATM require that software be installed on the client computer?

Question 37 Answer

A DOCSIS-compliant cable modem downloads its configuration file during power-on. Within the configuration file it is possible to specify that a software image should be downloaded on power-on and where that image should come from.

Question 38 Answer

PPP over Ethernet (PPPoE) requires that client software or native PPPoE support be present on the client computer. Since PPP over ATM terminates on the CPE and not the client computer, no client computer support is required.

Question 39

In which PPP over Ethernet session initiation and discovery packet is the Session ID transmitted?

Question 40

What series of commands enables an IOS router to serve as a PPP over ATM client?

Question 39 Answer

The PPP over Ethernet (PPPoE) Session ID is transmitted in the PPPoE Active Discovery Session (PADS) confirmation packet. This is the last packet used during PPPoE session establishment.

Question 40 Answer

The commands below enable the PPP over ATM client functionality on a Cisco router.

vpdn-group *group_name*

request-dialin

protocol pppoe

Interface configuration must take place in addition to these commands.

Question 41

An Ethernet interface using PPP over Ethernet can have an MTU no larger than what?

Question 41 Answer

The largest MTU that can be supported with PPP over Ethernet (PPPoE) is 1492 bytes. This is reduced from the standard Ethernet MTU by 8 bytes due to the addition of the 6-byte PPPoE header and the 2 byte PPP protocol ID field.

Section 10

Understanding Virtual Private Networks

Virtual private networks (VPNs) are an excellent mechanism to secure IP communications. VPNs fall into two categories: remote-access VPNs and site-to-site VPNs. Remote-access VPNs provide remote users secure access to information on a corporate or central network. To the benefit of the central site administrators, remote-access VPNs provide extensive options for remote-user authentication. Site-to-site VPNs are used to link sites across a less secure network, typically the Internet. These secure connections can also provide a significant cost savings by obviating the need for a traditional WAN. Regardless of the type of VPN, there are several common protocols that make up any IPSec VPN. Knowledge of these protocols is critical to becoming a successful CCNP.

The flashcards in this chapter challenge and expand your understanding of both types of IPSec VPNs. They cover not only the mechanisms used by the protocols but also their configuration.

Question 1

What is IKE?

Question 2

How many phases take place during a successful IKE negotiation?

Question 1 Answer

The Internet Key Exchange (IKE) protocol is used to negotiate, create, and exchange information needed to establish an IPSec connection. This negotiated information is called a security association (SA).

Question 2 Answer

There are two phases to an IKE negotiation. The first phase has two modes: aggressive mode and main mode. The second phase has a single mode named quick mode.

Question 3

How are main mode and aggressive mode different?

Question 4

How can you authenticate remote devices in a site-to-site VPN scenario?

Question 3 Answer

A successful main mode negotiation is made up of exactly six messages. First the keying material is negotiated. This keying material is used to encrypt the remaining messages.

Aggressive mode is less secure because the keying material and options are negotiated simultaneously using only three messages.

Question 4 Answer

There are the three options for site-to-site VPN authentication:

- Preshared keys
- RSA encrypted nonces
- RSA signatures

Question 5

Is it necessary that the ISAKMP policy and IPSec transform be configured to use the same encryption algorithm?

Question 6

What is the difference between tunnel mode and transport mode IPSec?

Question 5 Answer

No, it is possible to use one encryption algorithm for IKE and another for IPSec.

Question 6 Answer

In tunnel mode IPSec, the Cisco default, the entire original IP packet is encapsulated in a new IP packet. All routing takes place based on information in the outer most IP header—in essence hiding the internal IP addresses.

In transport mode IPSec, a new ESP header is placed between the existing Layer 3 and Layer 4 headers. The source and destination IP address of the original packet are used for routing the encrypted packet.

Question 7

Can AH and ESP be used at the same time?

Question 8

When AH and ESP are used together, what is the numeric value present in the protocol field of the IP packet?

Question 7 Answer

Yes. When AH and ESP are used together, the AH header is the outer most Layer 4 header. This is important to consider when designing access control lists that affect IPSec traffic.

Question 8 Answer

Since AH is the first Layer 4 header, its protocol value is in the Layer 3 IP header. The protocol value for AH is 51.

Question 9

Is it necessary that both ends of a site-to-site VPN have static IP addresses?

Question 10

How can a site-to-site VPN be established when one site acquires its IP address dynamically?

Question 9 Answer

No, a dynamic crypto map can be used when the remote peer has a dynamic IP address. Only one end of a site-to-site VPN configuration may use a dynamic crypto map.

Question 10 Answer

Dynamic crypto maps can be used when a single end of a site-to-site VPN uses a dynamic IP address. The dynamic crypto map must be configured on the IPSec peer with a static IP address.

Question 11

What command assigns a single ISAKMP key to all IPSec peers?

Question 12

What configuration commands create and apply crypto transform sets?

Question 11 Answer

To create a wildcard ISAKMP key, use the global configuration command **crypto isakmp key** *key* **address 0.0.0.0**.

Question 12 Answer

IPSec transform sets are created with the global configuration command **crypto ipsec transform-set** and are applied to crypto maps via the **set transform-set** command.

Question 13

What encryption algorithms are available for use with IPSec?

Question 14

What IP protocol values represent AH, ESP, and GRE?

Question 13 Answer

You can use one of the following encryption algorithms with IPSec:

- DES (56 bit)
- 3DES (168 bit)
- AES (128 or 256 bit)

Question 14 Answer

The IP protocol values for these protocols are

- AH: 51
- ESP: 50
- GRE: 47

Question 15

What command enables transport mode IPSec?

Question 16

Can multiple crypto maps be applied to a single router interface?

Question 15 Answer

Transport mode IPSec is enabled by issuing the **mode transport** command in transform-set configuration mode. The following is an example of a transform set configured for transport mode:

```
crypto ipsec transform-set TRANSFORM esp-des esp-sha-hmac
    mode transport
```

Question 16 Answer

No. However, it is possible to have multiple instances of the same crypto map. Similar to the configuration of route maps, each crypto map instance is given a unique numeric tag. When encrypting traffic, crypto map instances are evaluated in order, starting at tag 1. The tag value can range from 1 to 65535. Multiple instances are used when multiple remote peers exist in a site-to-site VPN configuration.

Question 17

How can routing protocols be used over a site-to-site VPN?

Question 18

What Layer 4 protocol and port are used for ISAKMP communications?

Question 17 Answer

To use a routing protocol in a site-to-site VPN environment, GRE tunnels must be utilized. With GRE tunnels, a virtual tunnel interface is used to represent the logical connection between peers. It is on this tunnel interface that a routing protocol can be utilized.

Question 18 Answer

ISAKMP uses UDP with source and destination ports equal to 500.

It should be noted that some implementations—especially remote-access implementations—use UDP source ports other than 500.

Question 19

When two peers begin IKE negotiations, how do they identify themselves?

Question 20

What command is used to configure the ISAKMP identity of a router?

Question 19 Answer

Either IP address or host name can be used as the IKE identity. The identity value supplied must match the ISAKMP key configured on the peer.

The global configuration command **crypto isakmp identity** {**hostname** | **address**} configures which identity is used.

Question 20 Answer

The global configuration command **crypto isakmp identity** {**hostname** | **address**} configures which identity is used during IKE negotiations.

Question 21

What is the difference between authentication provided by ESP and AH?

Question 22

How can you authenticate remote-access VPN connections?

Question 21 Answer

The authentication provided by ESP computes a hash based solely on a packet's payload. In contrast, the hash associated with AH is computed on the entire packet, headers included (this excludes fields like TTL that legitimately change in transit). AH, therefore, provides greater security by ensuring that the entire packet has not changed.

Question 22 Answer

Remote-access VPN connections can be authenticated using one of the following options:

- Preshared keys
- RSA signatures

In addition to the above options, remote-access users can be further authenticated using Extended Authentication (XAUTH). With XAUTH, users are authenticated against an external RADIUS server, such as Cisco ACS or Microsoft IAS.

Question 23

Within the context of certificates, what is a CRL?

Question 24

Can the same crypto map instance be used with multiple IPSec peers?

Question 23 Answer

A Certificate Revocation List (CRL) is used to verify that a certificate has not been revoked. If a certificate's serial number is listed on the CRL, it has been revoked and is no longer valid for any authentication purposes and is rejected.

Question 24 Answer

Yes, one crypto map instance can have multiple peers as long as both peers share an identical configuration. This is often used at a remote site to specify a redundant VPN device at the central site.

Question 25

Can different encryption algorithms be used with the same crypto map instance?

Question 26

How does the router determine which traffic to encrypt?

Question 25 Answer

No, a crypto map instance is associated with exactly one IPSec transform set, which is where the encryption algorithm is configured.

Question 26 Answer

An ACL is created and associated with a crypto map instance. This ACL, known as the crypto ACL, is used to select traffic that is to be encrypted. Traffic that is not selected by the crypto ACL (as permit entries) is not encrypted.

Question 27

What happens if the router receives traffic that matches a crypto ACL but is not encrypted?

Question 28

What is Perfect Forward Secrecy?

Question 27 Answer

Inbound traffic that should be encrypted and is not (as determined by evaluating the crypto ACL in reverse) is silently dropped.

Question 28 Answer

Diffie-Hellman Perfect Forward Secrecy (PFS) is used to generate new keying material for IPSec security associations. Without PFS, the IPSec keying material is derived from the IKE keying material.

Question 29

What does the command group 2 enable?

Question 30

What types of security associations exist?

Question 29 Answer

The **group 2** ISAKMP policy configuration command enables 1024-bit Diffie-Hellman key exchange during IKE negotiations. The default setting is **group 1**, which uses 768-bit encryption. It should be noted that larger keys require additional router CPU resources.

Question 30 Answer

There are two types of security associations (SAs): the ISAKMP SA and the IPSec SA. An SA is made up of a unidirectional connection and all of its associated security parameters. After the successful establishment of an IPSec session, each device has four SAs—an ISAKMP SA in each direction and an IPSec SA in each direction.

Question 31

What is an SPI?

Question 32

What command displays the number of existing ISAKMP security associations? What other information does this command display?

Question 31 Answer

A Security Parameters Index (SPI), is an index into the Security Parameters Database (SPD). Each security association has an SPI for each protocol (AH or ESP) in each direction (inbound and outbound).

Question 32 Answer

The EXEC command **show crypto isakmp sa** displays the number of existing ISAKMP security associations (SAs). In addition, this command displays the source and destination IP address of each SA.

Question 33

What is the name of the second IKE negotiation phase?

Understanding Virtual Private Networks

Question 34

When creating an IPSec transform set, you have selected the esp-sha-hmac option. What does this enable?

Understanding Virtual Private Networks

Question 33 Answer

The second IKE phase, called quick mode, is used to negotiate IPSec transform sets and establish IPSec security associations.

Question 34 Answer

This option enables ESP message authentication using the SHA hashing algorithm. Message authentication using MD5 can be enabled with the **esp-md5-hmac** option.

Question 35

What command links a crypto map with a crypto ACL?

Question 36

What command applies a crypto map to an interface?

Question 35 Answer

The crypto map configuration command **match address** *acl* is used to link an ACL to a crypto map.

Question 36 Answer

The interface configuration command **crypto map** *crypto-map-name* applies a crypto map to an interface.

Question 37

When creating an ISAKMP policy, which command enables the use of certificates for peer authentication?

Question 38

What settings make up the default ISAKMP policy?

Question 37 Answer

The ISAKMP policy configuration command **authentication rsa-sig** enables RSA digital signatures for the authentication of VPN peers.

Question 38 Answer

The following items make up the default ISAKMP policy:

- Authentication: rsa-sig
- Encryption: DES
- Diffie-Hellman: group 1
- Hash: SHA
- Lifetime: 86,400 seconds

Question 39

What are the main benefits associated with VPN technologies?

Question 40

Cisco offers two hashing algorithms for use with IPSec. What are they and which is more secure?

Question 39 Answer

VPNs have the following benefits:

- Reduced cost
- Improved data security
- Remote-access user authentication

Question 40 Answer

The two hashing algorithms available are SHA, which produces a hash 160 bits in length, and MD5, which produces a 128-bit hash. It is generally regarded that MD5 provides higher performance but, due to its larger resultant hash, that SHA is more secure.

BCRAN Quick Reference Sheets

Wide-Area Network Technologies

WAN Technologies

- Asynchronous Transfer Mode (ATM)
  - —Cell relay technology
  - —One physical interface can support many virtual circuits
  - —1.544 Mbps to 10 Gbps interfaces
  - —Uses fixed 53 byte cell
  - —Can support different traffic classes, such as variable bit rate (VBR), constant bit rate (CBR), unspecified bit rate (UBR), and available bit rate (ABR)
  - —Can support any Layer 3 protocol
- Dedicated Connections
  - —Typically 56 kbps or T1 connections
  - —Supported using circuit switching in the service provider network
  - —56 kbps to 45 Mbps interface speeds
  - —One-to-one mapping of physical to logical connections
  - —More expensive than packet or circuit switched connections of similar speeds
  - —Can support any Layer 3 protocol
- Frame Relay
  - —Packet switching technology
  - —Can support interfaces from 56 kbps to 45 Mbps
  - —Permanent virtual circuits (PVCs) are built between Frame Relay endpoints
  - —One physical interface can support many PVCs
  - —Can support any Layer 3 protocol
- Integrated Services Digital Network (ISDN)
  - —Circuit switching technology
  - —Two interface types
    - Basic Rate Interface (BRI)
      - One 16 kbps D channel
      - Two 64 kbps B channels
    - Primary Rate Interface (PRI)
      - One 64 kbps D channel
      - 23 64 kbps B channels in North America
      - 30 64 kbps B channels elsewhere
  - —BRI commonly used as a backup connection
  - —Can support any Layer 3 protocol

Working with Asynchronous Connections

Using Group-Async Interfaces

A Group-Async interface allows many asynchronous interfaces to share the same configuration. This is most widely used to support a remote access dialup solution.
This command creates a Group-Async virtual interface:

interface Group-Async *number*

This command associates a range of asynchronous lines to a Group-Async interface. This command is an interface configuration command and is available only under Group-Async interfaces:

group-range *start end*

Using the modemcap Database

The modemcap database contains a base configuration for many popular modems. The following commands use the modemcap database to configure modems.
This line configuration command automatically determines the modem type and then uses information in the modemcap database to configure it correctly:

modem autoconfigure discovery

The following line configuration command looks up the modem type specified and applies the configuration from the modemcap database:

modem autoconfigure type *modem-type*

It is also possible to add to or edit existing entries in the modemcap database. The following table details the relevant modemcap database editing commands.

Command	Description
modemcap edit *modem-name attribute value*	Edits a particular value within a modemcap entry
modemcap entry *modem-name*	Adds a modemcap entry to the modem database
show modemcap [*entry-name*]	Shows the current contents of the modemcap database

Using Reverse Telnet to Troubleshoot Modems

A *reverse Telnet* is a Telnet session that connects the user to an asynchronous serial line on the router. This can be used to interact directly with a modem for troubleshooting. A reverse Telnet is established by Telneting to any IP address on the router on a specific TCP port. The following ports ranges are used as the Telnet destination.

Character Mode Telnet	2000–2999
Line Mode TCP	4000–4999
Binary Mode Telnet	6000–6999
Xremote	9000–9999

To determine the exact port number to use, find the correct line in the output of **show line**. The leftmost column is the line number; simply add that number to the desired range in the preceding table.

For example, the command **telnet 192.168.1.1 2001** connects you to the first asynchronous line on a router whose IP address is 192.168.1.1.

NOTE For the Telnet session to successfully establish, you must Telnet to the IP address of an interface in an up/up state.

Once connected to a modem, you can enter AT commands directly. The following table lists some important and helpful commands.

AT&F	Reloads factory defaults
ATA	Answers the incoming call
ATDT *phone-number*	Uses tone dialing to place a call to the number specified
ATE0	Disables local echo
ATM0	Disables the modem speaker
ATS0=x	Specifies the ring on which to auto answer incoming calls
ATZ	Resets the modem

Physical Line Configuration

Many characteristics of a physical line can be manually configured. The following line configuration commands are used to specify the operation of router lines.

Command	Description
speed *speed*	Configures the speed of modem to router communication
flowcontrol {none | software | hardware}	Configures flow control between the router and modem
modem {dialin | dialout | inout}	Specifies the direction in which the modem can be used
stopbits {0 | 1}	Configures the stopbits on the physical interface
physical-layer async	Configures a synchronous/asynchronous interface for asynchronous operation
autoselect {ppp | during-login}	Enables the detection and use of PPP after a line is connected

Chat Scripts

Chat scripts are used to talk to or through a modem. Constructed using a simple expect-send syntax, chat scripts can prove useful. A chat script can be launched at several instances:

- Line activation
- Line connection
- Line reset
- New call
- Dialer startup

An example of chat script creation follows:

```
Router(config)# chat-script CS-SAMPLE ABORT ERROR ABORT BUSY "" "ATZ" OK
"ATDT14155551111" TIMEOUT 40 CONNECT \c
```

To associate a chat script to an interface or remote host, use one of the following commands:

- **dialer map**
- **script activation**
- **script connection**
- **script dialer**
- **script reset**
- **script startup**

Chat scripts can include escape characters. These escape characters are replaced when a script is executed. The following escape characters are supported.

Character	Description
\\	The \ character
\"	Sends the " in a double quoted send string
\c	Suppresses a carriage return at the end of the connect string
\d	Two-second delay
\K	Inserts a break
\n	A newline character
\N	Sends a null character

Character	Description
\p	Pauses for 1/4 of a second
\r	Sends a return
\s	Sends a space
\t	A tab character
\T	Replaced by the phone number from the dialer string or map

Configuring PPP with PAP and CHAP

Benefits of PPP

PPP offers many benefits, including:

- Bidirectional authentication through PAP or CHAP
- Multiprotocol support
- Flexible client IP address assignment
- Bandwidth aggregation with multilink PPP
- Link fragmentation and interleaving
- Link quality monitoring

Components of PPP

The following table describes the components of PPP.

Component	Description
LCP	The Link Control Protocol (LCP) is used to test, establish, and monitor the PPP connection.
Authentication	The Password Authentication Protocol (PAP) and Challenge Handshake Authentication Protocol (CHAP) are responsible for authenticating each end of a PPP connection; the implementation of these is optional, but strongly recommended.
NCPs	Network Control Protocols (NCPs) exist for each protocol supported over PPP; they establish and configure protocol specific parameters. Example NCPs include IPCP, IPXCP, ATalkCP, BridgeCP, and CDPCP.

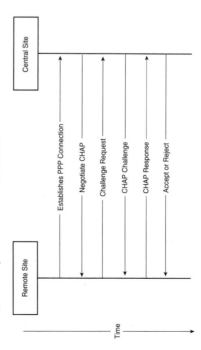

The state of LCP and any configured NCPs can be viewed with the EXEC command show interfaces.

Differences Between PAP and CHAP

The following table summarizes the differences between the Password Authentication Protocol (PAP) and the Challenge Handshake Authentication Protocol (CHAP).

CHAP	PAP
Passwords never sent over the network	Passwords sent as clear text
Provides two-way authentication	One-way authentication; can be run separately in both directions to establish two-way authentication

In CHAP, a three-way handshake authenticates users.

With PAP, because there is no attempt at secrecy, the process is much simpler.

Enabling PPP Encapsulation

The following interface configuration command enables PPP encapsulation:

encapsulation ppp

Configuring Authentication

Basic PPP authentication can be performed with the two following commands:

username *username* password *password*
ppp authentication {pap | chap | pap chap | chap pap}

In the following example, an access server is configured to attempt CHAP first, then fall back to PAP:

```
Router(config)# username jane password astro
Router(config)# username fred password dino
Router(config)# interface Group-Async 1
Router(config-if)# encapsulation ppp
Router(config-if)# ppp authentication chap pap
```

Configuring Compression

For compression to be successfully negotiated, it must be enabled in both directions. Compression is enabled using the following interface configuration command:

compress [predictor | stac | mppc [ignore-pfc]]

The state of compression can be viewed using the EXEC command **show compress**. If compression has been negotiated on a PPP link, the **show interfaces** EXEC command displays the CCP state as Open.

IP Address Assignment with PPP

An IP address can be assigned to a PPP client in several ways:

- TACACS+ or RADIUS server
- IP pool defined on the access server
- Dynamic Host Configuration Protocol (DHCP)
- Via the **ppp** EXEC command
- Via the **peer default ip address** interface configuration command
- PPP client configuration

The default address allocation method can be controlled with the global configuration command:

```
ip address-pool {dhcp-proxy-client | local}
```

An IP address pool is configured using the following command:
```
ip local pool pool-name start-address end-address
```

After the pool is created, it can be applied with the following interface configuration command:

```
peer default ip address pool pool-name
```

To configure the access server to use DHCP to determine addresses available for client assignment, use this global configuration command:

```
ip dhcp-server {ip-address | name}
```

After the DHCP servers are configured and the default address allocation method set to DHCP, the following interface configuration command enables IP address assignment from the DHCP retrieved addresses:

```
peer default ip address pool dhcp
```

A specific address can be assigned to users dialing into a particular access server interface with the following interface configuration command:

```
peer default ip address ip-address
```

Configuring Multilink PPP

The configuration of multilink PPP (MLP) depends on the implementation scenario. To properly bundle asynchronous interfaces, PPP authentication must be implemented. The following configuration example configures MLP on an ISDN BRI interface:

```
Router(config)# interface bri0
Router(config-if)# encapsulation ppp
Router(config-if)# ppp authentication chap pap
Router(config-if)# ppp multilink
```

To configure MLP on a dialer interface, the **ppp multilink** command must be applied to the physical and dialer interface. The following configuration sample shows this configuration:

```
Router(config)# interface bri 0
Router(config-if)# encapsulation ppp
Router(config-if)# ppp multilink
Router(config-if)# dialer pool-member 1
Router(config-if)# interface Dialer 0
Router(config-if)# encapsulation ppp
Router(config-if)# ppp authentication chap pap
Router(config-if)# ppp multilink
Router(config-if)# dialer pool 1
```

The configuration of MLP over synchronous interfaces can be accomplished in one of two ways. The first, shown here, uses virtual templates to configure the MLP group:

```
Router(config)# multilink virtual-template 1
Router(config)# interface Virtual-Template 1
Router(config-if)# ip address 10.1.1.1 255.255.255.252
Router(config-if)# ppp authentication pap
Router(config-if)# ppp multilink
Router(config-if)# interface Serial 0
Router(config-if)# encapsulation ppp
Router(config-if)# ppp multilink
Router(config-if)# interface Serial 1
Router(config-if)# encapsulation ppp
Router(config-if)# ppp multilink
```

The second MLP over synchronous interfaces option does not involve the creation of a virtual template interface. The advantage to this type of configuration is that multiple distinct MLP bundles can exist on the same router. This configuration is as follows:

```
Router(config)# interface Serial 0
Router(config-if)# encapsulation ppp
```

Verification of a PPP Configuration

The following commands can be used to view the status of a configured PPP configuration:

- show compress
- show interfaces [*type number*]
- show ppp multilink
- show users [all]

Configuring Dial-on-Demand Routing

Dial-on-Demand Routing Implementation Options

Dial-on-demand routing (DDR) can be implemented in one of two manners:

- **Legacy DDR**—In legacy DDR, the dialer configuration is placed directly on the physical interface. Although this simplifies the configuration somewhat, the lack of abstraction restricts the configuration possibilities.
- **Dialer Profiles**—With dialer profiles, virtual dialer interfaces are configured, and then bound to a group of physical interfaces. This permits more dialer interfaces to exist than physical interfaces. It also permits the router to operate around failed interfaces.

Configuring DDR

Many of the commands in legacy DDR and dialer profiles are shared between the two configurations. The following table details most of the commands shared between these two configurations.

Command	Description
dialer fast-idle *seconds*	Deactivates idle interfaces when physical interface contention exists
dialer idle-timeout *seconds*	Disconnects DDR sessions that are idle

---

```
Router(config-if)# ppp multilink
Router(config-if)# multilink-group 1
Router(config-if)# interface Serial 1
Router(config-if)# encapsulation ppp
Router(config-if)# ppp multilink
Router(config-if)# multilink-group 1
Router(config-if)# interface Multilink 1
Router(config-if)# ip address 10.1.1.1 255.255.255.252
Router(config-if)# ppp authentication pap
Router(config-if)# ppp multilink
```

Enabling and Using PPP Link Quality Monitoring

When PPP link quality monitoring (LQM) is enabled, link quality reports (LQRs) are sent instead of the regular interface keepalives. If LQM determines that the quality of an interface has dropped below the configured threshold, the interface is taken down. LQM can be enabled on one or both ends of the PPP connection.

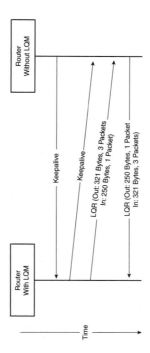

To enable LQM on a PPP interface, use the following interface configuration command:

ppp quality *percentage*

Client Host Route Creation

By default, the access server installs a host route (a route with a 32-bit mask) for each connected PPP client. To disable this functionality, use the interface configuration command as follows:

no peer neighbor-route

Command	Description
dialer load-threshold *load* [inbound | outbound | either]	Used with multilink PPP to establish additional dialer connections during periods of high network traffic
dialer map *protocol address phone-number*	Associates a Layer 3 address with a remote phone number
dialer string *phone-number*	Statically configures a remote phone number on an interface
dialer-group *number*	Groups a dialer list with a dialer interface for the selection of interesting traffic
dialer-list *number* protocol *protocol* [permit | deny] [*keyword value*]	Creates a dialer list that determines what traffic activates a dialer interface
encapsulation ppp	Enables PPP encapsulation on an interface

The following commands are specific to dialer profiles and provide much of their additional functionality.

Command	Description
dialer pool *number*	Associates a dialer interface with a pool of physical interfaces
dialer pool-member *number*	Places a physical interface into a dialer pool
dialer rotary-group *number*	Places a physical interface into a rotary group

Command	Description
interface dialer *number*	Creates a dialer interface; if this interface is to be associated with a configured rotary group, the interface number must match the rotary group number

The following configuration snippet configures two BRI interfaces as a member of a dialer pool and then configures two dialer interfaces for IP routing:

```
Router(config)# interface BRI 0
Router(config-if)# dialer in-band
Router(config-if)# dialer pool-member 10
Router(config-if)# interface BRI 1
Router(config-if)# dialer in-band
Router(config-if)# dialer pool-member 10
Router(config-if)# exit
Router(config)# dialer-list 1 protocol ip permit
Router(config)# interface Dialer 1
Router(config-if)# ip address 10.1.1.1 255.255.255.0
Router(config-if)# encapsulation ppp
Router(config-if)# dialer pool 10
Router(config-if)# dialer-group 1
Router(config-if)# dialer map ip 10.1.1.2 4155551111
Router(config)# interface Dialer 2
Router(config-if)# ip address 10.1.2.1 255.255.255.0
Router(config-if)# encapsulation ppp
Router(config-if)# dialer pool 10
Router(config-if)# dialer-group 1
Router(config-if)# dialer map ip 10.1.2.2 4155552222
```

Dialer Pools and Rotary Groups

Dialer pools and rotary groups have a similar goal; the separation of physical and logical interfaces. One difference to their implementation exists. With rotary groups, only one dialer interface is allowed to use the members of the group. In contrast, with dialer pools, many dialer interfaces are allowed to share the pool members.

To configure rotary groups, the dialer interface number must match the rotary group number, as shown in this abbreviated example:

```
Router(config)# interface BRI 0
Router(config-if)# dialer rotary-group 12
Router(config-if)# interface BRI 1
Router(config-if)# dialer rotary-group 12
Router(config-if)# interface Dialer 12
```

This one-to-one mapping is the downside of rotary groups. The following example updates the previous to use dialer pools with two dialer interfaces:

```
Router(config)# interface BRI 0
Router(config-if)# dialer pool-member 14
Router(config-if)# interface BRI 1
Router(config-if)# dialer pool-member 14
Router(config-if)# interface Dialer 1
Router(config-if)# dialer pool 14
Router(config-if)# interface Dialer 2
Router(config-if)# dialer pool 14
```

Determining Interesting Traffic

A router uses the idea of interesting traffic to determine if a dormant DDR link should be established. The **dialer-list** global configuration command defines interesting traffic. By using different dialer list numbers, interesting traffic can vary by interface. The complete syntax for the **dialer-list** command is as follows:

dialer-list *list-number* **protocol** *protocol* {**permit** | **deny**} [**list** *access-list-number*]

The **dialer-list** command is used regardless of the protocol you want to define as interesting. Valid protocols include appletalk, bridge, clns, clns_es, clns_is, decnet, decnet_router-L1, decnet_router-L2, decnet_node, ip, ipx, vines, and xns.

The **list** option to this command provides increased granularity through the association of an access list to a dialer list. Any traffic that is permitted by the access list qualifies as interesting and in turn enables the DDR interface.

NOTE Remember that ALL access lists include an implicit deny any as the last entry.

The following is an example access list that selects IP as interesting while excluding Open Shortest Path First (OSPF):

```
access-list 100 deny ospf any any
access-list 100 permit ip any any
dialer-list 1 protocol ip list 100
```

NOTE Although interesting traffic is used to establish a DDR connection, after the connection is established, all traffic is allowed to flow. The idle timeout, however, is reset only when interesting traffic is sent or received.

Dialer Map Classes

A dialer map class is a means to apply an identical configuration to multiple dialer interfaces or destinations. Map class configuration begins with the following command:

map-class dialer *map-class-name*

Once in map class configuration mode, a limited selection of dialer commands is available to you. The following table documents these commands.

dialer callback-server {dialstring | username}	Enables callback for the incoming connections
dialer enable-timeout *seconds*	Configures the time period before a router reuses a physical interface
dialer fast-idle *seconds*	The idle disconnect timeout used when Dialer interfaces are waiting for an available physical interface
dialer idle-timeout *seconds*	Configures when an idle DDR connection is disconnected
dialer isdn {speed *speed* | spc}	Sets the data rate of the ISDN B channel
dialer wait-for-carrier-time *seconds*	Determines how long the router waits after dialing for a connection to be established

To apply a map class use the class option to the **dialer-map** interface configuration command, as shown in the following example:

```
Router(config)# interface Dialer 1
Router(config-if)# dialer map ip 10.1.2.1 4155551111 class MC-EXAMPLE
```

Verification of a Dial-on-Demand Routing Configuration

The following commands can be used to diagnose and troubleshoot a DDR configuration:

• **show interfaces** [*type number*]
• **show dialer**

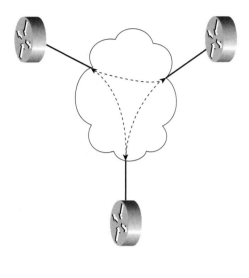

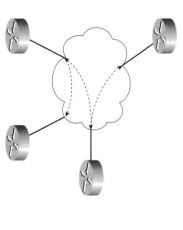

—In a partial mesh, endpoints are connected as needed.

- **show dialer map**
- **show dialer sessions**
- **show users**

Configuring Frame Relay

Characteristics of Frame Relay

- Packet switching—Packets from many connections are multiplexed onto a single physical circuit.
- High speed—Frame Relay typically supports connections from 56 kbps to 45 Mbps, with a full T1 (1.544 Mbps) being the most commonly deployed access port.
- No mechanism for retries—Frames that encounter errors in the network are dropped and left for the upper layer protocols to recover.
- Virtual circuits—One physical connection can support many virtual circuits (VC); each VC is identified by a data-link connection identifier (DLCI).
- Access and guaranteed data rates might be different—The port speed, the speed at which the router connects to the network, might be much faster than the committed information rate (CIR), a per-VC value that represents the amount of traffic guaranteed by the service provider to reach its destination.

Frame Relay Network Design Points

- Many VCs can be supported on a single physical interface.
  - Frame Relay subinterfaces can be multipoint or point-to-point.
    Advantages of multipoint interfaces include more efficient use of IP address space.
    Advantages of point-to-point subinterfaces include the following:
    Broadcasts are not replicated.
    Overcomes split horizon problems.
    Guaranteed routing protocol interoperability.
  - The physical interface always acts as a multipoint interface.
- Frame Relay networks can be fully or partially meshed.
  - In a full mesh, each Frame Relay endpoint has a VC to every other Frame Relay endpoint.
  - The number of VCs required is equal to n(n–1) / 2.

- A hub and spoke topology is essentially a partial mesh in which all the sites are connected to one central (hub) site.
- DLCIs are of local—router to Frame Relay switch—significance only.
  - Valid DLCI numbers differ according to the Local Management Interface (LMI) type used:
    ANSI: 16 to 991
    Cisco: 16 to 1007
    Q933a: 16 to 991
- Virtual interfaces, called subinterfaces, can be used to create virtual point-to-point connections on a per-VC basis.
  - Serial0.16 is an example subinterface name.
- Data sent in excess of the CIR has no guarantee of making it to the destination.
  - This traffic is marked with the Discard Eligible (DE) bit by the Frame Relay network.
- Frame Relay Traffic Shaping (FRTS) should be used to "smooth" traffic down to the CIR, or slightly above.
- Frame Relay map classes make it possible to apply the same configuration to many VCs.
- Must be mindful of routing protocol operation; things like split horizon, OSPF network type, and IS-IS requirements.

Configuring Frame Relay

To enable Frame Relay encapsulation on a serial interface, use the following:

`encapsulation frame-relay [cisco | ietf]`

The [cisco | ietf] argument specifies the LMI type for all VC connected to that interface. The default is cisco. For multipoint interfaces, the ietf option to the frame-relay map command enables IETF encapsulation on a per-VC basis.

To create a subinterface, use the one of the following two commands:

`Router(config)# interface Serial0.16 multipoint`

or

`Router(config)# interface Serial0.16 point-to-point`

Cisco routers support three Frame Relay LMI types. The LMI type can be configured on an interface basis with the following command:

`frame-relay lmi-type {cisco | ansi | q933a}`

When no Frame Relay LMI type is explicitly configured, the router autosenses the appropriate LMI type.

When configuring a multipoint Frame Relay interface, DLCI-to-address and protocol mappings must be manually configured. The following is an example using IP with two VCs:

```
Router(config-if)# frame-relay map ip 192.168.1.1 16 broadcast
Router(config-if)# frame-relay map ip 192.168.1.2 17 broadcast
```

NOTE   The broadcast argument indicates that the router should replicate broadcast packets over this VC. Without this argument, most routing protocols do not operate correctly.

When you use a point-to-point subinterface, only one VC can be used. The following command associates a DLCI with a point-to-point subinterface:

`Router(config-subif)# frame-relay interface-dlci dlci`

Configuring Frame Relay Traffic Shaping (FRTS)

While configuring FRTS, you should know a few variables (see the following table).

Variable	Meaning
Bc	Burst Committed: The amount of data to burst per Tc.
Be	Burst Excess: The amount of data to burst in excess of the contracted rate per Tc.
CIR	This is the contracted rate of traffic guaranteed to make it through the Frame Relay network.
EIR	The amount of traffic in addition to the CIR to send into the network.
MinCIR	The reduced transmission rate used when a BECN is received on a VC. By default MinCIR = CIR / 2.
Tc	This is the time interval used in tuning the performance of FRTS; it defaults to 1/8 of a second.

Two sets of commands can be used to configure FRTS. Both groups of commands are entered on a Frame Relay map class and then applied to a VC. Examples of both groups follow using a map class called MC-EXAMPLE, with a CIR of 128 k and EIR of 64 k:

```
Router(config)# map-class frame-relay MC-EXAMPLE
Router(config-map-class)# frame-relay traffic-rate 128000 192000
Router(config-map-class)# interface Serial0
Router(config-if)# frame-relay traffic-shaping
Router(config-if)# interface Serial0.16 point-to-point
Router(config-subif)# frame-relay interface-dlci 16
Router(config-fr-dlci)# class MC-EXAMPLE
```

or

```
Router(config)# map-class frame-relay MC-EXAMPLE
Router(config-map-class)# frame-relay bc 16000
Router(config-map-class)# frame-relay be 8000
Router(config-map-class)# interface Serial0
Router(config-if)# frame-relay traffic-shaping
Router(config-if)# interface Serial0.16 point-to-point
Router(config-subif)# frame-relay interface-dlci 16
Router(config-fr-dlci)# class MC-EXAMPLE
```

NOTE When the frame-relay traffic-shaping command is applied, all VCs without traffic shaping parameters set are shaped to 56 kbps.

When the command frame-relay adaptive-shaping becn is entered, the router automatically slows transmission on a VC upon receipt of a BECN. The new rate, called Min-CIR, is by default half of the CIR. This value can be changed with the map class configuration command frame-relay mincir mincir.

Configuring Compression

Compression can be applied to an interface or subinterface using the following command:
frame-relay payload-compression {FRF9 | data-stream | packet-by-packet} stac

or on a per-VC basis for multipoint interfaces with the following command:
frame-relay map protocol dlci compress [active | passive]

Verifying the Frame Relay Configuration

The following commands help you determine if your Frame Relay configuration is correct and operating properly:

- show frame-relay lmi [interface type number]
- show frame-relay map
- show frame-relay pvc [interface type number] [dlci]
- show frame-relay traffic
- show interfaces [type number]
- show traffic-shape [type number]
- show traffic-shape statistics [type number]

Network Redundancy and Backup Connections

Tools for Wide-Area Network Redundancy

- Backup interfaces
- Floating static routes
- Dialer watch

Backup Interface Design Points

- The backup interface is down and unusable until needed.
- The backup interface can be used to provide additional bandwidth.
- A delay can be configured before the backup interface is enabled and disabled.
- A dialer profile can be specified as a backup interface.

Configuring Backup Interfaces

The commands for enabling and tuning backup interfaces are detailed in the following table.

Command	Description
backup interface type number	Assigns an interface as a backup interface
backup delay {enable-delay	never} {disable-delay	never}	Configures the delay before enabling and disabling a backup interface
backup load {enable-threshold	never} {disable-threshold	never}	Configures a threshold for enabling and disabling the backup interface for additional bandwidth

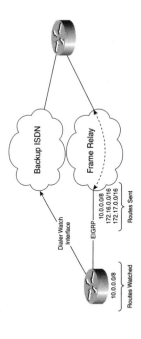

The following configuration example configures Serial 1 as a backup interface to Serial 0. This example also configures the router to enable the backup interface when the primary interfaces load exceeds 75 percent and to disable it once it falls below 50 percent:

```
Router(config)# interface Serial 0
Router(config-if)# backup interface Serial 1
Router(config-if)# backup load 75 50
```

Floating Static Route Design Points

- Care must be taken to ensure the route is not used unless a failure occurs.
- No provision for load balancing or delaying failover and fallback.

Configuring Floating Static Routes

A *floating static route* is a static route that has a higher administrative distance (AD) than a dynamically learned route. IBGP has the highest default AD of any routing protocol at 200. Setting the AD of a floating static route at 210 helps ensure that it is only used for redundancy purposes. The syntax used to create a floating static route is as follows:

```
ip route network mask {next-hop | interface-type number} distance
```

The following is an example of using this command to create a floating static route:

```
Router(config)# ip route 0.0.0.0 0.0.0.0 172.16.1.1 210
```

Once configured, the router uses this floating static route only during a failure of the primary dynamically learned route.

Dialer Watch Design Points

- Configures the router to monitor the existence of a dynamic route or routes
- No provision for load balancing
- Can delay fallback
- Backup interface activated after primary failure, without delay

Configuring Dialer Watch

The following commands configure dialer watch.

The following command defines the routes to watch. Multiple routes can be watched by entering multiple instances of this command. All watched routes must be absent before the dialer watch activates the backup interface:

```
dialer watch-list group-number ip ip-address address-mask
```

This command is applied to the dial-on-demand routing (DDR) interface to be used as a backup interface. The *group-number* argument must match that used in the dialer watch-list command:

```
dialer watch-group group-number
```

Applied to the dialer watch backup interface, this command configures the delay before the backup interface is shut down after the primary interface is restored:

```
dialer watch-disable seconds
```

The following configuration example implements dialer watch. This example monitors the route to 10.0.0.0/8 and waits 120 seconds before disabling the backup interface:

```
Router(config)# dialer watch-list 1 ip 10.0.0.0 255.0.0.0
Router(config)# interface Dialer 0
Router(config-if)# dialer watch-group 1
Router(config-if)# dialer watch-disable 120
```

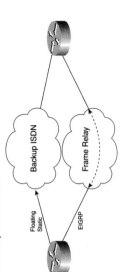

Verification of Network Redundancy

The following commands can monitor and verify the configuration of backup interfaces, floating static routes, and dialer watch:

* show backup
* show dialer [interface *type number*]
* show interfaces [interface *type number*]
* show ip route
* show ip route static

Configuring Compression

Types of Compression

* Frame Relay Payload Compression
* HDLC Link Compression
* PPP Link Compression (Microsoft Point-to-Point Compression [MPPC])
* RTP Header Compression

Applying Compression

To apply compression for all virtual circuits (VCs) on an interface, use the interface configuration command:

frame-relay payload-compress {packet-by-packet | frf9 stac
[*hardware-options*] | **data-stream stac** [*hardware-options*]}

To apply compression on a per-VC basis, use the payload-compress argument and the frame-relay map interface configuration command. The following is an example of the use of this argument:

Router(config-if)# **frame-relay map ip 10.1.1.1 16 broadcast**
payload-compress packet-by-packet

Compression can be applied to an interface with HDLC encapsulation using the following interface configuration command:

compress {predictor | stac}

To apply compression on a PPP link, use the following command in interface configuration mode:

compress [predictor | stac | mppc [ignore-pfc]]

RTP header compression can be used on point-to-point connections. It substantially reduces the overhead related to RTP. The following command enables RTP header compression on HDLC or PPP links:

ip rtp header-compression

RTP header compression can be enabled for Frame Relay at the interface level with this command:

frame-relay ip rtp header-compression

Monitoring and Verification of Compression

Use the following commands to determine the state of compression:

* show compress
* show interfaces [*type number*]
* show ip rtp header-compression [*type number*] [detail]

Configuring Queuing

Types of Queuing

* Class-Based Weighted Fair Queuing (CBWFQ)
  —Uses classes to group traffic types by protocol, by access lists, by IP Precedence, by IP ToS, by DiffServ bits, by packet length, and by input interface
  —Uses policy maps to apply queuing to classes
  —Integrates other queuing strategies
* Custom Queuing (CQ)
  —Uses access lists and protocol types to classify traffic
  —17 queues; queue 0 reserved for system use
  —Can set queue priority
  —All queues serviced eventually
* First-In, First-Out (FIFO) Queuing
  —Default for interfaces > 2 Mbps
* Low Latency Queuing (LLQ)
  —Strict priority queuing within CBWFQ
  —Can starve other queues
* Priority Queuing (PQ)
  —Uses access lists and protocol types to classify traffic
  —High priority queues always emptied first
  —Four queues: high, medium, normal, and low
  —Can starve lower priority queues
* Weighted Fair Queuing (WFQ)
  —Default for interface < 2 Mbps
  —Favors interactive traffic
  —IP Precedence aware

Implementing CBWFQ

The first step in configuring CBWFQ is to define traffic classes. To create a class, use the following command:

`class-map class-name`

Then, traffic can be placed in a class using one of the following commands:

`match access-group access-list`
`match input-interface type number`
`match protocol protocol`

After the class map is created, you can apply queuing techniques to the class using a policy map. The syntax to create a policy map is as follows:

`policy-map policy-map`

To configure a traffic class, enter the policy map configuration command as follows:

`class class-name`

The commands in the following table configure the queuing characteristics for a class within CBWFQ.

Command	Description
bandwidth [bandwidth | percent percent]	Assigns a bandwidth to the traffic class for CQ-like queuing; can be assigned as an amount of bandwidth or a percent of interface bandwidth.
Fair-queue	Enables WFQ for the traffic class.
no fair-queue	Disables WFQ and enables FIFO queuing for the class.
priority bandwidth	Assigns a maximum bandwidth for strict priority queuing; this is LLQ.

After a policy map is created and configured, use the following command to apply it to an interface:

`service-policy output policy-map`

The following is an example of a CBWFQ configuration that creates a strict priority queue (LLQ) for Telnet traffic, assigns 64 kbps for IPX traffic, and uses WFQ for any unclassified traffic types:

```
Router(config)# access-list 100 permit tcp any any eq 23
Router(config)# access-list 100 permit tcp any any eq 23 any
```

```
Router(config)# class-map MC-TELNET
Router(config-cmap)# match access-group 100
Router(config-cmap)# class-map MC-IPX
Router(config-cmap)# match protocol ipx
Router(config-cmap)# policy-map PM-E0-OUT
Router(config-pmap)# class MC-TELNET
Router(config-pmap-c)# priority 64
Router(config-pmap-c)# class MC-IPX
Router(config-pmap-c)# bandwidth 64
Router(config-pmap-c)# class class-default
Router(config-pmap-c)# fair-queue
Router(config-pmap-c)# interface Ethernet 0
Router(config-if)# service-policy output PM-E0-OUT
```

Configuring CQ

During the configuration of CQ, queue lists are created and then applied to an interface. To create, customize, and apply a custom queue list, use the commands shown in the following table.

Command	Description
queue-list list-number default queue-number	Assigns the default queue; traffic not explicitly place in a queue ends up here.
queue-list list-number interface type number queue-number	Assigns traffic to a specific queue based on the input interface.
queue-list list-number protocol protocol queue-number [queue-keyword value]	Assigns traffic to a specific queue based on the protocol, or several protocol keywords, including • fragments • list • gt • lt • tcp • udp
queue-list list-number queue queue-number byte-count byte-count	Limits how many bytes are emptied from the queue before moving on to the next queue; entire packets are taken until byte-count is exceeded.

Command	Description
queue-list *list-number* queue *queue-number* limit *queue-limit*	Configures the size of the queue in packets.
custom-queue-list *queue-list*	Applies a queue list an interface.

The following configuration example configures CQ to give 25 percent of available bandwidth to HTTP and HTTPS traffic:

```
Router(config)# access-list 100 permit tcp any any eq 80
Router(config)# access-list 100 permit tcp any eq 80 any
Router(config)# access-list 100 permit tcp any any eq 443
Router(config)# access-list 100 permit tcp any eq 443 any
Router(config)# queue-list 1 protocol ip 1 list 100
Router(config)# queue-list 1 default 1
Router(config)# queue-list 1 queue 1 byte-count 1500
Router(config)# queue-list 1 queue 2 byte-count 4500
Router(config)# interface Serial 0
Router(config-if)# custom-queue-list 1
```

Enabling FIFO Queuing

FIFO queuing is the default queuing method for interfaces faster than 2 Mbps. To enable FIFO queuing for other interfaces, use the following interface or policy map class configuration command:

`no fair-queue`

Configuring PQ

Similar to CQ, a PQ configuration entails the creation of a queue list and then application of that queue list to an interface. The commands to create and apply priority queue lists are detailed in the following table.

Command	Description
priority-list *list-number* default {high | medium | normal | low}	Configures the default queue for traffic not explicitly placed into another queue
priority-list *list-number* interface *type number* {high | medium | normal | low}	Places packets into a specific queue based on the input interface

Command	Description
priority-list *list-number* protocol *protocol* [high | medium | normal | low] [*keyword value*]	Assigns traffic to a specific queue based on the protocol, or several protocol keywords, including • fragments • list • gt • lt • tcp • udp
priority-list *list-number* queue-list [*high-limit* [*medium-limit* [*normal-limit* [*low-limit*]]]]	Specifies how many packets can be held in each of the queues
priority-group *list-number*	Assigns a priority queue list to an interface

The following configuration example creates a PQ configuration that gives strict priority to IPX traffic. The queue size is doubled for the high priority queue as well:

```
Router(config)# priority-list 1 protocol ipx high
Router(config)# priority-list 1 default normal
Router(config)# priority-list 1 queue-list 40 40 60 80
Router(config)# interface Serial 0
Router(config)# priority-group 1
```

Enabling and Tuning WFQ

WFQ is the default for serial interfaces slower than 2 Mbps. To enable WFQ for other interfaces or for traffic classes within CBWFQ, use the following configuration command:

`fair-queue`

The complete syntax for this command is

`fair-queue [congestive-discard-threshold [dynamic-queues [reservable-queues]]]`

Using the extended syntax lets you configure the number and size of the queues used by WFQ.

Monitoring and Verifying of a Queuing Configuration

Use the following commands to view the status a queuing configuration:

- **show queue** *type number*
- **show queueing** [interface *type number* | **custom** | **priority** | **fair** [interface *type number*]]
- **show policy-map** [*policy-map*]
- **show policy-map** *policy-map* **class** *class-map*
- **show policy-map interface** *type number* [**input** | **output**]

Configuring Network Address Translation (NAT)

Key NAT Terminology

Term	Definition
Inside global address	This is the inside IP address as seen outside the network.
Inside local address	This is the inside IP address as seen inside the network.
Outside global address	This is the outside IP address as seen on the outside network.
Outside local address	This is the outside IP address as seen inside the network.
Rotary pool	Used in TCP load distribution, the rotary pool is the group of internal servers that receive connections.

Types of NAT

- One-to-one NAT
- Many-to-many NAT
- Many-to-one NAT (also known as overload, Port Address Translation [PAT])
- TCP load distribution
- Translation of overlapping address spaces

Configuring NAT

Before a NAT configuration functions, the inside and outside of the network must be defined using the following interface configuration commands:

ip nat inside

and

ip nat outside

A simple one-to-one NAT can be configured with the command:

ip nat inside source static *inside-ip outside-ip*

The following command configures a range of outside addresses for use with many-to-many NAT or translation of overlapping address spaces:

ip nat pool *pool-name start-address end-address* **netmask** *netmask*

The syntax of the following **ip nat inside source list** command indicates which addresses on the inside interface should be processed by NAT and to bind those addresses to an outside pool:

ip nat inside source list *acl-number* **pool** *pool-name* [**overload**]

The **ip nat inside destination** command is used with TCP load distribution and has the following syntax:

ip nat inside destination list *acl-number* **pool** *pool-name* **rotary**

The following is an example of a one-to-one NAT configuration that maps 10.1.1.10 to 172.16.1.10, as shown in the figure.

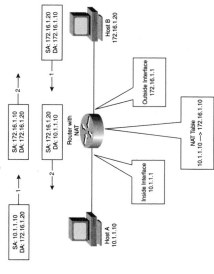

```
Router(config)# interface Ethernet 0
Router(config-if)# ip address 10.1.1.1 255.255.255.0
Router(config-if)# ip nat inside
Router(config-if)# interface Ethernet 1
Router(config-if)# ip address 172.16.1.1 255.255.255.0
Router(config-if)# ip nat outside
Router(config-if)# exit
Router(config)# ip nat inside source static 10.1.1.10 172.16.1.10
```

The following is an example of a many-to-many NAT configuration that translates 10.0.0.0 through 10.255.255.255 to 172.16.2.0 through 172.16.2.255, as shown in the figure.

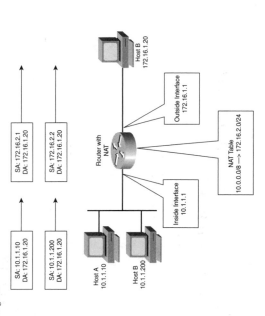

```
Router(config)# interface Ethernet 0
Router(config-if)# ip address 10.1.1.1 255.255.255.0
Router(config-if)# ip nat inside
Router(config-if)# interface Ethernet 1
Router(config-if)# ip address 172.16.1.1 255.255.255.0
Router(config-if)# ip nat outside
Router(config-if)# exit
Router(config)# access-list 1 permit 10.0.0.0 0.255.255.255
Router(config)# ip nat pool NAT-POOL 172.16.2.0 172.16.2.255 netmask
  255.255.255.0
Router(config)# ip nat inside source list 1 pool NAT-POOL
```

```
Router(config-if)# exit
Router(config)# access-list 1 permit 10.0.0.0 0.255.255.255
Router(config)# ip nat pool NAT-POOL 172.16.2.0 172.16.2.255 netmask
  255.255.255.0
Router(config)# ip nat inside source list 1 pool NAT-POOL
```

The following is an example of many-to-one NAT that translates addresses 10.0.0.0 through 10.255.255.255 to the address 172.16.1.10, as illustrated in the figure.

```
Router(config)# interface Ethernet 0
Router(config-if)# ip address 10.1.1.1 255.255.255.0
Router(config-if)# ip nat inside
Router(config-if)# interface Ethernet 1
Router(config-if)# ip address 172.16.1.1 255.255.255.0
Router(config-if)# ip nat outside
Router(config-if)# exit
Router(config)# access-list 1 permit 10.0.0.0 0.255.255.255
Router(config)# ip nat pool NAT-POOL 172.16.1.10 172.16.1.10 netmask
  255.255.255.0
Router(config)# ip nat inside source list 1 pool NAT-POOL overload
```

The following is an example of a configuration that leverages NAT to overcome the connectivity problems where two networks have overlapping address spaces. In this configuration, two networks have the 10.1.0.0/16 network. Traffic sent from inside to outside from the 10.1.0.0/16 network is translated to 172.17.0.0/16. At the same time, traffic from outside to inside from 10.1.0.0/16 (the other one) is translated to 172.16.0.0/16.

For this solution to work, the router performing NAT must also modify certain DNS responses. Specifically, the router passively waits for DNS responses and alters their contents to match the current NAT translations. As shown in the following figure, the router alters the DNS response, which includes 10.1.1.10 (a duplicate address) with the address in the NAT table of 172.16.1.1.

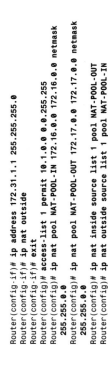

```
Router(config)# interface Ethernet 0
Router(config-if)# ip address 10.1.1.1 255.255.255.0
Router(config-if)# ip nat inside
Router(config-if)# interface Ethernet 1
```

```
Router(config-if)# ip address 172.31.1.1 255.255.255.0
Router(config-if)# ip nat outside
Router(config-if)# exit
Router(config)# access-list 1 permit 10.1.0.0 0.0.255.255
Router(config)# ip nat pool NAT-POOL-IN 172.16.0.0 172.16.0.0 netmask
255.255.0.0
Router(config)# ip nat pool NAT-POOL-OUT 172.17.0.0 172.17.0.0 netmask
255.255.0.0
Router(config)# ip nat inside source list 1 pool NAT-POOL-OUT
Router(config)# ip nat outside source list 1 pool NAT-POOL-IN
```

NAT can also be used to load balance TCP connections. The example that follows maps the virtual server IP address 10.1.1.1 to the servers 192.168.1.1 through 192.168.1.10.

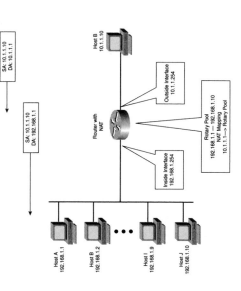

```
Router(config)# interface Ethernet 0
Router(config-if)# ip address 192.168.1.254 255.255.255.0
Router(config-if)# ip nat inside
Router(config-if)# interface Ethernet 1
Router(config-if)# ip address 10.1.1.254 255.255.255.0
```

```
Router(config-if)# ip nat outside
Router(config-if)# exit
Router(config)# access-list 1 permit 10.1.1.1 0.0.0.0
Router(config)# ip nat pool NAT-POOL 192.168.1.1 192.168.1.10 netmask
  255.255.255.0 type rotary
Router(config)# ip nat inside destination list 1 pool NAT-POOL
```

Tuning NAT Timeouts

The command used to tune NAT-related timeouts differs depending on the configuration. To change the timeout related to simple one-to-one NAT translations use the following:

ip nat translation timeout *timeout-seconds*

When your configuration includes overload NAT or PAT, use the following commands to tune protocol specific timeouts:

- ip nat translation udp-timeout {*seconds* | never}
- ip nat translation dns-timeout {*seconds* | never}
- ip nat translation tcp-timeout {*seconds* | never}
- ip nat translation icmp-timeout {*seconds* | never}
- ip nat translation pptp-timeout {*seconds* | never}

Verifying the NAT Configuration

The following commands help you determine if your NAT configuration is operating properly:

- clear ip nat translation {* | [inside *global-ip local-ip*] [outside *local-ip global-ip*]}
- clear ip nat translation *protocol* inside *global-ip global-port local-ip local-port* [outside *local-ip global-ip*]
- debug ip nat [detailed | *acl-number*]
- show ip nat statistics
- show ip nat translation [verbose]

Understanding DSL and Broadband Cable Technologies

Technology Goals

Although DSL and cable infrastructures are very different in their implementation, their goals are nearly identical. The following table lists goals and how each technology attains those goals.

Goal	DSL	Cable
Provide Internet or enterprise remote access	Provides Internet access or remote access to the enterprise	Provides Internet access only but can be teamed with a VPN solution for remote access to enterprise resources
Utilize existing facilities to reach as many potential customers as possible	Delivered over an existing telephone service to residential or business customers	Takes advantage of an existing cable television network that reaches nearly all potential customers

Modulation Techniques

ADSL uses one of two modulation techniques to allow the simultaneous transmission of voice and data over the same cable pair: CAP or DMT.

DSL Modulation Technique	Overview
Carrierless Amplitude Phase (CAP)	Data transmission uses one of two bands: 25 kHz to 160 kHz for upstream communications and 240 kHz to 1.5 MHz for downstream communications. Not an industry standard but widely deployed.
Discreet MultiTone (DMT)	Available bandwidth is divided into 256 4.3125 kHz channels. The DMT devices monitor the channels in use and utilize of channels that provide cleaner transmissions.

In a broadband cable network, the existing RF modulation technique transmits data as well as television programming.

Devices in the Network

A DSL or cable network consists of serveral devices, which are summarized in the following table.

DSL Access Multiplexer (DSLAM)	DSL	Aggregates many customer connections to a few ATM connections
DSL Customer Premise Equipment (CPE)	DSL	Provides Ethernet connectivity to the user within their residence or business
Cable Modem Termination System (CMTS)	Cable	Services many customer connections from the cable network
Cable Modem	Cable	Provides Ethernet connectivity from customer devices to the cable network

The DOCSIS Standard

The Data over Cable Service Interface Specification (DOCSIS) is a standard for cable modem CPE to CMTS communication over a cable network. DOCSIS has three versions: 1.0, 1.1 (widely deployed), and 2.0.

As part of DOCSIS, the cable modem downloads its configuration and, optionally, its software image from a centralized TFTP server. The following information is part of a DOCSIS-compliant configuration file:

- Radio frequency information
- Configuration details
- Vendor-specific information
- Management specifics
- Software upgrade information

RFC-Defined Standards

The following table lists the RFCs that are relevant to the configuration and deployment of DSL.

RFC	Relevance

ETHER_TYPE Field	Use
0x8863	PPPoE Discovery phase
0x8864	PPPoE Session phase

ATM Operating Parameters

When configuring an ATM interface, it is important to consider the following points:

Item	Valid Settings	Comments
Encapsulation	AAL5SNAP	All DSL CPEs should use this type of encapsulation. This becomes important when configuring the ATM PVC.
VPC	32-65535	Values 0-31 are reserved and are not used for PVCs. This is relevant when configuring a PVC.
VPI	0-255	This is relevant when configuring a PVC.

1483	Details the transmission of connectionless LAN data across an ATM network. Defines two modes of operation: bridged and routed. This is the basis of many legacy DSL CPE implementations.
2364	Defines PPP over ATM (PPPoA). PPPoA provides device authentication and service selection in a routed CPE configuration. With PPPoA, PPP terminates on CPE.
2516	Defines PPP over Ethernet (PPPoE). With PPPoE, a LAN-connected client can be authenticated and utilize the service selection capabilities inherent with PPP. Unlike PPPoA, PPPoE terminates PPP on the client computer and requires the CPE to be in a bridging mode.

PPP over Ethernet Session Establishment

The PPPoE session establishment process consists of four PPPoE packets: the PPPoE Active Discovery Initiation (PADI), the PPPoE Active Discovery Offer (PADO), the PPPoE Active Discovery Request (PADR), and the PPPoE Active Discovery Session (PADS) confirmation packet.

A fifth PPPoE packet is the PPPoE Active Discovery Terminate (PADT) packet. This is used to terminate an active PPPoE session.

PPPoE packets use one of the following ETHER_TYPE fields.

Understanding Virtual Private Networks

Types of VPNs

- Remote Access
- Site-to-Site

Remote Access VPNs

A Remote Access VPN allows remote users to securely access resources within an organization. The goals of a Remote Access VPN are simple:

- Secure access to internal resources
- User authentication and authorization
- Data confidentiality and authentication
- Cost savings through the utilization of local Internet connections

Site-to-Site VPNs

A site-to-site VPN provides secure connectivity between two networks over a less secure network, usually the Internet. The benefits of a site-to-site VPN include

- Secure access to remote resources
- Seamless access across sites
- Data confidentiality and authentication
- Cost savings through the utilization of local Internet connections

IPSec Protocols

The following protocols are relevant to the configuration of an IPSec solution:

- Internet Key Exchange (IKE)
- IPSec
- Encapsulated Security Payload (ESP)
- Authentication Header (AH)
- Generic Routing Encapsulation (GRE)

Layer 4 Protocols

The table below details the Layer 4 protocols that are relevant to an IPSec solution.

Protocol Name	Protocol Number	Description
Authentication Header	51	Verifies that a packet's contents have not been altered. This verification is computed based on the entire IP packet (legitimately changing fields [TTL, for example] ignored). This is enabled with the **ah-md5-hmac** or **ah-sha-hmac** transform set options.
Encapsulated Security Payload	50	Encrypts and authenticates information as it traverses the network. Authentication is provided on the Layer 4 payload only. ESP is enabled via the **esp-des** or **esp-3des** transform set options. ESP authentication is configured using the **esp-md5-hmac** or **esp-sha-hmac** transform set options.
Generic Routing Encapsulation	47	Creates a virtual point-to-point interface between IPSec peers. This interface aids in the deployment of routing protocols and redundancy.

Internet Key Exchange

The Internet Key Exchange (IKE) protocol negotiates IPSec security association information necessary to build an IPSec connection. IKE consists of two phases: phase one and phase two. Phase one has two modes: aggressive mode and main mode. In aggressive mode, IKE keying material is negotiated simultaneously with the IKE security associations. Aggressive mode uses three messages as opposed to the six used by main mode negotiations. In main mode, security is enhanced by first exchanging the keying material used by IKE and by then encrypting the remaining negotiations. Phase two of IKE negotiations has a single mode known as quick mode. In phase two, negotiations take place to establish the IPSec security associations. The following table details the default IKE policy configuration.

IPSec Tunnel Mode

IPSec has two operation modes: tunnel mode and transport mode. In tunnel mode, the Cisco default, each packet is completely encapsulated into a new IP packet with either an ESP or AH Layer 4 header. The following figure shows this encapsulation.

IP	TCP, UDP, Other	Payload

IP	ESP or AH	Payload

The following table lists the options available for each of the IKE policy configuration items following table.

Characteristic	Default Setting
Authentication	RSA Signatures
DH group	Group 1
Encryption	DES
Hashing	SHA
Lifetime	86,400 seconds

IPSec Transport Mode

In transport mode, a new Layer 4 header is added for either AH or ESP. This new header is inserted between the existing Layer 3 and 4 headers. The following figure shows how a packet is changed during transport mode operation.

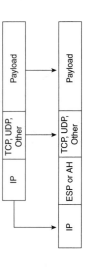

IP	TCP, UDP, Other	Payload

IP	ESP or AH	TCP, UDP, Other	Payload

Characteristic	Available Settings
Authentication	Preshared Keys, RSA Encrypted Nounces, RSA Signatures
DH group	Group 1, Group 2
Encryption	DES, 3DES, AES
Hashing	SHA, MD5
Lifetime	Time in Seconds, or Data in KB

Configuring a Site-to-Site IPSec VPN

First, an access control list (ACL) must be created to select the traffic to be encrypted. This ACL, known as the *crypto ACL*, controls exactly which packets are encrypted. The following crypto ACL encrypts all IP traffic from the 192.168.1.0/24 subnet to the 192.168.2.0/24 subnet:

`access-list 100 permit ip 192.168.1.0 0.0.0.255 192.168.2.0 0.0.0.255`

After creating the crypto ACL, the IKE policy must be configured. The following commands enable IKE and configure a policy with 3DES encryption, MD5 hashing, and authentication using preshared keys:

```
crypto isakmp enable
crypto isakmp policy 10
```

Hashing Protocols

Hashing Protocol	Characteristics
SHA	Generates a 160-bit hash from a message of any length. Considered more secure than MD5 due to the decreased likelihood of collisions.
MD5	Produces a 128-bit hash from an arbitrary length message. Considered to impose less of a performance hit than SHA.

```
authentication preshared
hash md5
encryption 3des
```

Next, a transform set is created that defines the IPSec encryption and hashing to be used:

```
crypto ipsec transform-set TRANSFORM esp-3des esp-md5-hmac
```

Now, create an IKE key for the remote peer. The following example creates a key for the peer at 10.1.1.2:

```
crypto isakmp key cisco address 10.1.1.2
```

After the crypto ACL, the IKE policy, and the transform set have been created and a key is assigned to the peer, they are all linked together using the crypto map:

```
crypto map CRYPTOMAP 10 ipsec-isakmp
set peer 10.1.1.2
set transform-set TRANSFORM
match address 100
```

Now that everything has been created, the crypto map is applied to an interface with the following commands:

```
interface FastEthernet 0/0
crypto map CRYPTOMAP
```

Verification of VPN Functionality

The following commands verify and troubleshoot IPSec VPN functionality:

- debug crypto ipsec
- debug crypto isakmp
- show access-list
- show crypto ipsec sa
- show crypto ipsec transform-set
- show crypto isakmp policy
- show crypto isakmp sa
- show crypto map

Notes

Notes

Notes

Notes

Notes

Notes

Notes

Notes

Notes